"Does HR enhance organizational success?' is a ques
policy-maker, employee and management scholar
important reading, because it describes what decades
does not, featuring a worldwide group of the most r
scholars in the HR field."

—**John Boudreau** – *University of South Carolina – South Carolina - USA*

This is a very timely book by an impressive array of international scholars. Here we
have – in one neat package – the intellectual impetus and insights that will take the HR
strategy literature to the next level".

—**Lee Dyer** – *Cornell University – Ithaca - USA*

"This is the book we have been waiting for. The distinguished author team provide a
tour de force of the HRM and performance debate. The coverage is comprehensive
and both advocates and critics will find much to inspire their research. I strongly
recommend this book to academics, managers, postgraduate masters students and
doctoral candidates worldwide."

—**Patrick Flood** – *Dublin city University – Dublin - Ireland*

"Written by leading scholars in the field, this book is a must-read for all who are
interested in further understanding the HRM-performance linkages from different
perspectives. Paauwe, Guest and Wright have done a great job via eleven chapters
in the book in picking-up the core issues in the field and propose a meaningful
way forward."

—**Pawan Budwhar** – *Aston Business School – Birmingham - United Kingdom*

"This is a must read book for everyone researching the subject of human resource
management and performance. Paauwe, Wright and Guest (three of the leaders in the
field) have put together an excellent volume with an outstanding international cast of
authors; it is a lucid and cogent coverage of the current state of research and sets up a
rich agenda for future scholary endeavour. It will become the standard reference in
this research area."

—**Adrian Wilkinson** – *Griffith University – Brisbane - Australia*

"Unraveling how HRM influences firm performance is one of those HARD research
problems that really is worth the effort. To crack this problem, we need to get beyond
generic HR systems research to the heart of how things work. This collection of
research from scholars both within and outside the U.S. is just the sort of critical work
that will help to advance the field."

—**Clinton Chadwick** – *University of Kansas - USA*

"Edited by three leading scholars long associated with this field, this book lays out all
the critical and supportive arguments that have arisen in the HRM-performance
debate. It is a powerful summary of what we know and what remains unanswered
and successfully starts a new conversation about, and creates a roadmap for, how we
can improve on theory, method and evidence."

—**Paul Sparrow** – *Lancaster University – Lancaster - United Kingdom*

HRM AND PERFORMANCE

HRM AND PERFORMANCE

ACHIEVEMENTS AND CHALLENGES

EDITED BY
JAAP PAAUWE, DAVID GUEST AND
PATRICK WRIGHT

WILEY

This edition first published 2013
© 2012

Registered office

John Wiley & Sons Ltd, The Atrium, Southern Gate, Chichester, West Sussex, PO19 8SQ, United Kingdom

For details of our global editorial offices, for customer services and for information about how to apply for permission to reuse the copyright material in this book please see our website at www.wiley.com.

The right of the author of this work has been asserted in accordance with the Copyright, Designs and Patents Act 1988.

Reprinted October 2013

Wiley publishes in a variety of print and electronic formats and by print-on-demand. Some material included with standard print versions of this book may not be included in e-books or in print-on-demand. If this book refers to media such as a CD or DVD that is not included in the version you purchased, you may download this material at http://booksupport.wiley .com. For more information about Wiley products, visit www.wiley.com.

Library of Congress Cataloging-in-Publication Data

A catalogue record for this book is available from the British Library.

ISBN 978-1-405-16833-5 (paperback)
ISBN 978-1-118-48261-2 (emobi)
ISBN 978-1-118-48262-9 (epdf)
ISBN 978-1-118-48263-6 (epub)

Set in 10/12pt Meridien by MPS Limited, Chennai, India.
Printed in Great Britain by TJ International Ltd, Padstow, Cornwall

CONTENTS

PREFACE

For more than two decades the three of us have been involved in the topic of HRM and Performance. We kept track of all the publications, both theoretical as well as empirical and also contributed to the field ourselves in various ways. We also tried to build bridges between the USA, UK and mainland Europe. And, we organized in various places and at various times seminars, meetings to discuss findings, developments and progress and . . . obstacles to further progress to ensure that academics from around the world can benefit from each other's insights. And we will continue to do so. More specifically the first meeting related to this book dates back to a seminar organized in 2004 at Erasmus University in order to celebrate and present the book *HRM and Performance: Achieving long term viability* (Paauwe, 2004). During that conference a number of interesting papers were being discussed, which led us to think it would be a good idea to collect these papers under the heading HRM and Performance: What's Next?. Since that time, papers were replaced by new papers, the field progressed and also young, bright scholars entered the domain. So, right now we finally have a collection of papers, which bundles both the achievements of the past two decades, but more importantly looks forward to future challenges. Moreover, we have been able to include generations of researchers as authors of the different chapters with a mixture of more established academics, the 'about to take over' generation and new upcoming academics. We also made sure to include the macro (organizational) perspective and the micro (individual) perspective as well as the multitude of linkages between these two perspectives; linkages that will take the field forward.

We hope you will enjoy reading this volume and that it will indeed inspire others to take up the challenges for future research. We - as editors- owe much to our contributing fellow-authors from across the globe, who also represent a global community of dedicated academics, always open to the debate, and always eager to take the field forward.

Jaap Paauwe
David Guest
Patrick Wright

EDITOR BIOGRAPHIES

Patrick Wright is Thomas C. Vandiver Bicentennial Chair in the Darla Moore School of Business at the University of South Carolina. Prior to joining USC he has served on the faculties at Cornell University, Texas A&M University, and the University of Notre Dame.

Professor Wright teaches, conducts research, and consults in the area of Strategic Human Resource Management (SHRM), particularly focusing on how firms use people as a source of competitive advantage and the changing nature of the Chief HR Officer role. For the past 8 years he has been studying the CHRO role through a series of confidential interviews, public podcasts, small discussion groups, and conducting the Cornell/CAHRS Survey of Chief HR Officers. In addition, he is the faculty leader for the Cornell ILR Executive Education/NAHR program "The Chief HR Officer: Strategies for Success" aimed at developing potential successors to the CHRO role. He served as the lead editor on the recently released book "The Chief HR Officer: Defining the New Role of Human Resource Leaders" published by John Wiley and Sons.

He has published over 60 research articles in journals as well as over 20 chapters in books and edited volumes. He has co-authored two textbooks titled Human Resource Management: Gaining Competitive Advantage (now in its third edition) and Management of Organizations. He has co-edited a special issue of Research in Personnel and Human Resources Management titled "Strategic Human Resource Management in the 21st Century," and Guest Edited a special issue of Human Resource Management Review titled "Research in Strategic HRM for the 21st Century."

He has conducted programs and/or consulted for a number of large organizations including Comcast, Royal Dutch Shell, KennaMetal, AstraZeneca, BT, and BP. He currently serves as a member on the Board of Directors for the National Academy of Human Resources (NAHR). He is a former board member of HRPS, SHRM Foundation and World at Work (formerly American Compensation

Association). In 2011 he was named by HRM Magazine as one of the 20 "Most Influential Thought Leaders in HR".

Department of Management
Darla Moore School of Business
University of South Carolina
1705 College Street
Columbia, SC 29208 USA
Tel: 1 803 777 5955
Email: patrick.wright@moore.sc.edu

David E Guest is one of the leading academic experts on human resource management and related aspects of work and organizational psychology. He has a first degree in Psychology and Sociology from Birmingham University and PhD in Occupational Psychology from London University.

His first job was a research officer in the Department of Occupational Psychology at Birkbeck College. He then spent three years as behavioural science adviser to British Rail before joining the London School of Economics in 1972. He moved to Birkbeck in 1990 and for ten years was Professor of Occupational Psychology and head of the Department of Organizational Psychology. During that period he had a spell as a Governor of Birkbeck and as Pro-Vice Master. He moved to King's College in 2000 where he has served as Head of The Department of Management and Deputy Head of the School of Social Science and Public Policy.

He has written and researched extensively in the areas of human resource management, employment relations and the psychological contract, motivation and commitment, and careers. His most recent book is "Psychological Contracts, Employment Contracts and Employee Well-Being: An International Study" (Oxford University Press, 2010). He is a member of the editorial advisory board of a number of journals. He has been a member of the NHS SDO Commissioning Board and of UK Skills and Employment Advisory Group. Over the years, he has worked closely with a range of companies including Shell, IBM, HSBC, Hong Kong MTRC, as well as with the UK National Health Service and a number of government departments.

His current research is concerned with the relationship between human resource management, organisational performance and employee well-being in the private and public sectors; the role of human resource departments; the individualization of employment relations and the role of the psychological contract; flexibility and employment contracts; partnership at work; and the future of the career. For five years up to July 2012 he was Programme Director for Workforce issues and also Managing Director of the King's NIHR Patient Safety and Service Quality Research Centre, engaged in research on human resource issues in healthcare.

Department of Management
King's College, London
150 Stamford Street
London SE1 9NH
Tel: 02078483723
Email: david.guest@kcl.ac.uk

Jaap Paauwe (PhD, Erasmus University Rotterdam) is Professor of Human Resource Studies at Tilburg University, The Netherlands. Before joining Tilburg he worked as a full professor of Organization at Erasmus University Rotterdam, School of Economics. At Erasmus University he is still involved in supervising PhD students in the area of HRM and performance in the health care.

He has written and co-authored books on human resource management and published more than 150 papers/chapters in international refereed journals and books. In 1991 he was Academic Visitor at the London School of Economics. In 1996 he was Visiting Professor at Templeton College, Oxford University. Before joining the university he worked for the trade union movement (Head of CNV Research Department 1983-1988) and a Dutch based multinational company (SHV 1980-1983). His main research interests are in the area of HRM, performance and well-being, HR function and -delivery, corporate strategy, governance and risk management, organizational change and industrial relations. These research and consultancy activities mainly take place in the market sector in close cooperation with internationally operating firms/MNC's.

Also active in the health care sector, with a special focus on the HR function and the relationship between HRM, organizational climate and performance.

In 2005 he joined Cornell University (Ithaca, USA) as a visiting fellow. In addition he is a fellow at the TIASNIMBAS Business school and fellow of the Judge Business School/Cambridge University (UK) and academic director of the executive Advanced Human Resource Program of the People Management Centre (PMC), which aims to build bridges between the university and the HR practitioners' community. In 2010 he spent his sabbatical leave at Pablo de Olavide University in Seville, Spain. His latest book is on HRM and Performance: achieving long term viability (Oxford University Press, June 2004), for which he received the Dutch HRM network Award in 2005. Together with Cambridge, INSEAD and Cornell University he is involved in a large scale international research project on improving the excellence of the HR function within multinational companies. Next to this project the research group at Tilburg has initiated a similar international project, but then focused on the role of the HR-function in corporate governance and risk management. In 2010 he received -together with his co-authors the international HRM Scholarly Research Award from the Academy of Management-HR Division. Next to his academic work Jaap is also involved in more practice oriented research, coaching and acting as a moderator for a leading group of HR directors.

Department of Human Resource Studies
Tilburg University, Tilburg
Warandelaan 2, 5000 LE Tilburg
Tel: +31 13 466 2851/2371
Email: paauwe@tilburguniversity.edu

AUTHOR BIOGRAPHIES

Beijer Susanne Beijer is a PhD candidate at the Department of Human Resource Studies at Tilburg University. Susanne's research interests and PhD project both focus on the concept of HR practices and their relationship with employee well-being and organizational outcomes. *S.e.beijer@tilburguniversity.edu*

Boon Corine Boon is Assistant Professor at the department of Human Resource Management and Organizational Behaviour of the University of Amsterdam Business School. Her research interests include strategic human resource management, person-environment fit, and job crafting. *c.t.boon@uva.nl*

Boselie Paul Boselie (PhD, MSc) is Professor in the Utrecht School of Governance at Utrecht University (The Netherlands). His research traverses human resource management, institutionalism, strategic management and industrial relations. *P.Boselie@uu.nl*

Boxall Peter Boxall is professor of human resource management in the department of management and international business at the University of Auckland and author, with John Purcell, of Strategy and Human Resource Management (Palgrave Macmillan). *p.boxall@auckland.ac.nz*

Den Hartog Prof dr. Deanne N. Den Hartog is professor of Organizational Behavior and head of the HRM-OB section of the University of Amsterdam Business School. Her research interests include leadership, proactive and innovative work behavior, HRM, trust, culture, and teams. *d.n.denhartog@uva.nl*

Federman Federman – Jessica E. Federman is a doctoral candidate in human resource management in the School of Industrial and Labor Relations at Cornell University. Her research interests include motivation, leadership, problem-solving, creativity and communication. *jef236@cornell.edu*

Gerhart Barry Gerhart is a professor at the Department of Management and Human Resources at the Wisconsin School of Business. His research interests include compensation, human resource management, incentives, and staffing. *bgerhart@bus.wisc.edu*

Harris Dr. Harris has teaching and research interests in the areas of human resource management and organizational behavior. Prior to joining Marietta

College, Dr. Harris gained international teaching and research experience as a professor in the Netherlands. He has taught a variety courses in the management field at both the undergraduate and graduate levels. *c.m.harris@tilburguniversity.edu*

Hermans Michel Hermans is working towards the completion of his PhD in Industrial and Labor Relations at Cornell University. His research interests include strategic human resources management, inter-organizational work arrangements and their implications for HRM, and HRM in Latin America. *mh597@cornell.edu*

Klein – Gemaild: fbk3@cornell.edu

Heavey Angela Langevin Heavey joined Florida International University as an Assistant Professor of Management and International Business after receiving her Ph.D. in Human Resource Studies from the ILR School at Cornell University. Angela's research interests include employee perceptions of HR practices, employee turnover and withdrawal, and age in the workplace. *aheavey@fiu.edu*

Martinson Brian Martinson is currently an Assistant Professor of Human Resource Management in the Department of Management, Marketing and Administrative Systems at Tarleton State University. Brian's research interests include human resource management practices, human capital, and leader/member exchange, and their linkages with employee behaviors and performance. *martinson@tarleton.edu*

McClean Elizabeth McClean is a PhD student in the Human Resources Department in the School of Industrial and Labor Relations. Elizabeth's research interests include employee voice, leadership, and strategic HR management. *ejm45@cornell.edu*

McMahan Dr. Gary C. McMahan is associate professor at the University of Texas at Arlington. His Current interests include strategic human resource management, work motivation, issues in organization change and development, empowerment/employee involvement, rewards, and job design. *gmcmahan@uta.edu*

Nishii Lisa Nishii joined the faculty of the Human Resource Studies department at the ILR School, Cornell University, after receiving her Ph.D. and M.A. in Organizational Psychology from the University of Maryland, and a B.A in economics and psychology from Wellesley College. Nishii's research focuses on diversity and inclusion, particularly in global organizations *lhn5@cornell.edu*

Peccei Riccardo Peccei is Professor of Organizational Behavior and Human Resource Management in the Department of Management at King's College London. He is also a Research Fellow in the Department of Human Resource Studies at Tilburg University. His current research interests, within a multilevel perspective, are in the areas of HRM, employee well-being and organizational performance. *riccardo.peccei@kcl.ac.uk*

Sels Luc Sels (Merksem, 1967) is Dean of the Faculty of Economics and Business. He joined the Faculty in 1996 as an assistant professor and became full professor in 2004. His research interests center around active ageing and (corporate) demography, individual and organisational career management, the relationship between investments in HR management and firm performance (ROI) and features of strong HRM systems. *Luc.Sels@econ.kuleuven.be*

Van Veldhoven Marc van Veldhoven joined Tilburg University/the department of HR Studies in 2002, and was appointed full professor there in November

2010 and his mainly interest is in occupational health psychology and organizational behavior literature. Before joining Tilburg University he worked as an independent consultant for larger companies. *M.J.P.M.vanVeldhoven@uvt.nl*

Van de Voorde Karina Van De Voorde is an assistant professor at the department of Human Resource Studies (Tilburg University). Her research is focused on aligning the Organizational Behavior/Occupational Health Psychology orientation towards the topic of HRM and organizational performance.

De Winne Sophie De Winne is associate professor at the Faculty of Business and Economics (University of Leuven, Belgium). Her main research interests include the relationship between HRM and firm performance, HRM system strength, the role of line managers in HRM, HR differentiation and the relationship between firm demography, employee turnover and firm performance. Sophie. *DeWinne@kuleuven.be*

1

HRM AND PERFORMANCE: WHAT DO WE KNOW AND WHERE SHOULD WE GO?

JAAP PAAUWE, PATRICK WRIGHT
AND DAVID GUEST

'Based on four national surveys and observations on more than 2000 firms, our judgment is that the *effect* of a one standard deviation *change* in the HR system is 10–20% of a firm's market value.' (Huselid & Becker, 2000, p. 851; emphasis added)

'The existing evidence for a relationship between HRM and performance should be treated with caution.' (Wall & Wood, 2005, p. 454)

'After hundreds of research studies we are still in no position to assert with any confidence that good HRM has an impact on organization performance.' (Guest, 2011, p. xx)

Practitioners interested in human resources management (HRM) have long sought to convince others of its value. Drucker (1954) referred to 'personnel' managers as constantly worrying about 'their inability to prove that they are making a contribution to the enterprise' (p. 275). More recently Tom Stewart described HR leaders as being 'unable to describe their contribution to value added except in trendy, unquantifiable and wannabe terms' (Stewart, 1996, p. 105).

In response to this longstanding and often repeated criticism that HR does not add value to organizations, academic research has exploded over the past 20 years, seeking to show that HRM practices are related to firm performance. Huselid's (1995) groundbreaking study showed that a set of HR practices he called 'high-performance work systems' (HPWSs) were related to turnover, accounting profits and firm market value. This study served as the springboard for a significant body of research confirming empirical relationships between HR and performance.

However, in spite of the vast body of research that has emerged over the past two decades, as these quotes from some distinguished academic researchers suggest, divergence exists regarding what we can conclude about the relationship

between HRM practices and firm performance. Is the HRM–performance relationship one that is strong, universal and causal, or is it potentially weak,
contingent and even spurious? More importantly, what is the underlying research
base from which we can answer that question, and how can we improve that base
in order to answer it in a way that is valid, reliable and practically important? The
purpose of this book is to attempt to bring together some of the leading researchers
in this area to provide insights into what we know, what we need to know, and
how we can begin on a journey to improve our knowledge of the relationship
between HR and firm performance.

In this chapter, we will first present an overview of what we seem to know about
this relationship. We will trace some of the streams of this research in an effort to
provide a foundation for how we have arrived at this point in our knowledge base.
We will then lay out some of the unanswered questions that have emerged from the
research to date on the relationship between HRM and performance. Within this
context we will show how the authors have attempted to provide some answers and
set out future directions as an overview to the rest of the book.

What do we know about the HRM–performance relationship?

The development of theory and research on the relationship between HRM and
performance began in the 1980s. A series of articles and books by authors such as
Fombrun et al. (1984) and Miles and Snow (1984) began to link business strategy
to human resource management. The Harvard group (Beer et al., 1984) and
Schuler and Jackson (1987) began to argue for a clear and systematic integration
between the strategy of the firm and the HRM practices used to manage the
workforce of that firm. In the UK, writers such as Guest (1987) and Storey (1992)
took a normative perspective, suggesting the need for external and internal fit of
HRM, contrasting it with the pluralism of an industrial relations perspective.

During this time, others such as Walton (1985), while less concerned with fitting
HRM to strategy, highlighted the need for a shift from control to commitment as the
basis for management of people at work. In parallel with this, authors such as Foulkes
(1980) and Peters and Waterman (1982) provided glimpses of evidence about successful organizations that seemed to apply the 'high commitment' HRM principles.
Thus, this early phase presented the foundational arguments that (a) HRM practices
should be integrated with the strategy of the firm in order to be maximally effective,
and (b) that certain 'high commitment' HRM practices were more effective for generating higher firm performance relative to control-oriented practices.

While these foundational arguments sparked thinking, they alone could not
provide convincing evidence of the potential value of HRM. However, the 1990s
served as the springboard for what would end up being a vast and growing
empirical literature. Huselid (1995) provided the seminal work in his study of more
than 800 corporations, revealing an empirical relationship between the HPWSs
(similar to the 'high commitment' practices discussed above) and important corporate performance variables such as the gross rate of return on assets (a measure
of accounting profits) and Tobin's Q (a measure of the value of the firm). This study

has become the central node in research on the HRM–performance relationship, but was by no means alone. Arthur (1994) found an empirical link between strategy of steel mini-mills and HRM practices. Ichniowski et al. (1995) found a relationship between HRM practices and operating performance of steel mini-mill manufacturing lines. MacDuffie (1995) presented evidence of 'bundles' of HRM practices and measures of manufacturing performance within the automobile industry. Finally, Delery and Doty (1996) explored universalistic, contingency and configurational models of HRM as predictors of firm performance among a sample of banks. They found support for the universalistic (i.e. a similar set of practices consistently related to performance) but little support for either contingency or configurational approaches. In Europe, and particularly the UK, a group of authors reacted strongly against this emerging stream of research, arguing that it represented a new and more subtle form of exploitation of workers (Keenoy, 1990; Keenoy & Schwan, 1990; Blyton & Turnbull, 1992; Legge, 1995). Their analysis was conceptual rather than empirical and partly as a result, received only limited attention among researchers (Keegan & Boselie, 2006). Nevertheless, they raised the important question, largely neglected in the early research on HRM and performance, about the impact of HRM on employees.

Since these early studies, the empirical research has continued unabated and expanded globally. For instance, Guthrie (2001) replicated Huselid's methodology in a sample of New Zealand firms and found a similar relationship between HPWSs and firm performance. Guest et al. (2003) related HR practices to both past and subsequent objective productivity and profitability data, as well as current subjective productivity and financial performance estimates, among a sample of 366 companies in the UK. Boselie et al. (2003) explored the role of sectoral/institutional factors in The Netherlands and showed that the effect of HRM on performance is lower in highly institutionalized sectors (like hospitals and local government) than in a less institutionalized sector like hotels. More recently Takeuchi et al. (2007) found a relationship between HPWSs and firm performance among a sample of Japanese firms. There is now a growing body of research on Chinese organizations that shows a similar pattern of results (e.g. Liao et al., 2009).

There is little doubt that in the past 20 years some progress has been made in the analysis of the relationship between HRM and performance. On balance, however, progress has been modest. This is reflected in the rather optimistic conclusions from some of the main overview articles that have appeared. Becker and Gerhart (1996), indicated that the conceptual and empirical work had progressed far enough to suggest that the role of human resources can be crucial. Similarly, Paauwe and Richardson (1997), based on an early review of 22 studies, concluded that HRM activities give rise to HRM outcomes that will influence the performance of the firm. More specifically and more positively, Huselid and Becker (2000) indicated that the effect of one standard deviation change in the HR system leads to a 10–20 per cent increase in a firm's market value.

However, on a more cautious note, Wright and Gardner (2003a), reflecting on the available evidence, concluded that HR practices are at least weakly related to firm performance. By 2005, Boselie et al. (2005), drawing on a comprehensive sample of 104 studies, concluded that much (though by no means all) of the empirical research shows that HRM is associated with organizational performance. Based on a selection of 25 mainly American so-called high-quality studies, Wall and Wood (2005) concluded – even more cautiously – that the evidence for an effect of HRM on performance is promising but only circumstantial due, for the most part, to inadequate research design. Thus, 19 of the 25 studies they examined reported statistically significant positive relationships between HR practices and performance, but the effect sizes are typically small and the majority of studies failed to consider whether it is the HRM system (the 'gestalt') generating the effects or just specific component/individual practices. Overall, therefore, they conclude that 'The existing evidence for a relationship between HRM and performance should be treated with caution' (Wall & Wood, 2005, p. 454).

On a more positive note, Combs et al. (2006) carried out a meta-analysis of 92 studies on the HR–firm performance relationship and found that an increase of one standard deviation in the use of high-performance work practices (HPWP) is associated with a 4.6 per cent increase in return on assets, and with a 4.4 percentage point decrease in turnover. Hence their conclusion that 'HPWPs' impact on organizational performance is not only statistically significant, but managerially relevant' (p. 518).

Whether examining individual studies, the systematic reviews or the meta-analytic summaries of this literature, what we do know is that HRM practices seem to be consistently related to performance. However, the reviews reveal different levels of confidence about the strength of the association, about the quality of the research on which it is based and about the practical conclusions we can draw from it about the impact of HRM. Therefore, before concluding that we have found the truth and there is no more need for research in this area, we may first want to look at it with a more critical eye. Such a critical view reveals that while this empirical body of research has consistently demonstrated a relationship between HRM practices and performance, it has revealed a number of problems. These centre around two basic themes: theoretical ambiguity and empirical invalidity.

Theoretical ambiguity

Regarding the theoretical ambiguity, Guest (1997) neatly summarized the challenge when he stated this literature needed 'a theory of HRM, a theory of performance, and a theory of how the two are linked.'

First, in attempts to articulate a theory of HRM, Guest (1997), along with others such as Becker et al. (1997) utilized expectancy theory (Vroom, 1964) to theorize about the core HRM practices. This basic framework was adopted and adapted to what has emerged as the AMO (ability, motivation, and opportunity) framework (Appelbaum et al., 2000; Purcell & Hutchinson, 2007). This framework suggests that HR practices can influence the skills, competencies and abilities of the workforce to provide a strong human capital base. Second, practices can affect the motivation and commitment of employees, engaging them to want to behave in ways that benefit the firm. Finally, HR practices such as job design and participative processes can provide the opportunities for the skilled and motivated workforce to positively affect organizational outcomes. This has become the most well-accepted framework for understanding HRM practices. However, while the framework has been widely accepted, there is no consensus about the specific practices that should be considered. This is a major problem. After all, how can we ever make progress in this field if we do not agree on what constitutes one of the main independent variables, namely HR practices?

Regarding a theory of performance, since Huselid's (1995) study, most of the research has focused on performance from the standpoint of the firm. For instance, in their meta-analysis on HPWSs and performance, Combs et al. (2006) noted that of the 92 studies they included, '[a]ccounting returns were most frequently studied (35 effects), followed by productivity (32), retention (23), multidimensional (22), growth (16), and market returns (8)' (p. 510).

However, a somewhat separate line of research on HRM has explored employee-centred outcomes, assuming a need to look beyond firm performance. For instance, Ramsay et al. (2000) suggested that HRM might not be in the workers' best interests, and some studies critical of HRM based on workers responses supported this (e.g. Cappelli & Neumark, 2001; Godard, 2004).

Recently, a more nuanced view is emerging, suggesting that worker outcomes can be considered a central issue, and that it is possible that HRM can lead to both enhanced workers' well-being and higher performance (Peccei, 2004; Guest, 2011). For instance, Kehoe and Wright (2010) found that HRM practices were related to employees' affective commitment to the firm, their willingness to exhibit discretionary behaviour, and their intent to stay with the firm. In a more complex analysis, Gardner et al. (2011) found that motivation and opportunity enhancing practices were positively related to affective commitment and negatively related to turnover. However, ability-enhancing practices, consistent with labour market theory, were unrelated to affective commitment and positively related to turnover. Thus, theory and research regarding what constitutes the various aspects of performance affected by HRM has expanded beyond the pure financial measures. This view is further reinforced by research in public sector organizations where conventional private sector financial indicators are not relevant (see, for example, Messersmith et al., 2011). This supports the view that the outcomes of HRM are multi-faceted and that we need to look beyond financial performance (Boxall & Purcell, 2003; Paauwe, 2004).

Finally, regarding the theory linking HRM and performance, Wright and McMahan (1992) presented six theories that had been used in exploring the relationship between the two. However, by far the most popular theory in the 1990s was the resource-based view of the firm, which argues that when a firm's resources are valuable, rare, inimitable, and non-substitutable, they can be a source of sustainable competitive advantage. Wright et al. (1994) explored how a firm's human resources could meet these criteria and thus constitute a potential source of sustainable competitive advantage. While popular, this theory provides only a very generic argument for how HR practices might be related to performance, and does not help to understand the specific nature of this relationship.

One of the challenges, therefore, is how far it can be adapted to offer more specific proposals.

Becker et al.'s (1997) box and arrows model presented a more specific theoretical framework for explaining the mediating mechanisms between HRM and performance. They suggested that HRM practices have their most direct impact on the employee skills and motivation, which, in turn, results in creativity, productivity, and discretionary behaviour. Employees' behaviour influences the firm's operating performance, which leads to profitability, growth, and market value.

The review by Boselie et al. (2005), concluded that up until then, the three most popular theories being used in HRM and performance research were contingency theory, the resource-based view (RBV) and the AMO framework. If we include papers published since 2000, more than half use AMO theory (Paauwe, 2009). Both RBV and contingency theory focus on the organizational level, whereas AMO theory focuses on the importance of taking into account employee-level factors. Overall we can discern a lack of attention being paid to the institutional context (Paauwe & Boselie, 2003).

Thus a number of attempts have been made to develop a theory of HRM, a theory of performance, and a theory of how the two are linked. However, all are 'works in progress' and none have achieved consensus support among researchers. There is therefore still a need for more theoretical and conceptual development.

Empirical invalidity

Even if there was consensus about theory, as the opening quotes illustrate, a number of researchers have taken issue with the validity of the research base exploring the HRM–performance relationship. Gerhart et al. (2000b) first suggested that the single respondent measures of HR practices lacked reliability. They noted that while low reliability could diminish the observed relationship between HR and performance, it could also inflate it, if much of the error variance was systematically biased. They suggested that the traditional point estimates of the dollar value gains associated with increasing HR practices by a standard deviation, if corrected, would be far beyond what seems reasonable, and thus suggested that some systematic bias might exist.

Later researchers investigated some of the potential forms of systematic bias. Guest et al. (2003) were the first researchers to note that while the assumed direction of causality was from HR practices to performance, this should not be taken for granted. Their own data suggested that performance causing HR practices was an equally plausible explanation of the association. Wright et al. (2005) followed up on this research and showed that their HR practice measures were as strongly related to past performance as to future performance. In addition, they found that when controlling for past performance, the relationship between HR practices and future performance was substantially reduced. Neither set of researchers suggested that HR had NO impact on later performance, but raised the question about how much of the observed relationship was directly causal. Wall and Wood (2005) argue that the lack of rigorous longitudinal studies on the HRM–performance relationship precludes any firm conclusions regarding the causal nature of this relationship. Some more recent studies have taken careful account of causality, using longitudinal research (van Veldhoven, 2005; van de Voorde et al., 2010b) and they also indicate reverse causation, that is, that performance influences subsequent HR practices and well-being.

Another issue that may call into question the strength of the HRM–performance relationship deals with response patterns of the people filling out surveys. Implicit performance theory, rooted in the leadership literature, has shown that respondents observing the same leader will report leadership behaviours consistent with what they are led to believe was the leader's group's performance (Rush et al., 1977). Gardner and Wright (2010) presented executives and students with descriptions of high and low-performing organizations and found that respondents reported greater use of HR practices in the high-performing firms. This opens up the possibility that in addition to actual performance causing HR practices, there might be an effect of performance on respondents' *reports* of HR practices.

The result of all this led Paauwe (2009) in his overview to conclude that in spite of the fact that we have made progress in the area of HRM and performance, we still face significant methodological and theoretical challenges with regard to furthering our understanding of this relationship. In a similar vein, Guest (2011) concludes that: 'the research is riddled with error both with respect to data on HRM and on outcomes. As some have argued, this may hide the size of any true effect (Gerhart et al., 2000b). But is also leaves room for considerable doubt about the processes at play. We therefore need to recognize the need for more careful formulation of research and perhaps less research with a wide sweep. Indeed, we probably need to move away from the "big research" concept.' (Wall and Wood (2005))

Thus, while research on the HRM–performance relationship continues to grow in popularity, a number of questions remain. The purpose of this book is to begin a conversation around some of these questions in the hope that future research might be able to answer a number of them. We would argue that some of the major unanswered (or at least not fully answered) questions must be addressed if this area of research is to lead to any firm conclusions. While more specific, each question deals with the three challenges laid out by Guest (1997) to develop a theory of HR, a theory of performance and a theory of how the two are linked.

Which HRM practices?

Returning to Guest's admonition that this field needs a theory of HR, one of the striking problems revolves around a lack of consensus regarding what constitutes the correct set of HRM practices. In the 1996 special issue of the *Academy of Management Journal* on HRM and performance, Becker and Gerhart examined the practices that were assessed in the papers making up that issue. They found that not a single practice appeared across all of the studies, and that only one (hours of training) appeared across a majority of the studies. This led them to conclude that 'even when the same HR practices are included in different studies, researchers may still use different measures, further hindering efforts to cumulate findings' (Becker & Gerhart, 1996, p. 793).

The review by Boselie et al. (2005) reveals an enormous variety of different practices being used in the 104 studies they analysed. There is no single agreed, or fixed, list of HR practices or systems of practices used to define or measure HRM. In total, Boselie et al. (2005) identified 26 different practices that are used in different studies, of which the top four, in order of popularity, are training and development, contingent pay and reward schemes, performance management (including appraisal), and careful recruitment and selection. The meta-analysis conducted by Combs et al. (2006) also noted a lack of consistency in which practices are assessed across a range of studies. Their review identified 22 practices that researchers had described as HPWPs. However, they narrowed these down to the 13 that they believed consensus had emerged around (incentive compensation, training, compensation level, participation, selectivity, internal promotion, HR planning, flexible work, performance appraisal, grievance procedures, teams, information sharing and employment security). Yet, they found that studies had employed a range from 2–13 practices, with the average and median number of practices studied being 6.2 and 5, respectively.

This problem of consistency extends beyond the specific practices, but is even evident in defining the goal of the system of HRM practices. For instance, authors have focused variously on high involvement work systems (Lawler, 1986), high performance work systems (Huselid, 1995), or commitment-based HR systems (Collins & Smith, 2006; Boxall & Macky, 2009). Such lack of consistency led Kepes and Delery (2007) to suggest that 'nearly all the empirical studies have measured different HRM practices and constructed HRM strategy and system measures in different ways.' (p. 57). Thus, in spite change of all the research conducted on the HRM–performance relationship, one is struck by the fact that the field has still not reached any consensus regarding what HRM is and which HR practices, arranged within which system, constitute the drivers of firm performance.

How should HRM practices be measured?

Even if consensus emerged regarding the specific set or system of HR practices that effectively drive higher performance, one next must address the question as to how to measure them. This entails making research design decisions regarding the source (who, individually or collectively, to ask about the HRM practices), the scale (what type of rating scale is used), and the scope (what employee group or groups are the focus) of the measurement.

For instance, in Huselid's classic study (1995) he sent surveys to the top HR person at corporate head offices (source). This respondent was asked to indicate the percent of employees (scale) covered by each practice. Then these ratings were made twice: once for managerial, professional and technical employees, and once for hourly and manual employees (scope). At the other extreme, Wright et al. (2005) surveyed between 20 and 100 per cent of employees (source), asking them whether or not (yes/no/don't know) each practice was used (scale) in their particular job (scope).

These differing measurement strategies suggest different assumptions regarding who can provide the most accurate reports of HR practices, what dimensions of the practices provide the most valid descriptions (e.g.; use, coverage, effectiveness, etc.) and the unit of measurement over which one can provide an accurate report of these practices. These different assumptions may each be right, and simply point to different constructs that are being assessed. For instance, Becker and Huselid (2001) and Gerhart et al. (2000b) distinguished between the HR policies (i.e. what the organization has defined as the practices that should be used by managers/supervisors) and HR practices (those actually used by a manager/supervisor and their subordinates). Each of these are quite valid and interesting constructs, and each may have different sets of antecedents and consequences. However, researchers need to carefully plan the measurement strategy to be consistent with the construct they seek to assess. The questions of which HR practices and how to measure them deal specifically with the challenge to develop a theory of HRM. Next we turn to the theory of performance.

What is performance?

One of the significant contributions of Huselid's 1995 study was the demonstration of an empirical relationship between HRM and corporate financial performance. This sparked a spate of studies examining some form of organizational performance such as accounting profits, economic profits, productivity, customer satisfaction, and so on. Many studies relied on accounting/financial/market measures of performance because such measures were publicly available through corporate reporting databases. However, whether using public data or self-report data, the vast majority of studies has defined performance from a strongly managerialist perspective, using performance measures most important to shareholders.

Rogers and Wright (1998) suggested that the use of public data was unnecessarily pushing research at a corporate level, with a narrow range of outcomes. They suggested performance information markets (PIM) as a broader alternative approach to assessing firm or unit performance. This approach entails identifying the extent to which the firm is satisfying important stakeholders. They proposed four main information markets relevant to HRM and performance research: the financial market, the labour market, the consumer/product market, and the political/social market. Such a stakeholder-oriented approach has been advocated by others such as Paauwe (2004) and Boxall and Purcell (2008). In fact, Panayotopoulou et al. (2003) used a competing values framework (similar to the PIM) and found different relationships between different aspects of HR and financial versus market performance. For public sector organizations in areas such as health and education, the relevant indicators of performance are unlikely to be financial. Yet public sector organizations have received relatively little attention in research on HRM and performance.

In addition, a number of researchers have rightly noted that much of the existing research carries managerialist assumptions, particularly in the choice of outcomes (e.g. Godard, 2004; Francis & Keegan, 2006; Keegan & Boselie, 2006; Delbridge & Keenoy, 2010). The question arises as to whether or not HRM practices might positively affect firm performance through exploiting workers in a way that has detrimental effects on their well-being. This suggests that a wider range of outcomes should be considered, including impacts on employees and customers, and, in public sector organizations such as hospitals, on patients. Thus the theory of performance seems to be an area ripe for conceptual and empirical analysis.

How are HRM practices implemented?

Related to the previously discussed difference between policies and practices is the question of implementation. Inherently assumed in much of the research on HRM practices and performance is that supervisors simply do whatever the organization policy requires them to do. If the policy says that supervisors give formal performance appraisal feedback once a year, they do. If hiring managers are supposed to use structured interviews, they use them. Such assumptions underlie the approach of asking the head of HR about the HRM practices that exist. However, these assumptions probably rarely, if ever, match reality. In some cases supervisors may be new or unaware of the plethora of HRM practice requirements. In other cases, they may be aware, but simply unwilling to implement them. For instance, many organizations track the percentage of completed performance appraisals, but these rarely reach 100 per cent, indicating that at least some supervisors are either unaware of or ignoring this job requirement.

In addition to the question of whether or not supervisors are actually implementing the practices comes the issue of how well they are implementing them. For instance, supervisors differ widely in their leadership and communication styles. So two supervisors conducting a performance appraisal session might vary in the effectiveness with which each communicates support, identifies development needs, and develops action plans. Such implementation issues have been largely ignored within the HRM–performance literature, yet they may be critical to developing a deeper understanding regarding this relationship. In fact, regarding the first three questions, Guest has concluded that 'we remain uncertain about how to measure HR practices and HR implementation. We have made little progress in establishing ways to measure an HR system' (2011, pp. 10–11).

How do HRM practices impact performance?

Earlier in the chapter we discussed the basic elements of a theory of how HRM and performance are related. However, many of the existing models of this relationship focus purely at the organizational or unit level of analysis, ignoring the individuals who constitute the focal actors in the process (Wright & Haggerty, 2005).

For instance, the Becker et al. (1997) model posits that HRM practices impact the creativity, productivity and discretionary behaviour of the workforce. However, in the context of the previously discussed issues, each individual employee may, in fact, experience a different HRM system. His or her supervisor may or may not implement the HRM policies, and when implemented, each may do so with different styles and different levels of effectiveness. In addition, each employee brings his/her own values and experiences as a lens through which to perceive, interpret and evaluate the practice. For instance, Nishii et al. (2008) found that it was employees' attributions about the HR practices that was the greater determinant of their reactions.

In other words, much of the earlier work on the HRM–performance relationship has been conducted at the unit level, simply assuming a set of individual level processes. More recent research and theorizing has begun to explore multi-level processes (e.g. van de Voorde et al., 2010b; Ployhart & Moliterno, 2011). In addition, van de Voorde et al. (2011) provide a systematic review of relationships between HRM, employee well-being and organizational performance. Empirical work by Kroon et al. (2009) compares two individual-level processes that might mediate the relationship between high-performance work practices implemented by organizations and employee burnout. Furthermore, Wood et al. (2012) utilize a multi-level model of well-being (including job satisfaction and job stress) as a mediator of the relationship between high-involvement management and organizational performance.

This line of research indicates that in order to clearly understand the relationship between HRM and performance, one must attempt to understand how practices impact individuals, who may then collectively impact performance.

How do we statistically model the HRM–performance relationship?

An additional challenge facing researchers in the HRM–performance arena revolves around the rigour of design and statistical modelling of the relationship. For instance, regarding design, Wall and Wood (2005) noted three generic types of designs. Cross-sectional designs assess all the variables at one time and, while efficient, provide a weak foundation for making causal inferences. Quasi-longitudinal designs assess HRM practices at one point and performance at some later point in time. Finally, most rigorous (for inferring cause) are 'authentic longitudinal' designs, which assess HRM and performance at multiple points in time, and are most valid for drawing causal inferences. However, they noted of the 25 studies they reviewed, 21 used cross-sectional designs. Two of the studies were quasi-longitudinal and two authentic longitudinal. However, the one authentic longitudinal design (Ichniowski et al., 2001) finding a positive relationship between HRM and performance suffers from a measurement issue in that it was what Wright et al. (2005) referred to as a 'retrospective' design where respondents were asked on a given date to recall and report the HR practices that existed at previous points in time. The remaining strong authentic longitudinal study (Cappelli & Neumark, 2001), as defined by Wall and Wood, found limited support for the efficacy of HRM in driving performance. More recently, van de Voorde et al. (2010a) studied longitudinal relationships between employee survey data on HRM-related change processes and objective business unit performance. Using two data waves, this study showed that business unit profits could be predicted by employee survey information on factors driven by HRM-related interventions after correcting for prior profits.

In addition to design issues is the actual statistical modelling of the relationship. Statistical modeling entails understanding all the types and sources of variance that exist in the measures and how each can lead to biasing the observed relationship. For instance, Gerhart et al. (2000b) discussed the various sources of measurement error (error due to items, source and time) that exist in measures of HRM practices. By showing that significant error due to source can exist, they suggested that more reliable measures of HRM practices could be procured by relying on multiple, as opposed to single, respondents. In addition, they showed how such error variance could bias, either positively or negatively, the observed relationship between HR and performance.

The modelling issue is not limited to single variables, but also to the relationship itself. For instance, Becker and Huselid (2006) note that omitted variable bias can occur when a variable is correlated with both the independent and dependent variables, and that failing to account for it can impact the magnitude and the direction of the observed relationship. Clearly, the statistical modelling of the HRM–performance relationship deserves further attention.

Answering the unanswered questions

The questions posed earlier frame a set of theoretical and research issues that need to be addressed if the HRM–performance relationship is to be better understood. The subsequent chapters allow some of the leading researchers in this area to begin to unravel the issues and questions posed, and to provide a set of guidelines and recommendations for future work that could enlighten the field.

The rest of the book is structured around two themes. The first section focuses on the theories and/or conceptual models for the processes through which HRM impacts performance. It begins in Chapter 2 with a detailed analysis and review by Riccardo Peccei, Karina van de Voorde and Marc van Veldhoven of the extent to which HRM can result in positive outcomes for both the organization and its employees. They therefore expand the view of performance beyond the narrow definition of financial performance to explore the impact of HRM on employee well-being. In Chapter 3, Peter Boxall presents a detailed analysis of the concept of high performance work systems and the role of HR practices and HR systems. One of the recurring themes in research on HRM and performance concerns the concept of 'fit'. This is central both to the link to business strategy but also to the analysis of the concept of an HR system. In Chapter 4, Jaap Paauwe, Corine Boon, Paul Boselie and Deanne den Hartog analyse in some detail the various ways in which fit has been used in the literature, and present an integrated framework to stimulate future research. In Chapter 5 the issue of HR processes is further explored by David Guest and Anna Bos-Nehles, who analyse the concept of implementation of HR and again present a framework within which future research might progress. Chapter 6, by Patrick Wright and Lisa Nishii, forms the last chapter of our first section and focuses on theories and/or conceptual models. They present the case for the incorporation of multi-level processes in studying how HRM impacts individual employees and, through this, affects organizational performance.

The second section explores more deeply some of the challenges in measuring constructs within the HRM–performance relationship. In Chapter 7, Gary McMahan and Christopher Harris focus on the measurement of human capital. In Chapter 8, Angela Langevin, Susanne Beijer, Jessica Federman, Michel Hermans, Felice Klein, Elizabeth McClean and Brian Martinson review the vast volume of HRM practices that have been measured in this vein of research, provide guidance regarding the most important HRM practices that should be included in research on the HRM–performance relationship and discuss in detail, drawing on best practice research evidence, the ways in which HR practices should be measured. In Chapter 9, Barry Gerhart explores a number of the challenges in statistically modelling the HRM–performance relationship and outlines the steps that need to be taken to arrive at more confident conclusions from our research. Chapter 10, by Sophie de Winne and Luc Sels, explores the evidence about the relationship between HRM and performance in small and medium-sized enterprises. This is a necessary antidote to the typical focus on research in large organizations. It also serves to broaden the perspective and, if there had been a larger body of relevant research, we might also have wished to include a chapter on HRM and performance in public sector and not-for-profit organizations. Finally, in Chapter 11 the editors bring the many ideas together to provide a clear roadmap for theory, research and application in the HRM–performance relationship.

Research and theorizing on the relationship between HRM and performance has the potential to have a significant impact on organizational performance and employee well-being. For these reasons, it is an important topic for research. It has already significantly influenced the credibility of HRM within organizations, as reflected in influential and widely sold books such as Huselid et al.'s *The Workforce Scorecard* (2005). As this research expands in terms of the issues addressed, extends the theoretical understanding of how HRM can impact performance and continues to grow in rigour, there is the potential for HRM to become more firmly established both as an academic discipline and a valuable business function. Our hope is that the ideas and suggestions provided in this book can be a springboard to furthering this evolution.

2

HRM, WELL-BEING AND PERFORMANCE: A THEORETICAL AND EMPIRICAL REVIEW

RICCARDO PECCEI, KARINA VAN DE VOORDE
AND MARC VAN VELDHOVEN

Introduction

Human resource management (HRM) is a relatively new field of inquiry, no more than about 25 years old. Over this period the primary focus of much of the literature in the area has been on the link between HRM and organizational performance; on the impact that human resource (HR) practices have on various aspects of firm performance (Huselid, 1995; Becker & Gerhart, 1996; Wright & Boswell, 2002; Combs et al., 2006). Starting in the late 1990s and spurred in part by critical writers in the area (e.g. Keenoy, 1990; Legge, 1995, 2000), researchers begun to focus more directly on employee-centred outcomes and to look explicitly at the effect that HR practices have on employee well-being, attitudes and behaviour at work. Important early contributions to this stream of research explicitly designed to 'build the worker into HRM' (Guest, 2002) include the work of Appelbaum et al. (2000; Appelbaum, 2002) in the US, of Godard (2001) in Canada, and of Guest (2001, 2002) and of Ramsay et al. (2000) in the UK. There is now a considerable body of research examining the effects of HRM on both employee and organizational outcomes and focusing specifically on the relationship between HR practices, employee well-being (WB) and organizational performance (OP) (Orlitzky & Frenkel, 2005; Wright et al., 2005; Vanhala & Tuoni, 2006).

Despite this growing body of work, there is still considerable debate about the precise nature of the relationship between HRM, well-being and organizational performance. An understanding of this relationship is important not only in its own right, but also in terms of the wider 'black box' (Boxall & Purcell, 2008) debate in the HRM literature. Despite the growing evidence of a positive association between HRM and various aspects of organizational performance (Boselie et al., 2005; Becker & Huselid, 1998; Combs et al., 2006), our understanding of the factors and processes that may help to mediate the HRM–performance relationship is still limited (Wright & Gardner, 2003b; Bowen & Ostroff, 2004; Wall & Wood, 2005). This so-called 'black box' problem is widely regarded as one of the key issues requiring further attention in the field of strategic HRM (Becker & Gerhart, 1996; Guest, 1997; Boxall & Purcell, 2008). In response, a number of models of the impact of HRM on organizational performance have been proposed. Central to many of these models is the idea that the effect of HRM on organizational performance mainly goes through people. In other words, employee psychological, attitudinal and behavioural outcomes at work, including employee well-being, are hypothesized to play a key role in understanding the impact of HR practices on organizational performance (Huselid, 1995; Becker et al., 1997; Guest, 1997; Paauwe & Richardson, 1997; Appelbaum et al., 2000; Wright & Gardner, 2003).

The present systematic review and analysis of the relationship between HRM, WB and OP is designed to clarify the extent to which HR practices do indeed have an effect on important employee, as well as organizational, outcomes. In the process, it is also designed to contribute to a better understanding of the role that employee well-being plays in mediating the impact of HRM on performance, thereby contributing to the wider 'black box' debate in the HRM literature. More specifically, our aim in this chapter is two-fold. First, we aim to look back and provide a systematic overview of extant theoretical and empirical work on the relationship between HRM, employee well-being and organizational performance. And second, based on this analysis, we aim to highlight key knowledge gaps in the area and identify important lines for future research that can contribute to a better theoretical and empirical understanding of the HRM–WB–OP relationship.

The rest of the chapter is organized as follows. In the next section we provide working definitions of the focal HRM, well-being and organizational performance constructs, and clarify and delimit the scope of our analysis. We then set out alternative interpretations and models of the HRM–WB–OP relationship, identifying key theoretical arguments and mechanisms underpinning current explanations of the impact of HR practices and systems on various aspects of employee well-being and organizational performance. This is followed by a systematic qualitative review of extant research that has examined the link between HRM and various aspects of both well-being and performance. We then extend and refine the theoretical and empirical analysis by adopting a contingency perspective on the HRM–WB–OP relationship and consider possible factors that may affect the links between the focal variables of interest. We conclude by first highlighting key open questions about the HRM–WB–OP relationship and then identifying important avenues of future research in the area.

Conceptual focus and definitions

Understanding the relationship between HRM, WB and OP is made more difficult not only by the complex multi-dimensional nature of the three constructs involved, but also by the lack of agreement about their actual meaning and coverage. As a result, when considering the relationship between HRM, WB and OP, it is not uncommon for researchers to focus on different aspects or dimensions of the constructs in question, thereby making cumulative theoretical and empirical progress more difficult in this area. To clarify the focus and conceptual boundaries of the present analysis, we start with a brief discussion and definition of the three focal constructs of interest.

Human resource management

Broadly speaking, HRM refers to 'all those activities associated with the management of people in firms' (Boxall & Purcell, 2008, p. 1). However, as is widely recognized in the HRM literature (Becker & Gerhart, 1996; Wright & Boswell, 2002; Boselie et al., 2005), there is no real consensus about 'the exact HR practices that make up a coherent HRM system' (Delery, 1998, p. 296). Here we adopt a broad approach to the notion of HRM; specifically, we conceptualize HRM systems as comprising a wide range of practices covering all main aspects of the management of people in organizations. This includes, for example, policies and practices in the areas of recruitment and selection, induction and socialization, training and development, job design, performance management, pay, rewards and recognition, upward and downward communication, numerical flexibility, job security, employee welfare, and so on. Importantly, our interest is not only in the range of more 'advanced', 'progressive' or 'high-road' HR practices commonly associated with high-performance work systems (HPWS) (Huselid, 1995; Appelbaum et al., 2000) and with high commitment (Arthur, 1994; Pfeffer, 1998) and high involvement (Batt, 2000) models of HRM. These practices include, for example, sophisticated recruitment and selection procedures, extensive training and development for employees, decentralized systems of job design coupled with extensive forms of offline participation, systematic performance management involving regular performance appraisals, goal-setting and feedback, high organizationally based comparative levels of pay, extensive non-financial benefits and rewards for employees, extensive information-sharing, status equalization and employee welfare policies, internal promotions systems and job security guarantees, and individual and collective grievance procedures. Our interest here is also in the low pay, long hours, tight monitoring, low job discretion and low job security HR practices usually associated with more 'exploitative', 'low-road', 'transactional' systems of HRM (Guest & Hoque, 1994; Tsui et al., 1997; Ramsay et al., 2000).

Employee well-being

Our focus is on employee work-related well-being, which, following Warr (1987), can be broadly defined as the overall quality of an individual's subjective experience and functioning at work. Two main dimensions of well-being at work are commonly identified in the literature (Grant et al., 2007). The first dimension refers to individuals' subjective experiences at work. This dimension, which is often referred to as 'happiness well-being' (Grant et al., 2007), covers elements such as overall and facet-specific aspects of job satisfaction, and both positive and negative work-related affect. Although more debatable, it is also said to cover broader positive attitudes at work, such as aspects of organizational commitment. Here we adopt this broader conceptualization and focus on employee affective commitment (AC) to the organization as a key additional indicator of well-being relating to individuals' broader sense of integration and belonging at the workplace.

The second dimension is concerned with physiological and psychological aspects of employee health at work, including, for example, job-related anxiety, stress, burnout and exhaustion (Danna & Griffin, 1999). A further distinction that is increasingly made in the occupational health and well-being literature is between negative/passive and positive/active aspects of employee health and well-being (Maslach et al., 2001; Spreitzer et al., 2005; Warr, 2007). At the negative/passive end the emphasis is on strain-related aspects of health and well-being, such as fatigue, anxiety and (lack of) satisfaction, while at the positive/active end the emphasis is not merely on the absence of 'unwell-being' but on more active constructs such as vitality, thriving, vigour and energy at work (Schaufeli & Bakker, 2004; Spreitzer et al., 2005; Dorenbosch, 2009). Our interest here is in both the happiness and health-related dimensions of well-being, covering both negative/passive and positive/active aspects of the phenomenon.

Organizational performance

Different aspects or dimensions of organizational performance are commonly distinguished in the HRM literature. In particular, drawing on Dyer and Reeves' (1995) original, four-fold classification of organizational performance outcomes, researchers often distinguish between proximal and distal outcomes (Guest, 1997; Paauwe & Richardson, 1997). Proximal outcomes are ones that, in causal terms, can be expected to be more closely and directly linked to the HR practices adopted by the organization. These include the so-called HR and organizational outcomes identified by Dyer and Reeves (1995), such as organizational absence and turnover rates, productivity, quality, and service performance. In contrast, distal outcomes cover aspects of the overall financial and market performance of the organization that are less likely to be directly affected by the HR practices in place, such as return on capital, market value, return on investment and market share (Dyer & Reeves, 1995). In the theoretical discussion we focus primarily on more proximal performance outcomes. In the empirical review section, however, we also cover studies that have focused on more distal financial and market performance outcomes.

When examining the HRM–WB–OP relationship it is important to bear in mind that, in addition to well-being, there are other employee-related factors that may help to mediate the effect of HR practices on performance. The employee ability, motivation and opportunity (AMO) framework (Becker et al., 1997; Appelbaum et al., 2000; Boxall & Purcell, 2008) suggests, for example, that while HR practices can influence performance by affecting employee well-being (and therefore motivation) at work, they may also affect performance through the impact they have on employee skills and on individuals' opportunity to use their skills at work. More specifically, human capital models of HRM, for example, emphasize the impact of high-performance work systems on performance through the enhancement of employee knowledge, skills and abilities (Snell & Dean, 1992; Crook et al., 2011), while relational models of HRM go beyond the AMO framework and suggest that HPWS can improve organizational performance by strengthening relationships and coordination between employees (Gittell et al., 2010). Similarly, the 'strong' model of HRM proposed by Bowen and Ostroff (2004) suggests that HRM system strength can significantly affect firm performance by creating strong, focused organizational climates that help to structure and direct employee effort and behaviour towards the achievement of key desired organizational goals. Moreover, not all motivational links between HRM and performance need necessarily go through employee well-being, including organizational commitment. Transactional models of HRM suggest, for example, that one key route through which HRM systems can affect organizational performance is by emphasizing extrinsic employee rewards and motivation, thereby enhancing individuals' willingness to engage in standard aspects of in-role performance (Tsui et al., 1997).

The alternative non-well-being-related pathways of the link between HRM, employee outcomes and organizational performance outlined above, together with the focal well-being-related pathway, are shown in Figure 2.1. Two points are worth noting about the different pathways: first, the pathways shown are not exhaustive, nor are they mutually exclusive; second, although analytically distinct, the various pathways are not always clearly distinguished in empirical studies of the relationship between HRM and performance.

Figure 2.1   Some alternative employee-related pathways linking HRM and organizational performance

Alternative models of the HRM–WB–OP relationship

Different overall models and interpretations of the relationship between HRM, employee well-being and organizational performance have been proposed in the literature. Here, we outline two main contributions designed to capture key alternative views of the link between the three variables of interest. The first is the typology of different perspectives on the HRM–WB–OP relationship proposed by Peccei (2004) and the second is the set of alternative models of this relationship identified by van de Voorde (2010). On this basis we then propose a more refined and articulated view of the relationship between the three variables of interest that synthesizes and extends Peccei's (2004) and van de Voorde's (2010) analyses.

Peccei (2004) identified two main perspectives on the HRM–WB–OP relationship in the extant literature. Central to the first, so-called 'optimistic' perspective is the idea that HRM is beneficial for employees and that it has a generally positive impact on their well-being. In particular, the adoption by management of more advanced and progressive HR practices (associated for example with HPWS or with high-commitment models of HRM) is expected to lead to higher levels of job discretion and empowerment for employees, and to the establishment of a generally more interesting, supportive and rewarding work environment. All this, in turn, should result in a better quality of work life for employees and contribute to maximizing employee positive affective reactions at work. In line with behavioural theories of HRM (Wright & MacMahan, 1992; Guest, 1997; Becker & Huselid, 1998; Appelbaum et al., 2000) and basic social exchange theory arguments (Gouldner, 1960; Blau, 1964), employees can then be expected to repay the organization by working harder, putting in extra effort and engaging in various forms of citizenship behaviour, thus actively contributing to enhance the overall productivity and performance of the organization. In brief, the optimistic view not only sees both employers and employees as directly benefitting from HRM; it also suggests that well-being itself plays a key role in enhancing organizational performance.

In contrast, according to Peccei (2004), the second, so-called 'pessimistic' perspective views HRM as essentially harmful to employees and as having a negative impact on their interests and well-being. Central to this view – and drawing on aspects of labour process theory (Godard, 2001; Appelbaum, 2002) – is the idea that the adoption of apparently more progressive and advanced high-performance practices by organizations normally leads to an intensification of work and to a generally more systematic exploitation of employees on the shop floor (Delbridge & Turnbull, 1992; Ramsay et al., 2000; Appelbaum, 2002), often accompanied by increased levels of surveillance and monitoring of work effort (Sewell & Wilkinson, 1992; Barker, 1993). Far from being better off, therefore, employees under HRM have to work harder, have less control and are under greater pressure at work. This may well help to enhance organizational productivity and performance, but it can be expected to have a negative effect on the overall well-being of the workforce. According to the pessimistic view, therefore, it is above all employers and not employees who are likely to benefit from HRM – although in many circumstances,

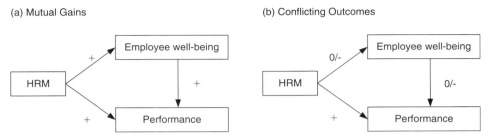

Figure 2.2   Alternative models of the role of employee well-being in the HRM-organizational performance relationship

according to some critical scholars (Willmott, 1993; Legge, 1995; Keenoy, 1997), employees may well be duped by the rhetoric of HRM into thinking that they too are better off.

Recently, van de Voorde (2010) updated and extended Peccei's (2004) analysis. She distinguished two main models of the HRM–WB–OP relationship that she labelled the 'mutual gains' and the 'conflicting outcomes' model respectively (see Figure 2.2). The mutual gains model, shown in Figure 2.2(a), basically corresponds to Peccei's (2004) optimistic interpretation of the HRM–WB–OP relationship. Specifically, based on behavioural theories of HRM (Wright & MacMahan, 1992; Appelbaum et al., 2000) and on social exchange arguments (Gouldner, 1990), the mutual gains model hypothesizes that HRM has a positive impact on both employee well-being and organizational performance. Importantly though, in her discussion of the mutual gains model, van de Voorde (2010) extends the analysis of the link between HRM and well-being to cover not only the type of individual-level mechanisms associated with the behavioural and social exchange theory arguments outlined here, but also aggregate-level mechanisms. In particular, she draws attention to Bowen and Ostroff's (2004) multi-level model of HRM and the idea that strong HRM systems can positively affect shared employee psychological states, attitudes and behaviours by reinforcing shared employee perceptions of their work environment and contributing to the development of a strong and positive organizational climate. More generally, the mutual gains model also hypothesizes a positive effect of well-being on performance, thereby suggesting that the HRM–OP relationship is at least partially mediated by employee well-being.

The alternative conflicting outcomes model, shown in Figure 2.2(b), links to aspects of Peccei's (2004) pessimistic perspective. Specifically, drawing on Paauwe (2009), Peccei (2004) and Boxall and Purcell (2008), as well as on Quinn and Rohrbaugh's (1983) competing values framework, van de Voorde (2010) notes that the HR practices that maximize employee well-being may not only be different from those that maximize organizational performance, but that there may be an active trade-off in terms of outcomes. In other words, the HR practices that contribute to organizational performance may have no effect – or even a negative effect – on employee well-being, and vice versa. In its strongest version, the competing outcomes model suggests that, in line with the labour theory arguments outlined earlier (Ramsay et al., 2000; Godard, 2001), enhancements in organizational performance are achieved at the cost of reduced employee well-being. To the extent that HRM has a positive impact on performance, therefore, this effect is established through negative employee well-being effects. In brief, the conflicting outcomes model suggests that while HRM has a positive effect on performance, it has either a negative effect or no effect on well-being, which, in turn, is also expected to have either a negative effect or no effect on performance.

By way of summary, we combine Peccei's (2004) and van de Voorde's (2010) analyses and propose three main overall models of the relationship between HRM, well-being and performance. These models are summarized in Figure 2.3. They include both a weak and a strong variant of a mutual gains interpretation of the HRM–WB–OP relationship and a conflicting outcomes model. It is worth noting that all models basically assume a positive relationship between HRM, in its various forms, and organizational performance. This direct HRM–OP link is consistent with the multiple pathways idea discussed earlier and summarized in Figure 2.1.

The weak version of the mutual gains model in Figure 2.3 (Model 1(a)) is a simple win-win model involving positive parallel, but unrelated, employee and organizational outcomes. Specifically, in this case HRM is hypothesized to have a direct beneficial effect on both the well-being of employees and the performance of the organization, but no additional link is hypothesized from well-being to performance. In other words, well-being is not assumed to mediate any of the effects of HR practices on performance. In contrast, in the strong version of the mutual gains model (Model 1(b)), the relationship between HRM, WB and OP is assumed to be more complex. In this case HRM is expected to have a positive impact on both WB and OP but, in addition, well-being itself is hypothesized to have a positive

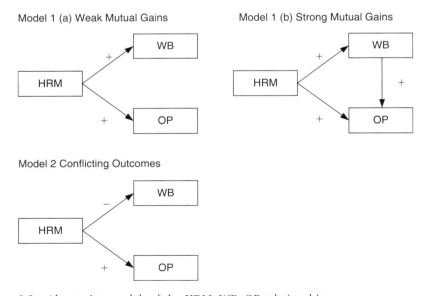

Figure 2.3   Alternative models of the HRM–WB–OP relationship

effect on performance. Here, therefore, the positive effect of HRM on performance is assumed to operate, at least in part, through the positive effect that HR practices have on employee well-being. Well-being, in other words, is assumed to partially and positively mediate the HRM-OP relationship.

The conflicting outcomes model (Model 2) is a simple win-lose model where HRM is expected to be beneficial to organizational performance but harmful to employee well-being. Specifically, this model suggests that, to a large extent, the positive impact of HRM on performance results from the adoption of exploitative HR practices that are likely to have a negative effect on employee well-being. In the medium- to long-term this negative effect on well-being may well undermine performance by, for example, leading to higher levels of absence and turnover. On the whole, however, proponents of a conflicting outcomes interpretation do not explicitly focus on the link between employee well-being and organizational performance. This is because they tend to view employee well-being more as a parallel outcome – as a by-product of management's pursuit of higher organizational performance – than as a causal mechanism mediating the HRM–OP relationship. As a result, we have not included an explicit link from WB to OP in the conflicting outcomes model.

Theoretical arguments and analytical approaches

Having identified key alternative models of the HRM–WB–OP relationship, we now develop the analysis further by examining some of the main theoretical arguments underpinning the different models. As background to this theoretical review, a number of preliminary points need to be highlighted. First, for the reasons already noted, our focus here is on possible explanations of the link between HRM and well-being and between well-being and performance, rather than on the direct link between HRM and performance. Second, explanations of the relationships of interest in studies that have focused explicitly on the HRM–WB–OP relationship are often quite general and/or compressed, and tend to draw on a limited range of theoretical perspectives. Here, therefore, we go beyond these more narrowly-focused HRM studies and highlight a fuller range of arguments in support of the WB-OP and HRM-WB relationship derived from the wider organizational behaviour (OB) and organizational/industrial psychology (OIP). literatures. For example, we consider arguments linked to broaden-and-build theory (Fredrickson, 2001), emotional contagion theory (Hatfield et al., 1994), the job demands-resources model (Demerouti et al., 2001), and conservation of resources theory (Hobfoll, 1989). For ease of presentation we work backwards and start with the well-being–performance relationship.

Well-being–performance relationship

Theoretically, a number of different explanations have been proposed for a positive effect of employee well-being on performance. One of the most common explanations, associated in particular with early versions of the 'happy-productive worker' thesis (Staw, 1986; Cropanzano & Wright, 2001) and with inducements-contributions conceptualizations of the employment relationship (March & Simon, 1958; Tsui et al., 1997), is in terms of social exchange theory (Blau, 1964) and the norm of reciprocity (Gouldner, 1960). Central to this explanation, as we have seen, is the idea that employees that are satisfied with their jobs and – because of the positive treatment and inducements they receive from the organization – are committed to the organization and enjoy high positive affect at work, are more likely to repay the organization by working hard and by engaging in various forms of discretionary effort and of organizational citizenship behaviour (OCB) (Organ, 1988; Meyer & Allen, 1997; Meyer et al., 2002) In the aggregate and over time, these OCBs are likely to enhance the overall effectiveness of the organization (Organ et al., 2006). This line of argument, as might be expected, is emphasized in particular in commitment-based models of HRM that suggest that a key route through which HR practices can affect organizational performance is by enhancing organizational commitment, thereby enhancing employees' willingness and motivation to engage in both in-role and discretionary behaviours at work (Arthur, 1994; Pfeffer, 1998; Appelbaum et al., 2000; Whitener, 2001; Kehoe & Wright, forthcoming).

An alternative explanation of the positive effect of well-being on performance that has attracted increasing attention in recent years is in terms of Fredrickson's (2001) broaden-and-build (B&B) theory of positive emotions. This theory suggests that unlike negative emotions that narrow an individual's immediate thought-action repertoire, such as fear or anxiety, positive emotions, such as joy, contentment and interest, broaden awareness and promote discovery of novel and creative behaviours, ideas and social bonds. For example, 'joy sparks the urge to play, interest sparks the urge to explore, contentment sparks the urge to savour and integrate' (Fredrickson, 2004, p. 1367). In turn, these more novel, varied and exploratory thoughts and actions help to build individuals' physical, psychological, intellectual and social resources, which they can later draw upon for more effective coping and survival. Accordingly, positive affect can be expected to contribute both to in-role and to discretionary performance (including, for example, various forms of prosocial and helping behaviour) by enhancing an individual's capacity to cope with job demands, heightening search and creative behaviour, and stimulating problem-solving and interaction with others, while at the same time building intellectual resources via learning processes and social resources by fostering relationships and networks (Fredrickson & Branigan, 2005; Salanova et al., 2010).

The performance predictions of B&B theory are consistent with earlier work by Isen and his colleagues (e.g. Isen et al., 1987; Isen, 2000), suggesting that positive emotions can enhance performance at work by increasing flexibility, creativity, integration and efficiency of thought. They are also consistent with 'feeling good, doing good' arguments (George & Brief, 1992) positing that, for a variety of reasons, including the desire to maintain their current positive mood, individuals that experience high positive affect are more likely to engage in altruistic and helping behaviours. These helping behaviours on the part of employees are particularly important in service contexts where they can make a significant contribution to customer satisfaction and, hence, to overall service performance (Bettencourt & Brown, 1997; Peccei & Rosenthal, 2001).

In service contexts, emotional contagion theory (Hatfield et al., 1994) is also of particular relevance for explaining the well-being–performance relationship. Specifically, emotional contagion refers to the transfer of positive or negative emotions from one person to another and the tendency, consequently, for inter-acting individuals to converge emotionally (Pugh, 2001). On this basis, employees with high positive affect can be expected to transmit their positive mood both to fellow employees that they interact with at work and to the customers that they are in contact with and serve. In turn, this contagion process should have a direct positive effect on customer positive affect following the service encounter and, therefore, contribute to more positive customer evaluations of the service received (Pugh, 2001). Moreover, it should also help to generate a more positive group affective tone (George, 1996), hence further enhancing aggregate-level customer satisfaction and service performance.

Two general points about the theoretical arguments outlined here are worth noting. First, some of the theories, such as Fredrickson's (2001) broaden-and-build theory, are couched more at the individual than the aggregate level of analysis. The extent to which arguments based on such individual-level theories can be trans-lated to the aggregate level and used to explain the relationship between employee well-being and organizational rather than individual level performance remains open to question. In other words, the extent to which individual-level theories can be used to explain cross-level well-being–performance effects needs further consideration.

Second, even though the theoretical arguments outlined earlier are explicitly designed to account for the impact of well-being on performance, both theoreti-cally and empirically, there is still debate about the order of causality between these two constructs. In particular, there is still considerable debate about whether individual and aggregate-level job satisfaction is an antecedent or outcome of individual and organizational performance respectively (Judge et al., 2001; Harter et al., 2002; Wright et al., 2005). Questions about direction of causality can also legitimately be raised with respect to B&B theory arguments, since high-per-forming individuals or units can be expected to be able to accumulate and enjoy more resources. This in turn, as we argue more fully next, should have a positive impact on well-being. More generally therefore, issues about the direction of causality between well-being and performance, like issues about cross-level well-being–performance effects, require further theoretical attention.

HRM–well-being relationship

Although a number of explanations of the impact of HRM on employee well-being have been proposed, this link remains under-theorized in the sense of lacking a systematic and well-articulated set of arguments able to explain how and why HR practices and systems may actually affect different aspects of employee well-being. Generally speaking, claims about the impact of HRM on well-being are based on the often implicit idea or assumption that HR practices ultimately affect well-being by structuring and affecting employees' experiences at work. Underpinning this idea, in turn, are two separate but interrelated arguments that are not always clearly distinguished or explicitly articulated in the HRM literature. The first argument is that the nature and quality of employees' experiences at work and their perceptions of these experiences, or perceived working conditions for short, have a significant positive or negative effect on their well-being. The second argument is that the nature and quality of these work experiences are significantly affected by the HR practices and systems adopted by the organization. Next, we consider each of these arguments in turn.

Perceived working conditions–well-being link

This link has been the subject of quite extensive theorizing in the OB and OIP literatures. One stream of theorizing is linked to notions of psychological and organizational climate. 'Psychological climate' refers to individual employees' own personal perceptions of their work environment (Hellriegel & Slocum, 1974; Carr et al., 2003; Patterson et al., 2005), while 'organizational climate' refers to employees' shared, collective perceptions of their work environment (Kopelman et al., 1990; Patterson et al., 2005). The climate literature suggests a clear beneficial effect of both a positive psychological and organizational climate on a range of employee attitudes and behaviours at work, such as trust, satisfaction, commitment, innovation and customer service (Schneider et al., 1998; Schneider et al., 2002; Carr et al., 2003; Parker et al., 2003). On the whole, however, employee well-being issues *per se* have received only limited attention in the climate literature.

A second overlapping but distinct stream of theorizing focuses specifically on the impact that work experiences – or what Crawford et al. (2010) refer to as perceptions of work condition – have on various aspects of well-being from the standpoint of job demands and resources. Central to this second stream of theorizing is the idea that, because of their potential contribution to the satisfaction of important individual needs at work, work experiences are significant predictors of both happiness (e.g. satisfaction, commitment, positive affect) and health (e.g. burnout and work stress) aspects of well-being. In other words, both happiness and health aspects of well-being are directly related to perceived characteristics of the job and of the wider work environment, including for example job demands, job control, social support, distributive and procedural justice, promotion opportunities, job security, and so on (Karasek, 1979; Brief, 1997; Meyer & Allen, 1997; Spector & Jex, 1998). More recently, the job demands–resources (JD–R) model has been proposed as a way of parsimoniously classifying key job attributes and other related work experiences into two broad categories – namely, demands and resources (Demerouti et al., 2001). Crawford et al. (2010) have extended this model by suggesting a distinction between resources (e.g. job autonomy, supervisor support, feedback, access to information, development opportunities) and two kinds of job demands: challenge demands (e.g. job complexity, job responsibility, subjective workload) and hindrance demands (e.g. role ambiguity, role conflict, role overload). In particular, they theorized (and empirically showed) that resources are positively related to employee work engagement and negatively related to burnout. Challenge demands, on the other hand, are positively related to both burnout and engagement, while hindrance demands are positively related to burnout, but negatively related to engagement.

More recently, the JD–R model has been linked to Hobfoll's (1989) conservation of resources (COR) theory, thereby providing a powerful theoretical lens for analysing and understanding the effects of work experiences on well-being. Specifically, Hobfoll (2002, p. 307) defines resources as those entities or conditions (e.g. job control, social support, job security) that 'either are centrally valued in their own right, or act as means to obtain centrally valued ends'. According to COR theory, resources are important to individuals because they contribute to the achievement of positive personal outcomes such as better coping, adaptation and well-being. In the work context, for example, resources like task discretion and social support help individuals cope more effectively with job demands, such as role stress and ambiguity – hence individuals strive to acquire, protect and conserve resources for their future needs. More generally, COR theory suggests that individuals who possess more resources and who work in a more resource-rich environment, are more likely to experience positive well-being outcomes and less likely to experience negative outcomes such as burnout and stress (Hobfoll & Freedy, 1993).

COR theory and the JD–R model have been successfully applied to the analysis of burnout and employee work engagement (Halbesleben, 2006; Salanova et al., 2010). More generally, however, in the context of HRM research, it would be useful to consider more systematically the extent to which established JD–R–well-being relationships may be affected by a range of individual, organizational and institutional factors. At the individual level these moderators may include, for example, the age, skill and educational level of employees (Kooij, 2010). At the organizational and institutional level they may include, for example, different organizational configurations (Mintzberg, 1995) and different systems of training and education, collective bargaining, labour market structures, and other legal and cultural arrangements that are capable of shaping employee values and expectations at work and that are likely to be associated with different industrial sectors, employment regimes and varieties of capitalism (Hall & Soskice, 2001; Paauwe, 2004; Gallie, 2007).

HRM–perceived working conditions link

The theoretical arguments in support of this link are generally less focused and compelling than the ones reviewed above in connection with the impact of work experiences on well-being. In the HRM literature it is not uncommon to assume, for example, that because of the supposedly more sophisticated and progressive nature of the HR practices associated with HPWs, or with high-commitment and high-involvement models of HRM, these practices and systems can automatically be expected to result in a more positive work environment for employees (Pfeffer, 1998; Appelbaum et al., 2000; Ostroff & Bowen, 2000; Peccei, 2004; Takeuchi et al., 2007). These practices and systems may well help to enhance the quality of working life of employees, while at the same time helping to create a more positive climate at the workplace by signalling to employees management's general concern with their well-being at work (Ostroff & Bowen, 2000). However, there is no clear theoretical reason for expecting this to be the case. On the contrary, there are a number of reasons for expecting the impact of HR practices on work experiences to be potentially quite varied and unstable, and therefore difficult to predict.

One reason, for example, is that the impact of HR practices on working conditions may well vary depending on how effectively the practices themselves are implemented (Purcell & Kinnie, 2007; Boxall & Purcell, 2008). A second and related reason is linked to the distinction made by Nishii and Wright (2008) in their process model of HRM between the HR policies and practices that are intended by management, and the HR practices that are actually implemented in the organization. To the extent that first-line supervisors, for example, implement HR practices (e.g. performance appraisals) differently both within and across workgroups, employees within the same organization can be expected to have non-homogeneous work experiences. Third, as noted by Appelbaum (2002), HR practices may have contradictory effects on different working conditions. For example, while greater delegation of responsibility to employees may increase job satisfaction, it may also increase job pressure, thereby cancelling out the positive effects of increased job autonomy. Finally, it is often difficult to map work experiences with any precision onto HR practices. As a result, it can be difficult to understand and trace through the impact that HR practices and systems have on key work experiences and conditions that are known to have a significant effect on well-being, such as role clarity or supervisor support.

Recently, Nishii et al. (2008) have contributed to more systematic theorizing in this area by focusing on employees' beliefs about the reasons why management adopts the HR practices that it does. Specifically, they identify five main so-called HR attributions, including attributions that HR practices reflect a managerial philosophy focused on quality, cost reduction, employee well-being, employee exploitation and union compliance. On this basis they then suggest that quality and well-being-related attributions are likely to be associated with higher levels of employee satisfaction and commitment, while cost reduction and exploitation attributions are likely to be negatively related to satisfaction and commitment. Although Nishii et al.'s (2008) contribution does not directly address the HRM–working conditions link, it helps to open a fruitful line of analysis for understanding why employees may view and react to HR practices more or less positively. Clearly, though, an important question that then needs to be asked is what affects employees' HR attributions in the first place. Important factors here are likely to include existing levels of trust in the organization, the history of labour management relations or the presence of unions and the availability of alternative interpretations of managerial motives and actions. The core point is that, once again, it may not ultimately be possible to gain a proper understanding of the effect of HRM on employee experiences, attitudes and well-being in isolation from the wider organizational, institutional and historical context within which HR systems are embedded and operate.

Conclusion

More generally, our theoretical review suggests that it may not be possible simply to read off the existence of more or less positive work experiences (and ultimately, therefore, of more or less positive well-being effects) from particular HR practices or particular systems of practices. Rather, the effect of HR practices and systems on working conditions (and, through these, on employee well-being) is likely to be complex, highly context-specific and contingent. In particular, relevant effects are likely to vary depending on a number of factors, ranging from the way particular practices are actually implemented by line managers to the wider institutional and historical context of the organization. We return to some of these contextual and contingency arguments later in our discussion; for now, however, we turn to a systematic examination of the empirical evidence about the HRM–WB–OP relationship.

Review of research on the HRM–WB–OP relationship

Prior reviews of HRM research concluded that HRM is positively related to performance (e.g. Combs et al., 2006). Appelbaum (2002), on the other hand, found that it is difficult to draw any definitive conclusions about the effects of HRM on employee well-being. A shortcoming of these reviews is that they focus solely on the associations between HRM and employee well-being or between HRM and organizational performance; therefore, they reveal little about the effect of HRM on multiple stakeholders simultaneously (organizational performance and employee well-being). We aim to provide an up-to-date overview of what is known about the HRM–employee well-being–organizational performance relationship by reporting a review of quantitative studies that investigate the effects of HRM, WB and OP simultaneously. This approach allows us to study the triangle of relationships between HRM, employee well-being and organizational performance. In addition, it allows us to draw conclusions on the role of employee well-being in the HRM–performance relationship by answering the question: is there more empirical support in the research literature for a mutual gains (optimistic) perspective or for a conflicting outcomes (pessimistic) perspective?

To select empirical studies, a systematic literature search in international refereed journals in management, organizational behaviour, work and organizational psychology, applied psychology, as well as other journals known for their explicit HRM-related focus was conducted. We completed our literature search by cross-checking this list with the reference sections of 11 review studies (i.e. Becker & Gerhart, 1996; Becker & Huselid, 1998; Ferris et al., 1999; Wood, 1999; Appelbaum, 2002; Wright & Boswell, 2002; Peccei, 2004; Boselie et al., 2005; Wall & Wood, 2005; Wright et al., 2005; Combs et al., 2006). Only articles published from 1995 to 2010 were searched. The year 1995 is chosen as the earliest date of interest because it was in 1995 that Huselid published his peer-reviewed empirical milestone study about HRM and performance.

As regards the measurement of HRM, only studies looking into multiple HR practices covering main aspects of the management of people in organizations are included in this review. The reason for this is that employee and organizational outcomes are influenced by multiple management activities at any point in time rather than by a single management activity (Wright & Boswell, 2002). With respect to employee well-being, in this review, empirical articles are classified by the following two types of work-related well-being: happiness and health-related well-being (Danna & Griffin, 1999; Grant et al., 2007). It is important to take the distinction between these dimensions of well-being into account because it is possible that trade-offs exist between the different dimensions (Campion & McClelland, 1993; Appelbaum, 2002; Grant et al., 2007). The happiness component of employee well-being is focused on subjective experiences at work (Grant et al., 2007). We distinguish between satisfaction and commitment. Satisfaction is targeted at the job (including contextual features), while commitment is targeted at the organization as a whole (Fisher, 2010). With respect to employee health-related well-being (i.e. physiological and psychological indicators related to employee health, see Danna & Griffin, 1999), no studies on active constructs (e.g. vitality, energy at work) are yet reported in the literature. We therefore relied on the dominant approach in the occupational health literature to differentiate between stressors and strain (Spector & Jex, 1998). Within this approach, stressors (e.g. workload, work intensification) refer to events or situations that give rise to stress, while strain (e.g. stress, burnout) refers to a response to stressors. Based on Dyer and Reeves (1995) we focus on two main indicators of organizational performance: operational outcomes and financial outcomes (including financial and market performance) (see Boselie et al., 2005 and Paauwe, 2009 for a similar approach).

In order to assess the quality of the included studies, four key criteria recognized for their relevance in the HR field (Wall & Wood, 2005; Wright et al., 2005; Gerhart, 2007a) were identified. These four criteria are: (a) sample size and response rate; (b) quality of research design; (c) reliability and validity of the HRM, well-being and performance measures, and (d) the adequacy of the statistical test performed. Studies obtained a score for each criterion and were subsequently classified as excellent quality studies, good quality studies or average quality studies.

To answer our question we calculated the ratio of data points supportive of each perspective to the total number of data points per well-being dimension. Data points are in line with a mutual gains perspective if there is a positive effect of HRM on well-being and on performance. Support for conflicting outcomes is established if there is no effect or a negative effect of HRM on well-being and a positive effect of HRM on performance. Furthermore, we checked whether the results of the excellent quality studies were in line with the outcome of this ratio. To distinguish between weak and strong versions of the mutual gains perspective (see Figure 2.3), we also report for each data point whether the mediating role of employee well-being in the relationship between HRM and performance is investigated. If the effects of single HR practices on well-being and performance or the effects of HRM on operational and financial outcomes were examined in a study, we based our conclusion on the results of the majority of reported effects.

The literature search resulted in 23 studies. A considerable number of studies were published in HR-focused journals, for example, the *International Journal of Human Resource Management*. Other studies were published in journals in management (e.g. *British Journal of Management*) as well as in psychology (e.g. *Personnel Psychology*). Table 2.1 gives information on the study population, the measurement of HRM, employee well-being and organizational performance, and the quality rating. Two studies could be classified as excellent quality studies, nine studies as good quality studies and 12 studies as average quality studies. As regards employee well-being, if multiple well-being dimensions or multiple measures of a single well-being type were examined in a study, results are reported separately in terms of data points. The results are summarized in Table 2.2.

Happiness well-being

In a total of 21 studies, associations between HRM and happiness well-being (commitment (9), satisfaction (6) or a combination of commitment, satisfaction, and other happiness at work-related attitudes (9)) were investigated, resulting in 24 data points for our review. As regards commitment, a positive HRM–commitment relationship and a positive HRM–organizational performance relationship was established in seven studies (Hoque, 1999; Ramsay et al., 2000; Ahmad & Schroeder, 2003; Gould-Williams, 2003; Wright et al., 2003, 2005; Riordan et al., 2005). HRM also proved a positive predictor of satisfaction and organizational performance in the studies of Hoque (1999), Varma et al. (1999), Gould-Williams (2003) and Riordan et al. (2005). Four studies (Vandenberg et al., 1999; Park et al., 2003; Katou & Budhwar, 2006; Nishii et al., 2008) found a positive association between HRM and a combination of satisfaction and commitment and organizational performance.

Two data points showed that HRM was associated with happiness well-being but not with organizational performance (Orlitzky & Frenkel, 2005; Akdere, 2009). Paul and Anantharaman (2003) established a positive HRM–performance effect; however, they found no HRM–commitment effect. Five data points did not show significant relationships between HRM and happiness well-being (measured by satisfaction (1), commitment (1) and positive attitudes (3)) and organizational performance. Although these studies showed positive associations between some of the included HR practices and happiness, the majority of the linkages studied between HR practices, happiness and organizational performance were found to be non-significant here (Godard, 1998, 2001; Guest & Peccei, 2001; van Veldhoven, 2005; Vanhala & Tuomi, 2006).

In short, no studies indicated a negative HRM–happiness well-being effect. Although one of the excellent studies found no associations between HRM and employee happiness well-being, more than 60 per cent of all data points indicated a positive association of HRM with happiness well-being and performance; hence the results are mainly in line with a weak version of the mutual gains perspective. Half of the data points investigated a strong model of the mutual gains perspective. A mediating role of employee well-being in the relationship between HRM and performance is mostly supported for commitment or a combination of satisfaction and commitment well-being.

Table 2.1 Description of studies

Reference	Sample	HRM	WB Ha	WB He	OP	Resp. rate	Design	Val. and Rel.	Stat. test	Quality
1. Ahmad & Schroeder, 2003	107 manufacturing plants	Security, hiring, teams, decentralization, compensation, training, status difference, sharing information	1		Organizational performance	> 30	CO	3	3	GQ
2. Akdere, 2009	Employees of 69 healthcare facilities	Supervision, empowerment, job design, coordination/ communication, training and development	1		Customer satisfaction Net margin Operating margin	> 30	CO	4	4	GQ
3. Chandler et al., 2000	23 manufacturing enterprises	Incentives, job descriptions, performance appraisal, training, recruitment, discipline system, orientation for new employees, employee participation		1	Firm profitability Sales growth	< 30	PP	2	3	AQ
4. Collings et al., 2010	340 firms in Turkey	Employee training, competence-based performance appraisal, performance-based compensation, merit-based promotion, internal communication, employee empowerment	1		Financial performance	> 30	PP	2	3	AQ
5. Godard, 1998	141 Canadian workplaces	Workgroup, multi-skilling, job enlargement, job or task rotation, autonomous group, profit or gain sharing, group incentive plan, ESOP, pay for knowledge	1		Costs improvement Output improvement	> 30	PP	1	3	AQ
6. Godard, 2001	78 Canadian workplaces	Teamwork, empowerment, participatory values, progressive HR, training, performance pay, job security	1		Costs improvement Output improvement	> 30	PR	1	3	GQ

Study	Sample	HR practices			Performance measures		Size				
7. Gould-Williams, 2003	191 employees in public sector	Training, information sharing, status difference, job variety, team-working, selection process, job security, internal promotion, pay for performance, involvement in decision	2		Organizational performance		> 30	CO	1	3	AQ
8. Guest & Peccai, 2001	54 firms in UK	Participation, job design and quality focus, performance management, communication, share ownership	1		Internal performance External performance		< 30	PP	3	3	AQ
9. Hoque, 1999	209 hotels in UK	Terms and conditions, recruitment and selection, training, job design, quality, pay system, communication and consultation	2		Labour productivity Quality of services Financial performance		> 30	CO	1	3	AQ
10. Katou & Budhwar, 2006	178 Greek manufacturing companies	Resourcing and development, reward and relations	1		Organizational performance		= 30	PP	1	3	AQ
11. Nishii et al., 2008	362 supermarket departments	HR attributions: service quality, cost reduction, well-being, exploitation, compliance with union	1		Customer satisfaction		NA	CO	3	4	GQ
12. Orlitzky & Frenkel, 2005	2001 Australian workplaces	Selection, training and development, participation, equal employment opportunity/affirmative action, job security, decentralized management, fair pay and procedures, good benefits	1		Labour productivity	2	NA	CO	2	4	GQ
13. Park et al., 2003	52 Japanese multinational subsidiaries in US and Russia	Performance oriented, strategic alignment, employee skills practices	1		Organizational performance		NA	CO	1	3	AQ

(Continued)

Table 2.1. Continued

Reference	Sample	HRM	WB Ha	He	OP	Resp. rate	Design	Val. and Rel.	Stat. test	Quality
14. Paul & Anantharaman, 2003	35 Indian software companies	Selection, induction, training, job design, work environment, performance appraisal, incentives compensation, career development	1		Operational performance Financial performance	> 30	PP	3	3	AQ
15. Ramsay et al., 2000	Around 1400 workplaces in UK	Profit-related pay, employee share ownership, employee consultation, TQM, problem solving groups, team autonomy, job control, job security, IP accreditation, internal labour market, upward communication, induction	1	1	Perceived labour productivity Perceived quality Financial performance	> 30	CO	2	3	GQ
16. Riordan et al., 2005	92 insurance companies in US and Canada	Employee involvement climate: participative decision-making, information-sharing, training, performance-based rewards	2		ROA NPW ROS	> 30	PR	4	3	EQ
17. Truss, 2001	single company compared with six other companies	Recruitment and selection, self-development scheme, promote and develop from within, total quality control, rewards, career management		1	Profit per employee ROA	NA	LO	3	2	AQ
18. Van den Berg et al., 1999	49 life insurance companies	Work design, incentives, flexibility, training opportunities, direction-setting	1		Effectiveness	NA	PR	4	4	GQ

19. Vanhala & Tuomi, 2006	91 companies in Finland	Formality, recruitment, development, motivation and reward, flexibility, team-working and participation, communication	1	1	Profit margin Performance Competitiveness Customer satisfaction	NA	LO	2	3	GQ
20. Varma et al., 1999	39 organizations	Team based and non-financial rewards, internal reward, selection, competency	1	1	Operational performance Financial performance	< 30	CO	1	3	AQ
21. Van Veldhoven, 2005	223 Dutch business units of financial organization	Pay, career possibilities, job security	1	1	Financial productivity	> 30	LO	4	3	EQ
22. Wright et al., 2003	50 business units of food service cooperation	Selection and staffing, training, pay for performance, participation	1		Quality, shrinkage Productivity Expenses, profits	NA	PR	3	2	AQ
23. Wright et al., 2005	45 business units of food service cooperation	Selection and staffing, training, pay for performance, participation	1		Quality, shrinkage Productivity Expenses, profits	NA	LO	3	2	GQ

Notes: NA = information not available; PP = post-predictive (1); CO = contemporaneous (2); PR = predictive (3); LO = longitudinal (4); Validity and reliability of measures (1 = subjective, single source data; 2 = subjective data, psychometrics reported for only one or two measurements; 3 = subjective data, all measurements psychometrics reported or objective outcome psychometrics not reported; 4 = objective outcome and psychometrics reported); Statistical test: 1 = no test; 2 = correlations; 3 = multiple regression or (M) ANOVA; 4 = multi-level analysis or structural equation modelling. Response rate: small sample size (below 50) and no information on or low response rate (less than 30 per cent) = 1; no information on or low response rate combined with medium sample size (between 50 and 100), or low sample size combined with high response rate (more than 30 per cent) = 2; no information on or low response rate combined with large sample size (more than 100), or medium sample size combined with high response rate = 3; large sample size combined with high response rate = 4. Quality = the number of quality criteria that are fulfilled (AQ (average) = scored 1 on two (or more) criteria; or scored 1 and 2 on two (or more) criteria; GQ (good) = studies that do not fall into average or excellent category); Ha: happiness well-being, He: health well-being.

Table 2.2   Results synthesis of evidence

Well-being type	Quality	Reference	HRM–WB	HRM–OP	Mediation
Happiness					
Commitment	AQ	7. Gould-Williams, 2003	+	+	+
	AQ	9. Hoque, 1999	+	+	Not tested
	AQ	14. Paul & Anantharaman, 2003	0	+	+
	AQ	22. Wright et al., 2003	+	+	Not tested
	GQ	1. Ahmad & Schroeder, 2003	+	+	+
	GQ	15. Ramsay et al., 2000	+	+	−
	GQ	23. Wright et al., 2005	+	+	Not tested
	EQ	16. Riordan et al., 2005	+	+	−
	EQ	21. Van Veldhoven, 2005	0	0	Not tested
Satisfaction	AQ	7. Gould-Williams, 2003	+	+	−
	AQ	9. Hoque, 1999	+	+	Not tested
	AQ	20. Varma et al., 1999	+	+	Not tested
	GQ	2. Akdere, 2009	+	0	Not tested
	GQ	19. Vanhala & Tuomi, 2006	0	0	Not tested
	EQ	16. Riordan et al., 2005	+	+	−
Commitment	AQ	5. Godard, 1998	0	0	Not tested
and satisfaction	AQ	8. Guest, 2001	0	0	−
	AQ	10. Guest & Peccei, 2001	+	+	+
	AQ	4. Collings et al., 2010	0	0	Not tested
	AQ	13. Park et al., 2003	+	+	+
	GQ	6. Godard, 2001	0	0	Not tested
	GQ	11. Nishii et al., 2008	+	+	+
	GQ	12. Orlitzky & Frenkel, 2005	+	0	−
	GQ	18. Van den Berg et al., 1999	+	+	+
Health					
Stressors	AQ	3. Chandler et al., 2000	−	0	Not tested
	AQ	17. Truss, 2001	−	+	Not tested
	GQ	12. Orlitzky & Frenkel, 2005	−	0	−
Strain	GQ	12. Orlitzky & Frenkel, 2005	−	0	−
	GQ	15. Ramsay et al., 2000	−	+	−
	GQ	19. Vanhala & Tuomi, 2006	0	0	Not tested
	EQ	21. Van Veldhoven, 2005	0	0	Not tested

Health-related well-being

Relatively few studies included a health-related component. Only six studies reported relationships between HRM and health well-being (indices of stressors: workload and work intensification and strain: need for recovery, emotional exhaustion and stress. Orlitzky and Frenkel (2005) included two measures of health-related well-being, resulting in seven data points for this well-being type in our review.

Support for a negative association between HRM and health-related well-being but no effect of HRM on organizational performance was found for three data points (Chandler et al., 2000; Orliztky & Frenkel, 2005). Van Veldhoven (2005) and Vanhala and Tuomi (2006) both found that the majority of relationships between HR practices and strain and organizational performance were non-significant. Two studies (Ramsay et al., 2000; Truss, 2001) reported a positive relationship between HRM and performance, and reported at the same time a negative effect between HRM and employee health well-being (workload and strain).

In summary, all the data points showed no relationship or a negative relationship between HRM and health-related well-being. The majority of the data points showed that HRM is negatively associated with employee well-being and is not associated with organizational performance. No evidence is found for a mediating role of health-related well-being in the relationship between HRM and performance. We conclude that the (preliminary) evidence obtained for health-related well-being is in line with a conflicting outcomes perspective. Due to the small number of studies including health-related well-being, however, this result should be interpreted with caution.

Conclusion

The main result of this review is that the role of employee well-being depends on the well-being type studied. For happiness well-being, we found more support for mutual gains than for conflicting outcomes. In contrast, for health we found more support for conflicting outcomes than for mutual gains. We also found initial support for the idea that the relationship between HRM and organizational performance is (partly) established through its effect on employee happiness well-being (a strong version of the mutual gains perspective). The reasoning that HRM has a positive effect on financial performance that is established through negative employee health effects does not seem to hold here. Employee health-related well-being and organizational performance seem to function more as parallel organizational outcomes. Only two studies included the two well-being types that we distinguished; although these studies investigated the effects of HRM on the two well-being types, no integrated model was tested.

Contextual and contingency factors

The theoretical and empirical picture of the processes and mechanisms linking HRM to employee well-being and organizational performance outlined previously is quite complex. This picture is further complicated by a multitude of contextual and contingency factors that may play a significant role in shaping the HRM–WB–OP relationship in specific organizational settings (Legge, 1995; Delery & Doty, 1996; Paauwe, 2004; Paauwe & Boselie, 2007). We have already touched on a number of these factors, but will now present a more systematic review. Given space constraints, our overview will necessarily be brief, focusing by way of illustration on a few key examples of contextual and contingency factors.

Role of national institutions and legislation

Based on historical differences, the frameworks for work and entrepreneurship differ across countries. These frameworks include institutions and legislation that may influence local HR settings to a greater or lesser extent. The wider institutional and legislative context, for example, strongly influences what is considered as normal HRM and/or high-performance HRM. It also sets restrictions on the agency of organizations and managers in how they can deal with HR practices, working conditions and employment relationships (Paauwe, 2004; Paauwe & Boselie, 2007). This is a research field in its own right, and one in which much still remains to be investigated. Some early empirical studies do exist, however; these have identified distinct groups of legal/institutional frameworks, such as the Anglo-Saxon and the Rhineland models, and have begun to investigate the effect of these different models on HRM and its impact on well-being and performance (Boselie et al., 2001; Paauwe, 2004; Gospel & Pendleton, 2005; Brewster, 2007).

Role of trade unions

Kochan and Osterman (1994) suggest that the effects of HRM on well-being and performance may only be strong in unionized workplaces, and perhaps unsustainable in non-unionized workplaces. In particular, they argue that in unionized workplaces there will be greater sharing of information. Without this, as is more likely to be the case in non-unionized workplaces, management will be mistrusted and HRM will lack credibility. Moreover, unions may enhance the impact of HRM on well-being through their agency role as monitors and enforcers of employment contracts, legal or implicit (Kaufman, 2004). Labour unions help in turning agreements on paper into organizational reality for workers. While there is some evidence of greater effects of HRM in unionized plants (e.g. Kelley & Harrison, 1992; Bryson et al. 2005), an alternative interpretation is that unions can raise worker expectations, thereby weakening any positive impact that HR practices may have on job satisfaction and other aspects of employee well-being. Whatever the specific role played by unions, however, they are likely to have an important moderating effect on key aspects of the HRM–WB–OP relationship and, therefore, deserve closer attention.

Sector/branch of industry

There are several reasons why the branch of industry or sector (e.g. public versus private, profit versus not-for-profit, service versus manufacturing) that an organization operates in may impact the relationship between HRM, well-being and performance. One reason, for example, is that not only can HR and management practices vary systematically across sectors, but the relative importance of specific practices may also differ across contexts. This is the case, for instance, with safety practices in chemical plants, nuclear installations or the construction industry (Zohar 1980; Zohar & Luria, 2005). Because of the centrality of safety in these contexts, safety practices and how they are managed can be expected to have a much stronger and wider effect on employee well-being and organizational performance in the chemical, nuclear and construction industry than in other sectors of the economy. A second reason is linked to patterns of attraction, selection and attrition (ASA) of employees in different sectors. According to Schneider's ASA model (Schneider, 1987; Brent-Smith, 2008), not only do organizations select employees, but employees also self-select themselves into certain jobs and organizations. Thus, sector-specific mechanisms of self-selection may exist, suggesting that employees in a specific sector are likely to have common profiles characterized by specific personal characteristics, orientations and expectations. This, in turn, may influence HR processes including, in particular, the effect that HR practices are likely to have on aspects of employee well-being.

Organizational turbulence

Organizations are not stable entities. Indeed, a substantial amount of HRM literature is devoted to analysing the nature and consequences of key processes of change in organizations, such as processes of growth, downsizing, relocation, outsourcing, acquisitions and mergers. Such dynamics and turbulence may greatly influence local HRM processes, although depending on the situation, the specific effects can be positive or negative. On the negative side, for instance, the uncertainty and job insecurity associated with downsizing or organizational mergers can be major sources of stress for employees (de Witte, 1999), significantly colouring their views of management and the organization, and potentially negatively affecting their HR attributions (Larson & Finkelstein, 1999; Morgan, 2009). On the positive side, however, organizational change and restructuring can create new opportunities for employees. It can, for example, result in promotions, more interesting redesigned jobs and expanded networks (Dean & Snell, 1991; Appelbaum & Grigore, 1997), all of which are likely to have a positive effect on local HRM processes.

Demographic characteristics and composition of the workforce

Workforce characteristics and demographic composition can be seen as important contingency factors moderating the relationship between HRM and employee well-being. The overall argument here is that employees with fundamentally different demographic backgrounds and profiles are likely to have different priorities and expectations at work and, consequently, are likely to evaluate and respond to HR practices differently. Essentially, this means that the extent to which particular HR practices are perceived in a more or less positive light by employees – and therefore the extent to which these practices are likely to have a more or less positive effect on their well-being – will depend, at least in part, on key demographic characteristics of the employees involved. Employee age provides a good example. For instance, Kooij et al. (2010) have shown how, because of differences in work motives and concerns, development-oriented (e.g. training) and maintenance-oriented (e.g. job security) HR practices are evaluated differently by older and younger workers and, consequently, have a differential effect on their well-being. Similarly, for workforces that are mainly female, some areas of HRM may acquire specific importance. In the Netherlands, for instance, many women work part-time in order to combine work with family. HR policies and practices in the area of work/family balance may be particularly relevant for employee well-being in organizations that mainly employ women (Perry-Smith & Blum, 2000).

Conclusion

As this section has made clear, there are many contextual and contingency factors that may shape the HR process at the local level. These relate to institutional, organizational and workforce factors. Indeed, some researchers have wondered whether it makes sense at all to think of HRM, well-being and performance in terms of universally valid relationships (Legge, 1995; Delery & Doty, 1996). The current consensus on the issue appears to be that both universalistic (best practice) and contingency (best fit) approaches are relevant to understanding the HR process in any workplace. In line with this consensus, we have tried to represent both approaches in this chapter. Now that we have reviewed both theory and empirical evidence, as well as context and contingencies, we have a grasp of where the area currently stands and can turn to discussing a series of possible ways forward.

Suggestions for future research

Based on our theoretical and empirical review, we conclude by highlighting a number of important gaps in our understanding of the relationship between HRM, well-being and organizational performance, and by identifying key lines of further research that can help to address these gaps. We focus on both theoretical and empirical issues, paying particular attention to areas of further research that, in our view, can make a significant contribution to a better understanding of the HRM–WB–OP relationship. We start with theory development.

The theoretical analysis presented above suggests that there are three main intervening links that can usefully be distinguished when considering the HRM–WB–OP relationship. These links can usefully be conceptualized at different levels of analysis in line with the multi-level approach to the HRM–WB–OP relationship recommended above. The relevant links are summarized in the multi-level 2–1–1–2 so-called 'bathtub' type model (Coleman, 1990) shown in Figure 2.4.

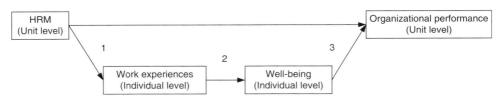

Figure 2.4   Key links in the HRM–WB–OP relationship

As can be seen in Figure 2.4, the first link is between HRM and perceived work experiences; the second link is between work experiences and well-being; and third link is that between well-being and organizational performance. As noted, the last two links have received a great deal of attention in the OB and OIP literatures. As a result we have a fair understanding not only of how and why well-being can affect performance, but also of what constitutes 'good work', that is, of the type of work environments and perceived working conditions that are likely to maximize employee well-being (Warr, 2007; Fisher, 2010). As we have seen, however, what is less well understood theoretically is the very first link in the hypothesized HRM–WB–OP causal chain: namely, the effect that HRM systems have on working conditions and employee experiences at work. This also happens to be the link that HRM scholars can be expected to be best placed to make a theoretical contribution to because of their direct interest and expertise in the analysis of HR practices. Nishii and Wright's (2008) process model of HRM, Nishii et al.'s (2008) notion of HR attributions, and Bowen and Ostroff's (2004; Ostroff & Bowen, 2000) concept of the strength of the HRM system all provide important starting points for the analysis of the effect of HRM on employee experiences and reactions at work. There is no doubt, however, that this area would benefit from further systematic theory development, building on but also going beyond the recent contributions of Nishii and Wright (2008), Nishii et al. (2008) and Bowen and Ostroff (2004).

One possibility for such theory development would be to try to theorize how HRM policies and practices translate into job demands as well as job resources (Bakker & Demerouti, 2007). The link from HRM to job resources may be relatively straightforward in terms of shared key concepts such as job autonomy, skill development, job security and participation in decision-making, for example. How HR policies and practices translate into job demands for employees, on the other hand, is less clear and may well be more complex, although the systematic application of signalling theory (Bowen & Ostroff, 2004) could provide an important way forward here.

A second key area requiring further theoretical development concerns possible contingency approaches to the analysis of the HRM–WB–OP relationship. Particularly important here is a better understanding of the factors that may affect the link between HRM and well-being. As noted in the empirical review section, the majority of studies to date have found a significant positive relationship between HRM and well-being. This positive main effect does not rule out the possibility of significant moderator effects operating in this area. There are quite strong theoretical reasons, in fact, for believing that the HRM–WB relationship may be moderated by a range of individual, processual, organizational and institutional factors of the kind discussed above. But to date these possible moderator effects have not received sustained attention in the HRM literature. We suggest that a systematic and theoretically informed programme of research along the lines outlined above, designed to identify and test key contingency effects in this area, is central to gaining a fuller understanding of the HRM–WB–OP relationship.

One strand of research that may be particularly promising in this respect would, for example, be to explore HRM, well-being and performance linkages in very specific circumstances, like in small enterprises, not-for profit organizations relying on professional volunteers or in highly regulated labour markets. In such cases, which represent extreme contingencies, it may then be possible to explore more systematically how and why general patterns of HRM–WP–OP linkages may still hold or be modified by the specific context involved. Importantly, a systematic programme of contingency-oriented research of the kind suggested above would push HRM scholars to incorporate theoretical insights from the micro-OB and OIP literatures, as well as from the wider macro-OB, institutional and sociological literatures, more explicitly into the analysis of the HRM–WB–OP relationship, thereby significantly expanding and enriching the scope of the analysis in this key area of HRM research.

A third area that requires more systematic attention concerns the effect that different combinations of HR practices and different types of HRM systems have on different aspects of both well-being and performance. On balance, as we have seen, the research evidence provides stronger support for a mutual gains (rather than for a conflicting outcomes) interpretation of the effect of HRM on employee well-being and organizational performance. At the same time the evidence also suggests that this may be the case more in terms of employees' subjective experiences at work (i.e. the happiness component of well-being) than in terms of the health-related aspects of well-being. In the case of health-related outcomes, the evidence suggests more of a conflicting outcomes interpretation, with the majority of studies indicating that HRM tends to be associated with negative health outcomes for employees and with no or a positive performance effect. As noted, however, the number of studies that have examined the link between HRM and both health-related outcomes and performance is limited.

Moreover, it is not clear the extent to which existing results are a function of the specific combination of HR practices and type of HRM systems examined. According to Ostroff and Bowen (2000), HRM can be anchored towards a specific goal. In the literature a distinction can be found between HRM focusing primarily on performance and HRM focusing primarily on employee well-being (Paauwe, 2004; Boxall & Purcell, 2008; Toh et al., 2008; Gong et al., 2009). However, Boxall and Purcell (2008) have recommended paying attention to the plurality of organizational goals; organizations might prioritize performance goals while simultaneously being concerned with maintaining some degree of employee well-being. Which specific combination of practices help to maximize which set of goals, however, remains unclear. It is also unclear whether the observed effects of HRM vary depending on how HR practices are operationalized and measured in the first place – whether, for example, the focus is on systems of HR practices as implemented and described by management, or as perceived by employees themselves (Nishii & Wright, 2008; Dorenbosch, 2009). In other words, further theoretical and empirical work is needed to explore the effect that different combinations and operationalizations of HR practices and different types of HRM systems simultaneously have on different aspects of performance and on both the happiness and health-related dimensions of well-being. This research should also seek to test more systematically for possible mediating effects of well-being in the HRM–OP relationship by explicitly tracing the effects of different combinations of HR practices through each of the more detailed steps in the multi-level causal chain shown in the 2–1–1–2 'bathtub' model in Figure 2.4. This more detailed and articulated programme of research clearly raises fundamental questions about the very nature, conceptualization and operationalization of HRM systems. These questions are beyond the scope of the present discussion, but they are clearly central to the further development of HRM research and are dealt with more fully in Chapter 8.

The fourth area requiring further attention concerns issues about the direction of causality in the HRM–WB–OP relationship and about the time it takes for different effects in the HRM–WB–OP causal chain to unfold. As shown in the empirical review, very few studies to date have examined this relationship longitudinally. At the same time, as we have seen, there remain a number of open questions about the causal order of the focal variables of interest. As noted, organizational performance may, for example, be seen both as an antecedent and as a consequence of well-being (Wright et al., 2005). It can also be seen as an antecedent or as a consequence of HRM itself, in the sense that successful organizations may be in a better position to invest in more elaborate systems of HR practices than less successful organizations (Siehl & Martin, 1990; Paauwe & Boselie, 2005b; Wright et al., 2005). In practice, HRM, well-being and performance may well mutually influence each other over time. The conservation of resources theory (Hobfoll, 2011) proposes so-called 'loss and gain spirals' to understand the dynamic processes between resources and well-being across time. Employees who lack resources attempt to employ their remaining resources and thereby deplete their resource reserves, while employees who gain resources increase their resource pool and acquire additional resources. Applying this theory to the HRM–WB–OP relationship suggests that successful organizations have financial resources to invest in HRM and in the well-being of their employees, resulting in higher well-being and higher performance (a gain cycle). Less successful firms do not have these financial resources to invest and might even adopt HR practices that lead to an intensification of work and negative well-being effects. But little is known about these potential non-recursive effects, about how long it may take for the variables involved to influence each other or about whether the time it takes for well-being to affect performance, for example, is the same as the time it takes for performance to affect HRM, or for HRM to affect well-being. Further theorizing is clearly needed in this area.

More generally, in order to be able to examine these more complex non-recursive relationships and temporal lags between the focal variables of interest, there is a need for more systematic, theoretically informed longitudinal studies of the HRM–WB–OP relationship. Ideally, these studies should include multiple waves of data collection over different time intervals, thereby allowing for a better understanding of the unfolding and dynamics of the HRM–WB–OP relationship over time. Detailed qualitative case studies tracing changes in the focal variables over time would also be particularly useful in this respect. Such studies might also help to clarify the reasons why certain organizations manage to stop and counteract a loss cycle whereas others fail to escape or even descend into a loss cycle when a gain spiral might be expected. In the OB literature, several constructs have been proposed for understanding such dynamics – including for example the idea of 'resource caravans' and 'caravan passageways' (Hobfoll, 2011) – which might provide useful advances in thinking also in the analysis of the HRM–WB–OP relationship over time.

A fifth area that requires further attention concerns issues about multi-level effects in the HRM–WB–OP relationship. By its very nature the analysis of this relationship involves a multi-level approach in that both HRM systems and organizational performance are commonly measured at the aggregate unit or organizational level, while well-being is an individual-level phenomenon. In principle, therefore, the analysis of the HRM–WB–OP relationship involves moving across different levels of analysis. In practice, however, measures of well-being are commonly aggregated to the unit level so that all aspects of the HRM–WB–OP relationship are examined at the aggregate level. Moreover, as we have seen, some of the theoretical arguments linking the variables of interest tend to be couched at the individual level of analysis, and the extent to which these arguments can actually be used to explain aggregate-level effects is not always clear. Overall, therefore, research in this area would benefit from a more explicit multi-level approach to the analysis of the focal relationships of interest, coupled with a clearer matching of theoretical arguments to the cross-level analytical strategies used.

Finally, and more generally, it is important to put the HRM–WB–OP relationship in context by examining the importance of this particular pathway compared to other employee-related pathways that have been proposed in the literature to explain the link between HRM and organizational performance. Alternative pathways that could usefully be compared to the well-being pathway are identified in Figure 2.1, some of which have recently been explored by Collins and Smith (2006), Takeuchi et al. (2007), and Chuang and Liao (2010). Such a multiple-pathway analysis would contribute to a better understanding of the relative importance of employee well-being as an underlying mechanism mediating the relationship between HRM and organizational performance, thereby directly contributing to the wider 'black box' debate in the HRM literature. Wall and Wood (2005) have suggested that the field of HRM research would benefit especially from large-scale studies that are specifically designed to pit such multiple pathways against each other and that can draw on longitudinal data to establish the relative contribution of different pathways.

Conclusions

In this chapter we have sought to provide a systematic, up-to-date theoretical and empirical review of the relationship between HRM, employee well-being and organizational performance. On the basis of this review we identified key gaps in the extant literature and suggested a number of important areas for future research. A number of our recommendations imply a 'big science' (Wall & Wood, 2005) approach to the analysis of the HRM–WB–OP relationship, based on large-scale, multi-level, longitudinal samples. As important as such a big science approach is likely to be in advancing knowledge in this area, we suggest that it might be best to start off more modestly. An important and fundamental first step in this respect, and one that can produce significant results in a relatively short period of time, involves focusing more directly on theory development. In particular, we believe that much is to be gained by focusing, at least initially, on our first two recommendations for further research. This means on the one hand giving priority to gaining a better theoretical understanding of the effect of HRM on employee experiences and reactions at work and, on the other, of key contingencies that are likely to affect the impact of HRM on different aspects of employee well-being. Improved theoretical understanding in these two key areas can then serve as the basis for a more fruitful, focused and cumulative programme of empirical research explicitly designed to test core theoretically based propositions about the HRM–WB–OP relationship.

3
BUILDING HIGHLY-PERFORMING WORK SYSTEMS: ANALYSING HR SYSTEMS AND THEIR CONTRIBUTION TO PERFORMANCE

PETER BOXALL

The way in which human resource management (HRM) contributes to business performance is at the heart of the field of strategic HRM, an area of academic studies that has grown enormously over the last 30 years. Why all the interest in this relationship? On one level, there is no need to justify the role of HRM because all organizations that grow beyond the capacities of a sole proprietor rely on a 'human resourcing' process (Watson, 2005). In any organization that starts to employ labour, there is an inescapable task associated with managing people and the work they do. HRM is therefore 'built into the wiring' of organizations. It is not something that needs an apology or an elaborate justification: without an HRM process of some kind, there is no basis for an organizational performance (Boxall & Steeneveld, 1999).

However, the fact that HRM is a necessary function in organizations does not mean that we understand it well enough or know how to improve it. As various reviews of strategic HRM (SHRM) attest (e.g. Lengnick-Hall & Lengnick-Hall, 1988; Paauwe, 2004, 2009; Boselie et al., 2005; Becker & Huselid, 2006; Boxall & Purcell, 2011), there are important, subtle and contentious questions that need serious study in the HRM–performance relationship. In recent years, much of the interest in the HRM–performance relationship has been wrapped up in the debate around high-performance work systems (HPWSs). The leading developers of the

HPWS literature have been researchers in industrial/employment relations (I/ER) (e.g. Appelbaum et al., 2000), but the terminology is now commonplace across I/ ER and HRM. The HPWS term has also won popular appeal. In the Anglophone world, it is used by government ministries, think tanks, HR professional associations and trade unions. In the UK, there is a raft of reports on how to foster 'high-performance working'.[1]

This chapter will examine how developments in this stream of work can help us to analyse the contribution of HRM to performance. It will challenge the notion that there can be an invariable set of context-free 'high-performance' HR practices. Instead it will argue that there are multiple HR systems in the world of organizations and that our first task is to understand this variety, analysing which ones perform highly in which contexts, how they do so and who benefits from them over time. It is only on this basis that we can become usefully prescriptive for the benefit of one or more of the stakeholders in HRM. This perspective rests on taking an analytical approach to HRM and it is here that we start.

The analytical approach to HRM

The fundamental premise in an analytical approach to HRM is that we should focus first on descriptive research, building a rigorous understanding of what managers try to do in managing work and people, of what motivates their actions, of what affects their success, and of the implications for organizational stakeholders of their actions (Boxall et al., 2007; Boxall & Purcell, 2010). This approach shares much with the dominant intellectual tradition in industrial/employment relations, which distinguished itself from neo-classical economic theory and its reliance on 'stylized facts' and committed to a rigorous process of descriptive research on employment institutions and workplace relations (Kaufman, 1993). One of the core insights from I/ER research on employers is that managerial philosophies are diverse and sensitive to the economic, political and social context in which they are embedded. I/ER research reminds us that expensive innovations in management practice do not necessarily diffuse nearly as far as their advocates imagine (e.g. Godard & Delaney, 2000; Blasi & Kruse, 2006). As Kaufman's (2010) perceptive critique of the SHRM literature emphasizes, most management strategies do not involve the high levels of investment in employees advocated by HRM 'best practice' writers because such strategies are not actually deemed profit-rational in most contexts. I/ ER research regularly illustrates the ways in which small and poorly resourced firms are different from big, well-endowed ones (e.g. Gittleman et al., 1998) and points to the existence of a large low-wage sector in most economies, including in the most advanced ones (e.g. Katz & Darbishire, 2000; Appelbaum et al., 2003; Kroon & Paauwe, 2013).

Careful descriptive research, then, is an antidote to what we might call 'best practicism', a syndrome with a long history in personnel management. Legge's (1978) landmark critique showed how the personnel textbook writers, in their urge to advocate particular 'best practices', sidestepped the troublesome issue of defining management goals and failed to examine the way in which their favourite prescriptions worked well in some contexts but not in others. This argument has been reinforced by similar critiques of best practice prescriptions in the HRM literature (e.g. Marchington & Grugulis, 2000), by systematic reviews of the relationships between contextual variables and HR practices (e.g. Jackson & Schuler, 1995), by studies of the social embeddedness of HR systems (e.g. Gooderham et al., 1999), and by simple observation of the contradictions among best practice writers who try to combine ideal practices into bundles (e.g. Becker & Gerhart, 1996).

The alternative to 'best practicism' is an analytical approach to HRM, one that starts from descriptive research addressing the 'what, why, how and for whom' questions that underpin the activity (Boxall et al., 2007; Boxall & Purcell, 2010). While an HRM process of some kind occurs in any organization with employees, there are critical questions of a contextual or contingency nature: *what* particular patterns or models characterize HRM in different societies, industries, occupations and organizations, and *why* do these different patterns arise? Which ones are more functional in which contexts and why? There are then questions that relate to the 'black box' (the *how*) of any particular model of HRM (Purcell et al., 2003; Wright & Gardner, 2004), questions that explore the critical linkages inside organizations that account for major differences in performance outcomes. This encompasses intrapersonal or psychological processes and interpersonal or social processes, the links between these levels, and the links from them to such economic outcomes as labour productivity and profit. This means that gathering data on how workers respond to management initiatives is essential to analytical HRM. It is not possible to understand whether HRM is working as intended, or how it is working, unless we have data on worker responses and attitudes, as Guest (e.g. 1999, 2002, 2007) has emphasized.

Furthermore, the inclusion of comprehensive data on worker outcomes enables an analytical approach to HRM to go beyond a focus on management interests and ask: to what extent do different stakeholders benefit from HRM? *For whom* does any particular system of HRM perform? Outcomes that are intermediate for the firm, such as skill development, job satisfaction and work/life balance, are actually important as ends in themselves for workers (e.g. Guest, 2002; Macky & Boxall, 2007). In an analytical approach to HRM, management can be understood as a political actor whose interests do not fully overlap with those of others (Boxall & Purcell, 2011). To a variable extent, management behaviour serves investor goals, worker needs and wider social outcomes, such as wealth generation and public services, but it can also be dangerously self-serving, as was illustrated in the staggering, short-term managerial and trader pay incentives in the banking and insurance sectors that contributed to the global financial crisis of 2008–2009 (Stiglitz, 2010). Performance-related pay practices, considered 'best practices' by some, were at the heart of the risk-taking behaviour that, in the end, contributed to major social costs. The potential for an uncritical or cynical use of HR practices to cause perverse consequences has never been better illustrated.

Thus, analytical research has the potential to make HRM relevant to the wider debate on worker and community well-being, in and across societies. It would be 'drawing a long bow' to argue that HRM research has so far made a major contribution to public policy on the labour market and social well-being. However, if studies are grounded in an analytical approach that is committed to gathering data on both worker and business outcomes, it has the potential to do so.

HPWSs: background and critique

What, then, does the literature on high-performance work systems (HPWSs) have to offer to an analysis of the role of HRM in building performance? If we are taking an analytical approach, we do not start by trying to identify a set of best practices as inherently highly performing, but begin by setting the HPWS phenomenon in its historical and social context (Boxall & Macky, 2009). There is a long history of interest in how to enhance organizational performance through improving the management of work and employment, including such well-known developments as scientific management, the human relations movement, socio-technical work systems, industrial democracy and job enrichment (for reviews, see Watson, 1986 and Karasek & Theorell, 1990, *inter alia*). The notion of high-performance work systems is the most recent turn of phrase; it is the present rallying point for those who see workplace reform as an answer to perceived economic and/or social problems.

The HPWS term originated in the USA, gaining traction in the debate over the decline of US manufacturing competitiveness (Cappelli & Neumark, 2001). A key stimulus of this concern was the rise of Japanese 'lean production' systems in the 1970s and 1980s, including such techniques as quality circles, just-in-time inventory and flexible, team-based production (Womack et al., 1990). Along with this challenge, another stimulus of change in work systems over the last 30 years was the advent of advanced manufacturing technology (AMT), which includes robotics, computer-aided design (CAD), computer numerical control (CNC) machine tools and electronic data interchange (EDI) systems (e.g. Snell & Dean, 1992). Most recently, the debate has been encouraged by the rise of 'off-shoring' to China, India and other low-cost producers. The need to reform US mass-production jobs (which were often low in responsibility and discretion) and invest in greater workforce skills and incentives was emphasized in leading studies, such as those in automobile manufacturing (MacDuffie, 1995), and in influential books such as *The New American Workplace* (Appelbaum & Batt, 1994) and *Manufacturing Advantage* (Appelbaum et al., 2000). While the initial focus was on the way production workers are managed in manufacturing, the topic of HPWSs became part of a larger agenda concerned with competitive performance in both manufacturing and services. There has been growing angst in the US over the location of services in a globalized production environment, spurring interest in how service firms might use HPWSs as a competitive asset (e.g. Batt, 2002, 2007).

If this is the nature of the problems that HPWSs are supposed to address, what is the nature of the solution? Here we encounter major difficulties because HPWSs are a fuzzy phenomenon in which three concepts are tied together: performance, systemic effects and work practices of some kind (Boxall & Macky, 2009).

Organizational performance, the dependent variable, can be understood in a variety of ways. Most researchers have focused on economic performance criteria, as Godard's (2004) evaluation of HPWS studies indicates. However, this may incorporate short- or long-run economic outcomes, and organizational performance can extend to wider notions of social legitimacy or corporate social responsibility (Edwards & Wright, 2001; Paauwe, 2004; Boxall & Purcell, 2011). Very importantly, a key premise that runs through the literature is that HPWSs depend on positive responses from employees. There is therefore a commitment to measure the impacts of HPWSs on worker interests, which has generated a debate in which some scholars see positive outcomes for employees (e.g. Appelbaum et al., 2000) while others call this sharply into question (e.g. White et al., 2003; Godard, 2004).

A second key element in the HPWS notion is the importance of systemic effects (e.g. Dyer & Reeves, 1995; Delery & Shaw, 2001). In MacDuffie's terms (1995, p. 200), 'bundling' of work practices is critical in HPWSs: 'it is the combination of practices into a bundle, rather than individual practices, which shapes the pattern of interactions between and among managers and employees'. What tends to have been variable in the HPWS literature is the extent to which the analysis of synergistic linkages has reached out to the companion elements of a business: its technology or proprietary knowledge, product or service mix, and financing, supply chain and governance, for example (Boxall & Macky, 2009). Narrowly conceived, bundling is an issue of design within the components of an HR system: making training consistent with a change to self-directed teams, for example. This tends to be the way that HR writers have thought about it, but it is only one part of the puzzle in strategic management terms.

Academic colleagues in operations management have generally done a better job of analysing systemic linkages across business functions. Scholars such as Boyer et al. (1997), Kotha and Swamidass (2000), Das and Narasimhan (2001) and Shah and Ward (2003) show, for example, that the performance of firms adopting advanced manufacturing technology is better when they make commensurate improvements in the human 'infrastructure' that enables the technology to function. They show the value of ensuring HR strategy fits with the goals and technological disposition of manufacturing strategy. Similarly, in an important longitudinal study (de Menezes et al., 2010) finds that British firms investing in Japanese-style lean manufacturing systems, such as integrated computer-based technology and total quality management, perform better when they integrate these costly changes in production strategy with a more empowering style of HRM and extensive employee training. Given the 'embeddedness' of work systems within wider production or operational strategies (MacDuffie, 1995; Purcell, 1999), we must acknowledge that the narrow conception of systems in HRM is much too limiting. It is essential that 'complementarity' is understood not only within the sphere of HRM but within the broader management system of the workplace or business unit (Boxall & Macky, 2009). Thinking about HPWSs in this way is likely to be much closer to the way that senior managers think about their businesses.

Finally, there is an independent variable: the work (and employment) practices that are deemed to constitute a high-performance system. These are subject to a confusing array of definitions and assertions. As early as the mid-1990s, Becker and Gerhart (1996) illustrated the diversity of conceptions of the relevant HR practices in a table of five leading HPWS studies, all conducted in the US. These studies listed as many as eleven and as few as four practices, with no one practice common to all five studies and some disagreement as to whether particular practices, such as variable pay, had positive or negative effects. As subsequent events in the finance sector have shown, there ought to be debate about this!

This brings us to the major weakness with the HPWS literature: it is hard to define the nature of the proposed solution and the term itself is not inherently descriptive.[2] On top of the disagreement over what constitutes an HPWS in a given society, there is the fact that when one moves from any one national context, socio-cultural variations in HR practices have to be accommodated (e.g. Paauwe & Boselie, 2003, 2007). For example, a practice such as an employee grievance procedure, which Huselid (1995) considers a high-performance indicator in the US, is simply a legal requirement in various other countries, and therefore not something that differentiates top performers. Some practices considered high performing in the US context are simply 'table stakes' in other countries, not a source of high performance (Boselie et al., 2001; Boxall & Purcell, 2011). The kind of contextual variations we need to recognize include legal differences, which are the more straightforward aspects of socio-cultural variation, and their underpinning cultural assumptions, which are much more challenging.

Approaches to constructing the independent variable in HPWSs in which writers aggregate their perceptions of 'best practices', without regard to their specific context, either historical or geographical, are therefore 'fundamentally flawed', and 'arguments that a particular set of practices is self-evidently highly performing are not defensible' (Boxall & Macky, 2009, p. 6). Even if a set of context-delineated practices could be agreed upon, there is the problem that data that simply counts HR practices – or even the proportion of the workforce covered by them – does not account for variations in *how* the practice is implemented (Purcell, 1999). These can be decisive. For example, do workers experience genuine improvements in their involvement as a result of a set of 'high-performing' HR practices or do they experience them as work intensification (e.g. van den Berg et al., 1999; Macky & Boxall, 2008; Godard, 2010)?

Where does this leave us? It should, arguably, convince us of the need to adopt more descriptive terminology in our discipline. We need to identify the major philosophies or dominant themes that management is pursuing in particular workplace contexts, measure how they are perceived by workers, and find some more meaningful terms for them.

The HPWS literature is not totally unhelpful in this respect, but it takes much more than a superficial engagement with it to uncover the gems. There are, as it happens, two main variations on the HPWS terminology that are more meaningful (Wood, 1999; Wood & Wall, 2007; Boxall & Macky, 2009). One traces back to Lawler (1986) and is concerned with high-involvement management. This term describes efforts to redesign jobs to enhance worker responsibilities and authority. It thus involves some reverse-engineering of Taylorist job design and is associated with companion improvements in skill development and incentives to participate.

The other term traces back to Walton (1985) and is concerned with high-commitment HR practices. This term involves practices that aim to enhance employee commitment to the organization rather than practices that are narrowly focused on control or compliance. Whether or not we talk of practices, processes, systems or management, these two terms are both more descriptive for HR systems because they indicate the dominant theme underpinning managerial action. Something descriptively helpful is conveyed when we draw a contrast between work processes in which managers try to control operating decisions and those that seek to give workers greater responsibility and involve them more fully in decision-making (e.g. Ramsay et al., 2000; Godard, 2004). Similarly, it is helpful to contrast employment practices that seek little employee commitment from those that seek a much stronger connection with the organization. The other virtue of using terms such as 'high involvement' and 'high commitment' is that they do not *assume* that 'the particular configuration of management practices is necessarily performance-enhancing' (Bryson et al., 2005, p. 460). This has to be demonstrated in specific contexts, not asserted in a generalized way.

Going forward: studying HR systems and their contribution to performance

With this critique in mind, what can we take out of the HPWS literature that can assist, and should inform, our ongoing analysis of the HRM–performance relationship?

Contexts and business models

Clearly, the first lesson is about the importance of identifying different kinds of HR or work systems, developing reasonably descriptive terms for them, and examining which are 'highly performing' in which contexts and why. A fundamental premise is that there is great diversity in the paths that managers follow in their pursuit of higher performance (Orlitzky & Frenkel, 2005; Boxall & Macky, 2009). Not only are there major variations across organizations, but there are also often major variations within any one organization (Lepak & Snell, 1999). As an initial categorization, Boxall and Purcell (2011) construct a typology of HR systems that traverses familial HR models, informal models, industrial models, salaried models, high-involvement models, craft-professional models and outsourcing models, and that relates these to organizational and industry contexts. Similarly, but using more technical language, Toh et al. (2008) identify five major HR systems – cost minimizers, contingent motivators, competitive motivators, resource makers and commitment maximizers – and relate each of them to key contextual variables in a study of 661 US organizations. Their unsurprising conclusion was that 'HR bundles are adopted that fit with the context in which the organizations are embedded' (Toh et al., 2008, p. 874).

The value of studying HR systems in their specific contexts can be illustrated through reference to two recent studies. Both studies examine a particular employee group (as advised by Lepak et al., 2006), identify the HR system used to manage them and examine the links to performance. The first is Siebert and Zubanov's (2009) analysis of HR systems inside a large UK retail chain. Stores in the chain have some full-time managers and experienced employees who are managed on a 'commitment system' (20 per cent of the workforce). However, there is also a large periphery of part-time workers who are managed in a 'secondary system'. These employees have 'less responsibility, less specialist training and fewer promotion opportunities . . . (and) their pay is flat' (Siebert & Zubanov, 2009, p. 297). This is not an unusual story in retail because the seasonality of the business, and therefore its staffing needs, generates part-time jobs, often held by student workers and new migrants. In many parts of retail, it is highly unlikely that a high-commitment model will be economically rational across the board. Siebert and Zubanov (2009) demonstrate this econometrically, showing that labour productivity is higher the lower the turnover of the core group (who provide the organization with continuity of skills and training), while there is an inverted U-shaped relationship between employee turnover and productivity for the part-timers. They calculate that a full-time equivalent turnover of up to 15 per cent for part-time employees enhances productivity. The dual HR systems in this organization operate on different principles: one is high commitment (relative to typical HR practices in the retail sector) and the other is low.

The second study (Boxall et al., 2011) also investigates an area of lower pay and lower skills. It examines the management of casual employees, who make up the majority of the operating workforce, in an Australian cinema chain. Qualitative data from managers, and analysis of critical HR policy documents, provides insight into management's goals for this workforce group. The study measures workers' experience of this official HR model and of managerial behaviour, and assesses their attitudinal and behavioural responses, relating these responses to subsequent supervisory ratings of performance. The results speak to an environment in which customers are served in a highly programmed way. They show that the company's HRM process fosters employee compliance with established, efficient scripts, as in similar service contexts where the 'product' is highly standardized and offered in a brief time-window. While customer-oriented behaviour is an important value, it is willing engagement with a Taylorist work process that makes it happen, not a more empowering form of work design. Like the work of Siebert and Zubanov (2009), this study shows us what managers consider profit rational in a particular business context. It is not about measuring a generic model of 'best practice', but about understanding the way in which HRM contributes to business strategy in a particular environment.

These sorts of studies show that it is unwise to imagine that we can generalize at the practice level from sectors like capital-intensive manufacturing or professional services to mass, standardized services. This does not, however, rule out lessons about how to improve HRM in different contexts that are formed at the level of general principles (Boxall & Purcell, 2011). At this level, it is possible to argue that there are cost-effective forms of empowerment that can lift performance in most jobs. In their interesting study of a retail chain in Finland, for example, Jones et al. (2010) show that greater employee participation in decisions about item display, and a greater willingness to be helpful when they are approached by customers for information, can bring an a productivity gain (see also Guy's (2003) study of Safeway stores in Califiornia). What their work reveals, however, is that this model of empowerment is relative to the lower pay/lower skill context of retail; the scale of HR investment is radically different from what one finds in capital-intensive manufacturing or professional services. There is no 'incentive pay, there are no "self-managed teams" and recruitment is not "selective" in this organization' (Jones et al., 2010, p. 8). There is a kind of employee involvement that is helpful in these retail jobs but it does not hinge on the expensive lists of 'best practices' that are more relevant to the economics of high-skill contexts.

Advancing the analytical approach to HRM, then, depends on studies that enable us to identify meaningful differences in HR systems and relate them to particular business priorities. From the management perspective, what is 'highly performing' is going to depend heavily on the economics of the business model. This does not rule out questions of social legitimacy and issues of internal politics in managerial choices, which play an important role, but underlines the inevitable discipline of profit-seeking in markets, as Kaufman (2010) has emphasized. The metaphor of the 'business model', increasingly used in the strategy literature, is helpful here. It conveys the idea of putting all the pieces together in a way that will deliver customer value at an acceptable profit (e.g. Johnson et al., 2008). The notion of a business model is built on a configurational understanding of strategy (e.g. Short et al., 2008): one in which marketing, operations/IT management, HRM, and finance all interact to serve the business goals in a particular context. The contingency approach, which is central to strategic management, leads naturally into a configurational understanding of strategy because making a business viable is likely to depend on much more than simply aligning two management variables. In fact, one should be careful about any kind of alignment between two variables until one has a sense of all the main variables that need some kind of integration in the business model.

Mediators and methods

A second important lesson from the HPWS debate is the way it has fostered an understanding of mediating variables in HRM. On one level, the role of HR systems in influencing individual abilities (A), motivations (M), and opportunities (O) to perform (the 'AMO' model of individual performance) has been at the heart of HPWS thinking from the outset (e.g. Huselid, 1995; MacDuffie, 1995; Appelbaum et al., 2000). The lesson here is that every HR system works through its impacts on the skills and knowledge of individual employees, their willingness to exert effort, and their opportunities to express their talents in their work. However, this is true irrespective of whether the model is high- or low-involvement, high- or low-skill, high- or low-commitment, etc. The AMO variables are an inevitable set of mediators through which management attempts to foster individual performance need to be transmitted. Within this essential framework, theoretical progress relies on developing a more focused set of theoretical propositions around mediators involving employee perception, cognition, emotion and well-being. The notions of ability and motivation cover a complex cluster of attributes, attitudes and behavioural variables that can be investigated through a variety of theoretical perspectives (e.g. expectancy theory, equity theory, social exchange theory, self-determination theory, goal-setting theory, job characteristics theory or engagement theory).

More than one level of analysis is involved here. The HPWS literature has helped to underline the fact that HR systems affect both individual employee responses and help to build the organizational capabilities, culture and climate in which they are embedded (e.g. Evans & Davis, 2005). The individual and collective levels are inextricably linked because the performance opportunities of individuals and their motivations are influenced by the physical and interpersonal resources in their working environment. HR systems that help to enhance trust in management and/or among peers improve an organization's 'social capital' – the quality of relationships within and across groups (Leana & van Buren, 1999). The work of Nishii et al. (2008) illustrates these linkages. In a study of some 4500 employees and 1100 department managers in a supermarket chain, they show how individual-level attributions about the managerial motives underpinning HR practices are linked to individual satisfaction and commitment levels, and thence to unit-level organizational citizenship behaviours and social climate.

The importance of studying how HR systems affect organizational climates is a growing focus in strategic HRM theory and research (e.g. van Veldhoven, 2005; Veld et al., 2010; Mossholder et al., 2011). As Lepak et al. (2006) explain, it is important to conduct research that identifies the kind of performance 'climate' that management is trying to create in specific organizational contexts. Management's intentions can be diverse: some management teams seek to create a climate for service, others a climate for innovation, while yet others may be seeking to build a climate of occupational safety, and so on. Describing HR systems in relation to management's desired psycho-social climates has the virtue of enabling us to recognize 'equifinality': the idea that companies will most likely adopt an idiosyncratic set of practices in their particular context in an effort to achieve a certain kind of climate (Delery & Doty, 1996; Kehoe & Collins, 2008).

This trend is important but we should not imagine that management seeks just one kind of psycho-social goal in HRM or a climate that we can sum up in one simple theme. For example, Veld et al. (2010) examine management attempts to build both a climate for quality and a climate for employee safety in a Dutch hospital. Management often seeks a blended set of HR goals containing strategic tensions or elements of paradox (Evans & Genadry, 1999; Boxall & Purcell, 2011). In the cinema chain studied by Boxall et al. (2011), for example, management strongly emphasized customer-oriented behaviour but supervisory ratings of employees showed that this hinged much more on employee compliance with behavioural scripts than on empowerment to depart from them. In Korczynski's (2001) terms, this is an example of a 'customer-oriented bureaucracy', a pattern of HRM that contains a variable tension between routinized efficiency and personalized service. Where the balance falls differs across particular companies and service contexts: contrast, for example, Peccei and Rosenthal's (2001) supermarket case, in which employees were given greater service discretion, with Boxall et al.'s (2011) cinema chain.

HPWS studies that have addressed the mediational questions inside the organizational 'black box' have helped to underline a number of important methodological lessons. They have emphasized the fundamental importance in HRM research of gaining management data on what is intended but employee data on what is experienced. Reviews of the HRM–performance literature have now come together around a range of important methodological lessons. These include identifying the target employee group in any study (rather than assuming that all employees in an organization are subject to the same HR system); gathering multiple responses from well-informed managers on their particular theory of HRM for this group; obtaining data from employees on their perceptions of, and responses, to management goals, practices and behaviours; locating proximal outcome measures that are not provided by the source(s) used for the independent variables and that are measured subsequent to them; and building longitudinal data sets, wherever possible (e.g. Wall & Wood, 2005; Wright et al., 2005; Gerhart, 2007a; Lepak et al., 2006; Nishii & Wright, 2008; Paauwe, 2009; van de Voorde et al., 2010a). As a result of these critical reflections on methods, the standard for what constitutes good data in any study of HR processes and outcomes has risen, and this is a good thing.

Mutuality and sustainability

A final issue that the HPWS literature has stimulated, and that we must carry forward, is the question of whose interests are served by any particular HR system. The notion of HPWSs has appealed to politicians because of the win-win arguments advanced by leading writers such as Appelbaum et al. (2000). Among academics, as noted earlier, this has stimulated a vigorous debate around who benefits from HPWSs. The nub of the question is: for whom is a 'highly-performing' work system highly-performing? In appraising what this means for workers, we should avoid assuming we know better than they do what is in their interest, as Guest (e.g. 1999, 2007) and Rosenthal (2004) emphasize in their critiques of writers who have a 'critical' perspective but not much data. What constitutes job quality is actually a complex question requiring measures of a range of factors, and should turn on major studies of worker attitudes and experiences (e.g. Green, 2006; Gallie, 2007; Warr, 2007). Arguably, the most sustainable HR systems serve investors well while also serving employees and their communities well (Boxall & Purcell, 2011; van de Voorde et al., forthcoming). This is *mutual* high performance and it is here that many of us would like to make a prescriptive contribution: we would like to be able to assist the parties to build mutually satisfying HR systems based on a good analysis of when, why, how and for whom they will work.

Problems of poor mutuality can arise around a number of variables, such as work intensity, wage levels, employment security, job control and skill development. Writers in political economy argue that the potential for mutuality at work is affected by the kind of capitalism under which we are working (e.g. Belanger et al., 2002; Konzelmann et al., 2004). In the Anglophone world, the 'liberal market' model is dominant (Hall & Soskice, 2001); in this variety of capitalism, shares are widely traded in share markets, corporate takeovers are commonplace and labour-market regulation offers fewer job protections than is true in 'coordinated market economies' such as those in the eurozone (Gospel & Pendleton, 2003).

However, the global financial crisis has illustrated the way in which more protected economies in the eurozone, such as Spain, Portugal and Greece, are not immune from major shocks and can pay a high price in unemployment levels and public-sector restructuring.[3] In any system of capitalism, the mutuality of HR systems will be challenged by economic cycles (Kaufman, 2010). The fact that management does not always wish to build long-term mutuality with every employee group or workforce is evident in any contemporary analysis of the corporate strategies of multidivisional and multinational companies (Boxall & Purcell, 2011). In order to cope with threatening change, some firms have fostered what Kelley (2000) calls the 'participatory bureaucracy', in which managers have tried to develop greater corporate resilience through higher levels of employee involvement. The participatory bureaucracy is common in capital-intensive, high-tech or professional service firms seeking to respond to high-quality competition through higher skills, learning and innovation. On the other hand, we have also seen the growth of the 'flexible bureaucracy' (Boxall & Purcell, 2011) that combines an inner core of salaried managerial and specialist staff whose contracts have been heightened in terms of performance expectations and rewards, with out-sourced HR systems and a willingness to dispense with workforces that cease to be cost-effective. It is common among multinational firms responding to severe cost pressures in international markets, large service firms in deregulated industries (e.g. airlines, telecommunications) and public sector organizations that have been required to adopt greater emphasis on financial control or, most recently, adjust to a lower level of government funding due to fiscal imbalances resulting from the global financial crisis of 2008–2009.

At the present time, analytical HRM is making its key contributions to the mutuality debate at the workplace and company levels. It is showing, for example, that 'many worker groups can enjoy positive outcomes' when managers foster high-involvement processes (Boxall & Macky, 2009, p. 16). This is not a generalization about *particular* HR practices, which can have variable effects, but a claim about the value of enhancing the extent to which individuals experience more meaningful empowerment at work. When individuals sense a growth in their scope for discretion coming through whatever HR practices their managers use (or don't use), they generally respond positively.

A greater contribution to public policy debate will hinge on relating these sorts of findings to the analysis of social well-being. How this can be done is illustrated in the multi-disciplinary work of Karasek and Theorell (1990), who relate the nature of work demands, control and social support to employee well-being as well as productivity levels (the 'demand-control-support' model). Their general argument is that enhancing employee control over work methods and pacing will improve both personal health and operating performance. Work demands may be high but this can be positive for worker learning and satisfaction if workers have commensurately high levels of skill utilization and job influence (an 'active job'). It must be said, however, that their case is strongest, and most enduring, on the way in which work organization can affect stress, cardiac health and life expectancy. Globalization of markets over the last 20 years has affected their analysis of the economic benefits of 'work reconstruction', which now needs to take account of the rationalization of production sites between high-cost countries and low-cost ones. There are various kinds of high-skill and capital-intensive productive activity that can survive in western countries, but multinationals have increasingly shifted labour-intensive and assembly-line operations to China, India and other developing economies (Boxall & Purcell, 2011). The question of how we build work systems that serve both productivity and employee well-being in the established economies, which contain a shifting mix of high- and low-wage jobs, has therefore evolved.

Conclusions

There are many kinds of HR system and the primary task of analytical HRM is to understand which ones perform in which contexts, how they do so and who benefits from them over time. What is highly performing in HRM is variable and depends on whose perspective is being considered. It is not set in the stone of any particular writer's conception of 'best practices' or 'high-performance' practices. We need to describe the multiple goals that management pursues in particular contexts (both geographical and historical), understand what drives them, and analyse their underpinning processes and outcomes for the parties. This mission has been stimulated by the boom in studies of HPWSs, despite the nebulous, non-descriptive nature of the term. The HPWS literature has rightly fostered a systemic view of HRM and this is useful – providing we understand it broadly. HR strategy is part and parcel of a larger business model, and it fails if it does not serve the economic imperatives that are essential to that model. The HPWS literature has also fostered a multi-level understanding of the mediators inside the 'black box' of HRM; we are now more attuned to the need to study how HRM affects both psychological and social climates inside organizations. Again, this is invaluable – providing we realize that organizational climates involve strategic tensions or elements of paradox. The HPWS literature has also pushed along the methodological debate so that we are now much more sensitive to data quality in HRM studies. Finally, it has stimulated us to think about who is best served by the diverse HR systems we see in action in today's world. We can improve our modelling and measurement of mutuality in HRM and, through this, our discipline has the potential to contribute to a larger debate around economic and social well-being.

Notes

1   See, for example, the CIPD's website, http://www.cipd.co.uk/hr-resources/research/high-performance-work-practices.aspx (accessed 8 July 2012).

2   Other non-descriptive terms are 'innovative', 'new' and 'alternative' work systems, usually contrasted with 'traditional' ones.

3   Spanish unemployment reached 20 per cent in 2010 – see http://www.bbc.co.uk/news/10093123 (accessed 8 July 2012).

4

RECONCEPTUALIZING FIT IN STRATEGIC HUMAN RESOURCE MANAGEMENT: 'LOST IN TRANSLATION?'

JAAP PAAUWE, CORINE BOON, PAUL BOSELIE
AND DEANNE DEN HARTOG

Abstract

To date, studies that focus on the concept of 'fit' in strategic human resource management (SHRM) fail to show consistent evidence. A variety of fit approaches are available, but there is no general consensus about what constitutes fit. This chapter aims to reconceptualize fit through a literature review and a critical reflection on the general findings to date. We reflect on what has been achieved up until now, identify what is still missing and present an alternative framework for conceptualizing fit, resulting in a set of propositions on SHRM and fit that can be tested in future research.

Introduction

The field of strategic human resource management (SHRM) has paid considerable attention to the concept of 'fit'. The premise underlying the concept of fit is that organizations are more efficient and effective when organizational parts (for example practices, structure and systems) are aligned than when alignment is absent (Nadler & Tushman, 1980; Wright & Snell, 1998). In SHRM, fit notions are mainly applied to studying the alignment or fit between human resource management practices and the fit between human resource management systems and the organizational context (e.g. Arthur, 1994; Huselid, 1995; MacDuffie, 1995).

To date, empirical testing of the fit propositions in SHRM fails to show consistent evidence (Gerhart, 2004). In other words, although the importance of alignment of

HRM with the organizational context (among which the business strategy) for increasing performance seems theoretically plausible, there is a lack of evidence supporting most theoretical claims (Wright & Sherman, 1999; Paauwe, 2004; Boxall & Purcell, 2008). There are some possible explanations for the lack of evidence. For example, insufficient attention has been paid to improve the measurement of fit in empirical studies in the fit area (Wright & Sherman, 1999; Gerhart, 2004). In addition, the concepts and indicators used for both HRM and fit are underdeveloped and there is no general consensus about what constitutes either HRM or fit. This last issue of what constitutes fit in the HRM field is the main subject of our chapter.

There is a variety of fit approaches available in SHRM. These focus, for example, on content (e.g. Gratton et al., 1999), process (e.g. Golden & Ramanujam, 1985), implementation (e.g. Becker & Huselid, 2006), strength of interactions (e.g. Delery, 1998), and dominant goals (e.g. Bowen & Ostroff, 2004), and are illustrative of the different lenses (perspectives) for studying HRM and fit. We argue that the field of SHRM, in particular with regard to the notion of fit, is about to get 'lost in translation' as a result of the lack of integration of these different perspectives. The aim of this chapter is to reconceptualize fit in SHRM through a thorough literature review and a critical reflection on the findings to date.

Below, we first describe the available 'best-fit' approaches in HRM. These approaches include both what we label the 'early fit models' (e.g. Schuler & Jackson, 1987), mainly focused on horizontal fit (internal fit) and vertical (strategic fit), and what we label the 'next generation fit models' which include other HRM fits such as organizational fit and institutional fit (e.g. Wood, 1999; Paauwe & Boselie, 2003; Boon et al., 2009). Next, we review what the different perspectives such as the content and process models contribute to the field. We reflect on what has been achieved up until now and what is still missing. Finally, we present an alternative framework for conceptualizing HRM and fit in future research. In the discussion section we apply our alternative fit framework and illustrate our framework using examples of two retail organizations. This results in a set of propositions on HRM and fit that can be tested in future research.

Best-fit approaches in human resource management

The key question in the fit debate in the HRM field is: does achieving a fit between HRM and its context increase organizational performance? This approach is often placed opposite to the 'best practice' hypothesis, which argues that certain HR practices will be effective in any context (e.g. Pfeffer, 1994, 1998; Delery & Doty, 1996). The 'best-fit' approaches, mainly rooted in the strategic contingency approaches of the 1970s and 1980s, emphasize the importance of internal and external organizational context for the shaping of HRM in an organization (e.g. Miles & Snow, 1978; Porter, 1985). A number of studies have shown evidence for the best-fit approach (e.g. Jackson & Schuler, 1995; Gooderham et al., 1999; Marchington & Grugulis, 2000; Toh et al., 2008).

Beer et al. (1984) were among the first to apply fit to SHRM in their Harvard 'map of the HRM territory'. In their model, situational factors (for example, workforce characteristics, task technology, laws and societal values) and stakeholder interests (for example, shareholders, management, employee groups, government and trade unions) are thought to affect HRM policy choices and organizational performance. Organizational success is achieved through optimal alignment (fit) between the situational factors and HRM policy choices, and between stakeholder interests and HRM. Two central notions emerged from the early 'fit' models in strategic human resource management:

- The notion of horizontal fit in HRM, also known as internal fit.
- The notion of vertical fit in HRM, also known as strategic fit.

Horizontal fit refers to the proposition that individual HR practices need to be aligned together in a consistent and coherent way, such that the HR practices work together as a system to achieve organizational objectives and enhance performance (Delery, 1998). Vertical fit refers to the proposition that a system of HR practices needs to be aligned to the business strategy of an organization, which should help to more effectively execute strategy and achieve optimal organizational performance). The 'early fit' model by Schuler and Jackson (1987) is noteworthy because they were among the first to connect specific HR practices to competitive strategies, including cost leadership, differentiation and focus.

The early fit models and the next generation fit models in HRM

In the early 1990s the first attempts to empirically test horizontal and vertical fit (e.g. Arthur, 1994; Huselid, 1995; MacDuffie, 1995) mainly failed to provide convincing evidence that better fit results in superior performance. In a response to this first wave of empirical studies testing the impact of fit, new conceptual work was published that highlighted multiple relevant fits in HRM, besides horizontal and vertical fit. Wood (1999) distinguishes four different fits in SHRM, which reflect the 'next generation fit models':

- Strategic fit focuses on the link between the HR system and business strategy.
- Internal fit focuses on the link between different HR practices within the HR system.
- Organizational fit focuses on the link between the HR system and other relevant systems in the organization including technological systems, production systems and control systems.
- Environmental fit focuses on the link between the HR system and the external institutional environment.

Since the overview provided by Wood (1999), even more different approaches to fit emerged in HRM research. Several have interesting and relevant findings, but there is little overall coherence and consistency – which might also have to do with the fact that in the majority of cases, researchers tried to establish fit at the principles level of HR practices, which according to Wright et al. (2004) is at a too high level of abstraction. They argue that establishing the fit between business strategy and HR would benefit from focusing more specifically on the HR practices or techniques instead of the underlying principles (see also Chapter 8). And in many cases, authors did not concentrate strongly on further developing operationalizations of the different fits they proposed. In that sense, the field of SHRM at this stage can be said to be 'lost in translation'.

Reviewing the literature makes clear that there is quite a variety in approaches to fit and HRM. These conceptualizations of fit in SHRM have mainly focused on either the *content* (e.g. Gratton et al., 1999) or the *process* (e.g. Golden & Ramanujam, 1985). Other perspectives for studying fit in HRM are focused on the *strength of interaction* between HR practices (e.g. Becker et al., 1997; Delery, 1998), the *alignment of dominant goals* with the HR system (e.g. Bowen & Ostroff, 2004), alignment with *organizational systems and work systems* (e.g. MacDuffie, 1995), the *institutional setting* (e.g. Paauwe & Boselie, 2003), *dynamic capabilities* and HRM (e.g. Wright & Snell, 1998), and more recently the *implementation* of the HR strategy (e.g. Becker & Huselid, 2006). These different approaches are all valuable, but at the same time they do not offer a coherent and consistent overall approach. Such an overall approach would be useful in starting to test fit propositions more systematically. We review these approaches next and use insights from them for a new framework of fit in SHRM that encompasses contemporary insights while at the same time aiming to bring back coherence in the fit debate. In this way our approach resembles that of Mintzberg et al. (2008) in the field of strategic management, who distinguish 'splitters' (different and diverging approaches to strategic management) and 'plummers' (bringing it all back together to see the coherence again).

Content approaches

Related to the concept of strategic or vertical fit, Gratton et al. (1999) define strategic fit as the alignment between HR practices and a set of strategic objectives unique to the organization. These HR practices 'create and support individual behaviour and competencies that have the potential to be a source of competitive advantage' (Gratton et al., 1999, p. 21). In their approach the extent to which HR practices are aligned with the business objectives of the organization (i.e. content) is considered as important. They discern five levels of strategic fit, varying from a weak to a strong linkage. A strong link between individual objectives and business goals implies that the business objectives are transformed into clear individual objectives. A weak linkage implies no clear communication of the business strategy to individual employees, and no mechanisms through which individual tasks and behaviour are discussed and linked to strategic objectives (Gratton et al., 1999).

This approach resembles the one that Schuler and Jackson (1987) developed earlier, which also focuses on content as they examine the fit between three types of strategy – innovation, quality enhancement and cost-reduction – and HR practice 'menus' that elicit needed employee behaviours for successfully implementing these strategies. For example, a cost-reduction strategy implies the need for a short-term focus, high concern for quantity and low risk-taking, which would

fit with narrow job descriptions, short-term results-oriented performance appraisals and minimal levels of employee training and development. In summary, the
content approaches mainly focus on:

- The extent to which different HR practices aim at achieving specific business
  goals.
- The degree of integration of business strategy with individual goals and HR
  practices.

Process approaches

Other researchers have emphasized the process of establishing fit (e.g. de Wit &
Meyer, 1998; Paauwe, 2004). The underlying idea of these process approaches is
that the integration of business strategy and HRM processes positively affects the fit
between the human resources required (following strategy) and employee skills
and behaviours that are elicited by HR practices (Bennett et al., 1998).

The role of the HRM department in the organization, which can vary from an
administrative to a strategic role, is an important focus of process approaches.
Golden and Ramanujam (1985), for example, studied the process of strategy formulation and the role of the HR department in this process. They distinguish four
linkages: the administrative linkage, the one-way linkage, the two-way linkage
and the integrative linkage. In an administrative linkage, human resources are
mainly considered necessary costs and not potential contributors to organizational
success. The HR department only has administrative tasks, but no influence on
strategy development. A one-way linkage implies that business goals are the
starting point for formulating the HR practices, but the HR department or function
has little influence on this process. If the strategy affects HRM and vice versa, it is
called a two-way linkage. In this linkage, human resources are seen as success
factors for the organization. The strongest fit in the Golden and Ramanujam (1985)
model is created through an integrative linkage. This linkage represents the highest
degree of alignment between strategy and HRM, in which the HR function is fully
integrated with strategy, formally as well as informally. HR professionals are
represented at the highest level of the organization (e.g. through membership of
the top management team). In summary, the process approaches mainly focus on:

- The extent to which the HR department is involved in strategy formulation.
- The role of the HR department in the organization.

The strength of interaction

The strength of interaction approaches are mainly related to, or inspired by, the
horizontal or internal fit between HR practices. The assumption is that 'certain HR
practices blend better than others do, and it is sensible to select practices in conjunction with and not in isolation from each other' (Wood, 1999, p. 368). The
strength (or weakness) of the aligned practices is defined in terms of the type of
connections that exist between individual HR practices, as it is seen as important to
know how HR practices support each other (Delery, 1998; Baron & Kreps, 1999).

Different HR practices can be additively or interactively (synergistically) related. In an *additive* relationship, HR practices have independent effects on outcomes. For example, teamwork and pay for team performance may both stimulate team performance, but in different ways. In an *interactive* relationship, the effectiveness of one practice depends on the level of the other practices (Delery, 1998). Becker et al. (1997) make a distinction between two types of interactive relationships between HR practices: powerful connections, which represent a positive synergy, and deadly combinations, which represent a negative synergy.

Powerful connections represent combinations of HR practices, such as employee involvement and extensive employee development, which strengthen each other and can create a high performance work system (HPWS) in an organization. A HPWS stimulates employee abilities and motivation, and provides opportunities to participate (Boxall & Macky, 2009), which is supposed to enhance employee job performance (for example, through organizational citizenship behaviour) and organizational performance (for example, through high levels of cost-effectiveness) (Boselie et al., 2005). Deadly combinations reveal a negative synergistic connection between individual HR practices. Here, combining practices such as teamwork and pay for individual performance leads to unintended negative consequences. Therefore, the impact of a deadly combination is most likely to be negative for the individual employee and the organization, as it can cause frustration, low motivation levels and low levels of trust. Internal fit models assume the effectiveness of powerful connections as opposed to deadly combinations (Becker et al., 1997, p. 43). In summary, interaction approaches in strategic HRM highlight:

- The extent to which the HR practices generate synergies.
- The number of powerful connections and deadly combinations that can be identified within the HR system of an organization.
- A systems approach emphasizing coherence among HR practices based on AMO theory.

Alignment of dominant goals

Literature on HR systems and internal fit stresses the importance of a focus on dominant business goals (Baron & Kreps, 1999). HR practices communicate messages to the employees, and higher consistency and clarity of these messages is associated with higher effectiveness (Rousseau, 1995; Baron & Kreps, 1999; Bowen & Ostroff, 2004). In other words, focusing an HR system on dominant, consistent messages is likely to be effective as employees are selected, trained, developed and rewarded to accomplish a dominant business goal. Bowen and Ostroff (2004) label this the 'strength' of the HR system, which is associated with a strong climate. Boxall and Purcell (2008) remark that usually not one, but several desirable themes can be communicated through the HR system. Sometimes these goals can be competing, forcing a trade-off between different goals within the HR system. HR systems thus need a clear focus, but this focus is often a set of goals or themes because of the complexity involved.

Different models propose that an HR system is likely to be effective when it is focused on dominant consistent messages that relate to both a strategic (vertical) and an internal (horizontal) fit of the HR system. Recently we start to see empirical evidence about the importance and effectiveness of signalling a consistent message through HR practices in order to achieve goals; for example, in healthcare settings we refer to Scotti et al. (2007), Stanton et al. (2010) and Veld et al. (2010). Most authors agree that alignment with dominant business goals and alignment between the HR practices are needed in order to achieve a strong HR system. This suggests that 'internal fit without external fit will have little strategic value' (Becker & Huselid, 2006, p. 909). If the HR architecture as a whole supports strategic business processes, this automatically implies that this HR architecture is internally aligned (Becker & Huselid, 2006). In summary, alignment of dominant goals highlights:

- The number of HR practices that focus on a set of dominant goals.
- The extent to which the HR practices support each other in bringing across a consistent message and in this way helping to achieve a set of dominant goals.

Organizational fit

Following Wood's (1999) arguments on the relevance of organizational fit in HRM, researchers have suggested that an organization should align its HR practices and employees' skills and motives with organizational structures, systems and processes (Wright et al., 2001a), and integrate the HR system with strategically important business processes (Becker & Huselid, 2006). In order to be effective, 'an HR bundle or system must be integrated with complementary bundles of practices from core business functions' (MacDuffie, 1995, p. 198).

Studies in HRM covering the relationship between organizational systems, structures and processes, and HR practices focus on various types of organizational systems. Research in the manufacturing sector has shown that HRM is affected by the dominant technology used in the sector and firm (MacDuffie, 1995; Youndt et al., 1996; Appelbaum et al., 2000). For example, Snell and Dean (1992) focused on alignment between advanced manufacturing technology, total quality management, just-in-time management and HRM. Shaw et al. (2001) examine the interactive relationship between integrated manufacturing and compensation practices, and find moderate support for the effectiveness of this congruence model. Cooke (2007) found that alternative workplace strategies differed by the degree of integration of technological and HR capabilities. These studies indicate the effectiveness of aligning different types of systems used in manufacturing with HR practices and strategies, and the same is found in other sectors (e.g. Verburg et al., 2007).

Recently, different authors make a plea for more explicitly incorporating the relevance of work design and work systems in addition to the aforementioned focus on technology, production systems, key business functions and processes. Cordery and Parker state that a work system is 'a particular configuration of interacting subsystems, including work content, technology, employee capabilities, leadership style, and management policies and practices' (Cordery & Parker, 2007, pp. 188–189). Organizational fit from a work system and work design perspective highlights the relevance of alignment between the design of work and (a) the HR systems in place and (b) the broader organizational context (e.g. culture, technology and production techniques). MacDuffie (1995), for example, studied HR practices and work system practices such as work teams, problem-solving groups, job rotation and decentralization of quality-related tasks. Up until now, the majority of HR research has paid little attention to these work systems (Boselie et al., 2005), although Boxall and Macky (2009) bring work system and work design notions back into the HRM and HPWS debate. In summary, organizational fit focuses on:

- Alignment between HR practices and organizational structure and systems.
- Alignment between HR practices and technology and production systems.
- Alignment between HR practices and the work system and work design.

Institutional fit

Environmental fit in Wood's (1999) approach is similar to the concept of institutional fit (Paauwe & Boselie, 2003; Paauwe, 2004). Although widely acknowledged, particularly in European HR models, only a few empirical studies take the institutional context into account (e.g. Boselie et al., 2003; Boon et al., 2009; van Gestel & Nyberg, 2009). Paauwe and Boselie (2003) present an HR model based on DiMaggio and Powell's (1983) institutional mechanisms for organizational isomorphism, namely coercive mechanisms, normative mechanisms and mimetic mechanisms. In their model, institutional fit is achieved when the HR policies and practices are aligned with legislation and the interests of social partners (coercive mechanisms) and the values of professionals, professional bodies and professional development networks (normative mechanisms), and not just the result of adopting HR fads and fashions (mimetic mechanisms).

Institutional fit in HRM may positively affect organizational performance, for example when an organization is better and faster in adopting institutionalized HR practices than competitors (Boon et al., 2009). These HR leaders (Mirvis, 1997) can benefit from the so-called 'first mover' advantage and strengthen their reputation towards stakeholders, including (potential) employees, customers, suppliers, government, financiers, and social partners (e.g. trade unions). Perhaps even more important is the risk of institutional misfit in HRM, potentially causing negative media attention and reputation damage (Paauwe & Boselie, 2005a). In summary, institutional fit in HRM is focused on:

- Aligning HR practices with legislation and other regulations (for example CBA) to avoid negative organizational effects (e.g. reputation damage).
- Early adoption of institutionalized HR practices to achieve unique positive outcomes (in some cases).

Implementation

SHRM traditionally mainly focuses on policies and HR intentions (Guest, 1999; Purcell, 1999; Wright & Boswell, 2002; Boselie et al., 2005; Legge, 2005). Over the last decade the interest in employee perceptions of HR practices has grown; however, little is known about the translation from HR strategies and HR policies (reflecting the organization's intentions) to actual HR practices applied in the organization (Chapter 6). Gratton and Truss (2003) argue that when there is a strong linkage between strategy and HRM in formulation but not in implementation, no positive performance effects can be expected.

Becker and Huselid (2006) focus on the role of key strategic business processes in HR implementation. These key business processes contain strategy and the systems to execute strategy. HR strategies can only be successful through an appropriate HR infrastructure, HR architecture and HR execution. According to Becker and Huselid (2006), strategic alignment of HRM not only plays a role at the organization level, but at the shop floor level as well. Strategy implementation includes strategic, tactical and operational elements to 'make HRM work in practice'. An organization with an extensive training and development infrastructure not only has the HR instrument called training, but the structure to make it work throughout the organization as well. In combination with a general organizational culture for continuous employee development, this company would possess an implementation strategy that can be a source of superior performance. Also, the degree to which employees participate in the process of setting objectives can foster desired employee behaviours. If employees have the opportunity to be involved in the process of setting business objectives, they will probably more committed, which will further implementation (Gratton et al., 1999). Thus, consistent implementation of strategy through HR practices is also necessary for HRM to be effective. In summary, implementation is focused on:

- The presence of an HR infrastructure and HR architecture throughout the organization for distributing HR interventions.
- The extent to which first-line supervisors and employees are involved in implementation of (HR) strategy.

Dynamic capabilities

Wright and Snell (1998) and Wright et al. (2001a) highlight the importance of flexibility in fit with regard to SHRM. Fit in HRM is a rather static concept, often not taking organizational dynamics fully into account. However, organizations do not operate in a vacuum; rather, they are confronted with dynamics in the internal and external context that require adaptation. Wright et al. (2001a) apply the resource-based view to HRM and highlight the importance of dynamic capabilities for HRM. Dynamic capabilities can add value to HRM because they function as a renewal component for resources. 'Such dynamic capabilities require that organizations establish processes that enable them to change their routines, services, products and even markets over time' (Wright et al., 2001a, p. 712).

Wright and Snell (1998, p. 758) use the term 'flexibility' referring to 'a firm's ability to quickly reconfigure resources and activities in response to environmental demands'. While strategic fit focuses on the match between an internal (HR practices) and an external characteristic (strategy), and is therefore strategy-focused, flexibility can be labelled as internal – encompassing employees as well as organizational systems (Wright & Snell, 1998, p. 757). Flexibility can be seen as a characteristic that can be stimulated in employees and integrated in the HR system, which can lead to successful adaptation to organizational changes (Wright & Snell, 1998). Wright and Snell (1998) argue that both strategy- and flexibility-focused HR practices should be present in an HR system in order to achieve both fit and flexibility. Empirical evidence shows that HR flexibility is associated with superior firm performance (Bhattacharya et al., 2005; Beltrán-Martín et al., 2008). HPWS can help develop flexibility of the workforce (Beltrán-Martín et al., 2008). HR flexibility implies adapting employee characteristics such as knowledge, skills, attitudes and behaviour to a changing environment (Bhattacharya et al., 2005). Essential characteristics of flexibility or dynamic fit are:

- The firm's ability to integrate and reconfigure internal and external competences to rapidly address changing environments.
- The extent to which both strategy- and flexibility-focused HR practices are present.
- The extent to which employee attributes (skills, competences, etc.) can be adapted to changing environmental (market) conditions.

Dynamic fit refers to an important contemporary organizational feature: change. Both the early and the next generation fit models in SHRM paid little attention to organizational change and the impact of ongoing change on HR systems.

The eight different perspectives on fit in SHRM presented here all highlight relevant elements of fit in SHRM, including content, process, strength of the interaction, alignment of dominant goals, organizational systems and work systems, institutional context, implementation, and dynamic capabilities.

Missing elements

The overview in the previous section highlights the broad set of insights on fit that authors have put forward in the last decade. However, we argue that several issues that should be part of a comprehensive view of fit have not yet been covered sufficiently. First, several authors (den Hartog et al., 2004; Purcell & Hutchinson, 2007; Wright & Nishii, Chapter 6) have emphasized the relevance of the line manager in the process of HR implementation or HRM enactment. Fit approaches in SHRM have not paid sufficient attention to the role of line managers. While HR professionals or managers are mainly involved in HR policy formulation, line managers play a crucial role in the HR implementation process.

Second, the *role of the employee* is not prominently present in many of the approaches of fit. This in spite of the fact that over the last decade, following the plea by Guest (1999) and Purcell (1999), HR studies have paid increased attention to the individual employee (Boselie et al., 2009). However, this is mainly reflected in the inclusion of employee data and the application of multi-level research techniques in contemporary HRM and performance research (Croon & van Veldhoven, 2007). Little attention in SHRM is paid to the notion of *person–environment fit* (van Vianen, 2000; Kristof-Brown et al., 2005; Boon et al., 2010). Person–environment fit (PE fit) refers to the extent to which certain types of people fit with certain types of organizational environments (Bretz & Judge, 1994). Research, mainly in the area of recruitment and selection, shows that PE fit positively affects employee attitudes and behaviours (Kristof-Brown et al., 2005). The two most studied types of PE fit are person-organization (PO) fit, and person-job (PJ) fit. PO fit focuses on the alignment between the individual employee and the organization's values, culture and goals. PJ fit focuses on the alignment between employees' skills, abilities and needs, and the characteristics of the job (Kristof-Brown et al., 2005). The relevant findings of PE fit studies have not been embedded in SHRM approaches and we argue that this is a missing link that could strengthen fit approaches in SHRM.

Third, there has been insufficient attention to aligning *intended* with *actual* and *perceived* HR practices, based on the insights of Wright and Nishii (Chapter 6). These authors draw our attention to the need for consistency among different actors. HR professionals and the HR department are involved in the development and design of HR policies and practices (intended); as mentioned, implementation is often carried out in close cooperation with line management at the various levels of the organization, which leads to 'actual' HR practices. The actual practices will only result in change of behaviour and subsequent outcomes if employees also perceive those practices. Where the aforementioned notion of implementation mainly focuses on the HR practices and the need for processes and infrastructure to support implementation, this notion of intended, actual and perceived HR practices emphasizes the actors involved and the need for them to act in a consistent way in order to strengthen fit (see also Chapter 5).

Integration of fit approaches and discussion

As described above, there is a broad diversity in fit approaches available. There are, however, clear links between the different approaches that have not been focused on to date. For example, the notion of internal or horizontal fit is reflected in the 'strength of interactions between practices' approach, which often occurs together with 'alignment with dominant goals'. As mentioned, the 'alignment with dominant goals' in turn highlights the importance of the relationship between internal or horizontal fit on the one hand, and strategic or vertical fit on the other hand, which makes this approach closely related to 'process' and 'content' approaches, which are both labelled as strategic fit approaches. However, as the different approaches have not been studied simultaneously, little is known about how exactly the different approaches to fit are related.

Another area that has not received much attention is the temporal order or hierarchy in achieving fit. Some elements of fit need to be achieved first as a basic condition or 'hygiene factor' for organizational survival; for example, achieving an institutional fit by complying with legal and CBA requirements. Other elements of

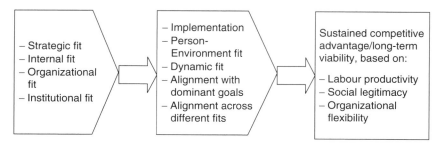

Figure 4.1   A two-stage framework for fit in SHRM

fit might not be a basic requirement but can be implemented or realized later in order to achieve a sustained competitive advantage; for example, aligning a competence management system with job characteristics and the requirements of a service delivery work system.

The ultimate goal in most fit theories is to enhance performance. However, when focusing on the various forms of fit, we run the risk of overlooking this desired relationship of fit with performance. And which types of performance is fit supposed to increase? We argue that in order to move the field forward, we need an integrated perspective on fit, which takes into account:

• How the different approaches to fit are related (forming a unique gestalt or configuration).
• Temporal order and hierarchical relationships between the different types of fit.
• The relationship between fit and performance.

We propose a two-stage framework of fit in SHRM (see Figure 4.1), which will be explained next.

In the first stage, the main aim is to achieve a basic level of fit. This stage includes the four types of fit that were distinguished by Wood (1999). Strategic fit covers both content and process approaches. Internal fit covers the strength of interaction between HR practices. Organizational and institutional fit are included to incorporate the importance of alignment of HRM with organizational systems and the institutional environment. Focusing on achieving these four types of fit enables the formulation of a sound HR system, which should lead to safeguarding organizational continuity.

However, we can't just say the more forms of fit, the better; nor can we say the higher the level of fit, the better. There could be tensions between different forms of fit, such that a high level of one fit can only be achieved at the expense of another type. For example, in SHRM, both competitive and institutional forces are often captured in one 'external environment' construct, as for example seen in the notion of external fit (e.g. Baird & Meshoulam, 1988; Miles & Snow, 1994). However, a complex interaction exists between the demands of a competitive environment and institutional pressures, and therefore we incorporate institutional and strategy dimensions separately, as outlined in the 'contextually based human resource theory' (Paauwe, 2004). In a similar vein, Deephouse (1999) argues in his 'strategic balance theory' that organizations face a trade-off between institutional and competitive pressures. Because of institutional forces, organizations are 'pressured' to become more similar, and so conformity increases legitimacy. However, competitive pressures lead to the need for differentiation of organizations; a firm with a different strategy benefits because it faces less competition for resources (Deephouse, 1999). Both legitimacy and financial performance are needed for long-term survival, so organizations face the challenge of balancing legitimacy and efficiency goals. Strategic balance theory thus suggests that strategic and institutional fit might be contradictory. Organizations have to achieve a certain degree of differentiation as well as conforming in order to be perceived as legitimate and get access to required resources like finance, labour, and so on. (Deephouse, 1999). This suggests that for achieving optimal performance, a minimum satisfactory level of institutional fit is needed (i.e. 'satisficing': Simon, 1979), whereas strategic fit is optimized. Therefore, we expect:

Proposition 1: An effective HR system requires optimizing the level of strategic fit and 'satisficing' the level of institutional fit

We will illustrate this first stage of the framework using an example of RetailCo, a Dutch retail organization selling products for daily use, with almost 300 stores in The Netherlands. In RetailCo, the first stage of the framework is implemented. The HR director of RetailCo has little strategic decision-making power because they are not a member of the management team. The HR department is, however, involved in strategic issues after strategic decision-making and supports these strategic decisions with HR practices, thus achieving a strategic fit. Internal fit results for example from the use of an employee planning system, which maps the level of employees' skills and knowledge relative to the desired level, and ties training, appraisal and selection together: Employees are recommended to engage in training based on the gap between current and desired skills, and they are appraised on their progress. Also, new employees are selected in order to fill a gap in knowledge or skills in the store. The employee planning system also contributes to an organizational fit, as it seeks to align work content and employee capabilities (part of the work system) with HR practices. RetailCo also achieves institutional fit by conforming to institutional pressures in order to achieve legitimacy. RetailCo conforms to trade union pressures after having had a problematic collective bargaining process because it wanted to decrease wages for new employees.

The first stage of our two-stage model concerns the 'basic' types of fit, which can be seen as necessary preconditions (or requirements) for organizational survival. The second stage includes fit approaches that can enhance the effectiveness of the HR system and help to achieve a sustained competitive advantage. First, implementation highlights the importance of not only designing an HR system that fits well, but also draws attention to the execution of this system. Without good implementation, the expected performance effect of the HR system cannot be achieved. Second, person–environment fit includes the role of the employee in the framework by taking into account employees' values, preferences and competencies, in order to get the right people in the right place, which is expected to increase performance (Kristof-Brown et al., 2005). Third, dynamic fit emphasizes the need for the HR system to focus on both strategy and flexibility in order to achieve a sustained competitive advantage (Wright & Snell, 1998). Thus, while achieving fit can lead to short-term success, a dynamic fit is needed to cope with changes and achieve fit in the long run. Fourth, as mentioned, aligning HR practices with dominant goals requires the integration of strategic and internal fit, as alignment of the HR system as a whole with organizational goals (i.e. strategic fit) implies that the HR system is internally aligned as well (Becker & Huselid, 2006). In line with this, the fifth element in the second stage of the model is alignment across different fits. When the different types of fit are aligned (i.e. a 'fit between the fits'), they all aim for the same overall goals, which makes it more likely for an organization to achieve superior performance. Thus, we expect:

Proposition 2: Both the first and second stages of the framework are needed for effectiveness

FurniCo is the Dutch part of an international furniture company, which owns 11 stores in The Netherlands. FurniCo is very successful and outperforms competitors in the market, which is reflected by its number one ranking (in 2011, but also in preceding years) on the list of Dutch retail department stores. FurniCo is an example of an organization that has been able to implement the second stage of the framework in addition to the first stage. For example, FurniCo takes into account the importance of good implementation by involving employees in strategic planning. One illustration is that employees have an input in goal-setting for the store and their department. Employee values and preferences are also taken into account because FurniCo selects new employees based on their fit with the company culture (i.e. PE fit). FurniCo also aims to achieve dynamic fit. For example, because the busiest hours in the stores are from 6 p.m. to 9 p.m., FurniCo has trained employees in each department to be employable in other departments in the store where assistance is needed during that period, increasing flexibility. Employees move through the store in parallel to the customers such that around closing time, many employees from different departments work at the cash register, where most of the customers are at that time. Alignment with dominant goals is achieved, for example with the 'appraisal cycle' of FurniCo where individual goals are set based on the contribution an employee can make to departmental goals. Employees are then trained to be better able to contribute to these goals, and are evaluated and rewarded based on the accomplishment of these goals. The appraisal cycle thus aligns HR practices such as training, appraisal and rewards into a coherent HR system (internal fit), and aligns these HR practices with strategic goals of the organization (strategic fit). Besides this alignment of internal and strategic fit, FurniCo also achieves other alignments across fits. Some examples are that flexibility, which is focused on to achieve a dynamic fit, is also considered as an important organizational goal. Also, FurniCo's innovative approach to achieving institutional fit by establishing a company union with which a company-specific CBA is negotiated has resulted in a close alignment with strategic fit, since organizational goals and values are incorporated in the CBA. FurniCo has thus managed to overcome part of the contradiction between strategic and institutional fit. In summary, FurniCo has implemented the second stage of the model. Two examples are, however, not enough to illustrate performance effects of fit. Possible relationships between fit and performance proposed by the model will be discussed below.

Inherent in the concept of fit is the assumption that achieving a high level of fit is associated with high effectiveness (Nadler & Tushman, 1980; Wright & Snell, 1998). But what type of performance is relevant as an indicator of effectiveness? Performance has a different meaning, depending on which perspective is used, and HRM could be more or less helpful depending on how performance is defined (Francis et al., 2005). In SHRM, researchers have mainly used financial performance measures in order to examine the effectiveness of HRM (Boselie et al., 2005; Francis et al., 2005); however, little attention has been paid to the meaning of performance from the perspective of other stakeholders. Therefore, we argue for using a multidimensional concept of performance (e.g. Paauwe, 2004), taking different types of stakeholders into account. Here, we follow Boxall and Purcell (2008) and make a distinction between three critical HR goals: labour productivity (cost-effectiveness), social legitimacy (employment citizenship) and organizational flexibility. For each type of fit, different performance categories might be most relevant.

Strategic fit has been associated with achieving strategic goals and gaining a competitive advantage in order to outperform competitors in the sector. Internal fit has a more inward focus. Research suggests that a coherent and consistent HR system is used in order to send messages to employees regarding desired behaviours (Bowen & Ostroff, 2004). The concept of organizational fit highlights the importance of integrating HR practices with organizational systems in order to achieve organizational goals more effectively. These three types of fit all aim at achieving desired goals and stimulating desired behaviours, which are all directly related to enhancing productivity of employees. Therefore, we expect:

Proposition 3: Aligned strategic, internal and organizational fit will be positively related to labour productivity

As mentioned, the goal of achieving institutional fit is achieving legitimacy, such as a high reputation and to be seen as a fair employer to employees. Organizations that do not conform to institutional pressures face higher legitimacy risks. Therefore, we expect that the performance effect of institutional fit will be geared towards achieving social legitimacy:

Proposition 4: Institutional fit will be positively related to social legitimacy

Authors suggest that in order to achieve superior performance, an organization needs adaptive or dynamic capabilities (i.e. Helfat & Peteraf, 2003; Colbert, 2004; Datta et al., 2005). Besides fit, flexibility is also needed to achieve sustainable performance. A dynamic fit focuses on coping with change and has the aim of increasing organizational flexibility. Aiming for achieving a dynamic fit can turn short-run performance into long-run agility or viability (Paauwe, 2004; Boxall & Purcell, 2008). Therefore, we propose:

Proposition 5: Achieving a dynamic fit is positively related to organizational flexibility

Overall, our framework proposes that a sustained competitive advantage can be gained by achieving all three types of performance: high labour productivity, social legitimacy and organizational flexibility (Boxall & Purcell, 2008). The first stage of the framework focuses on basic types of fit in HRM, which are considered as necessary but not sufficient for achieving a sustained competitive advantage. The second stage of the framework introduces a focus on the factors that are expected to enable the development of a sustained competitive advantage from these fits by increasing the focus on implementation, preferences of employees, coping with change and complementarities between the different types of fit, such that overall, the sum will be larger than the parts. This corresponds with achieving a configuration or 'gestalt' (Guest, 1997): finding an appropriate combination of practices of which the sum is greater than the parts. All separate practices are chosen or evaluated in the context of the other practices in place, which results in a unique 'gestalt' or configuration for an organization that is hard to replicate by other organizations and is therefore supposed to lead to long-term successfulness. In line with this, we expect:

Proposition 6: The different types of fit together can form a unique gestalt or configuration, which could lead to a sustained competitive advantage

Many performance measures cannot be exclusively related to HRM. Therefore, an organization could be successful without achieving any HRM-related fit or with only one or a few forms of fit in place, for example, in a situation of market growth, or as a result of an increase in labour supply. This possibility needs to be taken into account in future research, for example by choosing a research design that controls for other influences on performance. Moreover, besides the possibility of 'performance without fit', more research is needed into the effects of misfit or a lack of fit on organizational performance.

In summary, the proposed two-stage framework of fit in SHRM incorporates the classic and early fit models, and shows how all different perspectives on fit can be integrated within one framework. Also, it draws attention to links and relationships between different elements and types of fit, and to how fit could affect performance.

Conclusion

A variety of fit approaches are available in SHRM, including content, process, the strength of interaction and the alignment of dominant goals within HRM, and alignment of HRM with organizational systems and work systems. Next to these we have emphasized the importance of the institutional setting, dynamic capabilities and implementation. These different approaches are all valuable, but they do not offer a coherent and consistent overall approach for fit, since there is a lack of integration of these different perspectives. The aim of this paper was to integrate current fit approaches into a new framework, which includes available fit approaches, missing elements and the link between fit and performance. We derived propositions from this framework to guide future research.

Several issues for future research can be identified. First, future research needs to incorporate different types of fit in one study, as different types of fit could strengthen or contradict each other. Looking at each type of fit separately might thus not give an accurate picture. Second, research needs to take into account the distinction between basic types of fit, which are a necessary condition for organizational survival and have to be achieved first, and the fit approaches that – on top of the basic types of fit – could lead to a sustainable competitive advantage, as emphasized in our two-stage approach. For example, an organization that achieves the various types of fit in the first stage, but does not achieve the second stage types of fit, is not expected to perform well. It might survive, but it does not achieve a sustained competitive advantage. Third, our framework and propositions highlight the importance of using a multidimensional performance concept in future research, since different types of fit are likely to be related to different types of performance, which are all needed in order to achieve a sustained competitive advantage. Our framework could thus be useful in starting to more systematically test fit propositions.

As the different approaches to fit incorporate a range of contextual factors, a combination of research methods is needed to test the impact of fit. For example, Boxall et al. (2007) suggest the analytical approach, emphasizing (a) evidence based research, (b) contextually based research and (c) the application of rigorous methods and techniques. Both qualitative and quantitative research methods and techniques are required to explore the different fit types in specific contexts and to test the impact of fit on performance in future research. In summary, in this chapter we have offered a next step towards uncovering how fit affects performance; further research is needed to test our framework and hypotheses.

5

HRM AND PERFORMANCE: THE ROLE OF EFFECTIVE IMPLEMENTATION

DAVID GUEST AND
ANNA BOS-NEHLES

Since the pioneering work of researchers such as Arthur (1994), MacDuffie (1995) and Huselid (1995), a large number of studies have explored the link between human resource management (HRM) and performance. Reviews a decade later by Boselie et al. (2005) and Combs et al. (2006) confirm that there is considerable evidence to support an association. However, they also note a number of limitations in the research and in particular a failure to consider why or how this association comes about. This has led to calls to 'open up the black box' to explore how HRM and performance might be related.

Writers who have considered this issue generally focus on two broad and overlapping classes of within-organization explanation. The first addresses what might be termed a 'linkage model', which places at the centre of its analysis the impact of HR policy and practice on employees' attitudes and behaviour. An optimistic version proposes that HRM has a positive association with performance because workers respond positively to it (Becker et al., 1997; Guest, 1997; Appelbaum et al., 2000). An alternative, more pessimistic view is that HR practices result in intensification of work and it is this that leads to the performance gains (for a fuller discussion of these perspectives, see Chapter 2).

The second approach to the more detailed explanation of the relationship between HRM and performance considers the effectiveness of HR practices and of their implementation. For example, Huselid et al. (1997) explored the perceived effectiveness of different approaches to HRM, while Khilji and Wang (2006) highlighted the gap between intended and implemented practices. These two perspectives, seeking to explain the determinants of the HRM-performance relationship, are not independent: indeed, a positive worker response is a key indicator of effective implementation. The role of employee responses to HRM is a central focus of other chapters; in this chapter we focus on effective implementation.

In strategic human resource management theory, effective implementation is seen as the result of an appropriate fit between the HR architecture and strategic choice. According to Barney (2001), the resource-based view initially regarded implementation as a 'theoretical convenience' because 'implementation follows, almost automatically' (p. 53). However, Barney (2001) recognizes that 'the ability to implement strategies is, by itself, a resource that can be a source of competitive advantage (p. 54). Becker and Huselid (2006) locate effective HR strategy implementation as a key mediating variable between the HR architecture and firm performance. Recently, Guest (2011) noted that 'it is not enough to have good practices if they are not properly implemented' (p. 6). This implies that we need to improve our understanding about what determines effective HR implementation. The central aim of this chapter is therefore to analyse and improve our understanding of factors shaping effective implementation of HRM and to assess their implications for the relationship between HRM and performance. The chapter starts by presenting an analytic framework within which to consider implementation. Using this framework, we then review research findings, addressing each stage in the implementation process. This is followed by a section examining evidence about the roles of the key actors in the implementation of HRM. Finally, we outline some future research priorities.

A framework for the analysis of effective implementation of HRM

The analytic framework that we have developed to explore the implementation of HRM has three core dimensions and two contextual dimensions. It is presented in Table 5.1. The first core dimension identifies four stages in the implementation process, the second identifies the key actors in HR implementation and the third considers who evaluates the effectiveness of HR implementation. The model also highlights the importance of two core contextual dimensions, simply labelled 'internal context' and 'external context'.

Stages of HRM implementation

We adopt a broad view of HRM implementation, identifying four 'stages' where the effectiveness of implementation can affect the HRM–performance relationship. Strictly speaking these are not always sequential stages or entirely separate processes; but we argue that they are analytically distinct elements in the implementation process and can usefully be considered as such. These four stages are first, the decision to introduce or significantly change an HR practice or set of practices; second, the design and quality assurance of the practice; third, the core decision to implement the practice; and fourth, the quality of implementation. To take a typically cited example, a firm may, as a first step, decide to introduce an appraisal system. At the second stage, it has to ensure that the appraisal system is of sufficient quality to be fit for purpose. Thirdly, although it may be official policy to conduct appraisals of all staff, line managers have to choose whether or not to do so. Finally, at the fourth stage, line managers can choose to conduct high-quality

Table 5.1   A model of HR implementation

Stages	Primary implementers	Primary evaluators
Stage 1: decision to introduce HR practices	HR managers Senior executives/CEO	Senior executives External bodies/groups
Stage 2: quality of HR practices	HR managers	Senior executives HR managers Line managers
Stage 3: implementation of HR practices	Line managers	Senior executives Line managers HR managers Employees
Stage 4: quality of implementation	Line managers	Senior executives Line managers HR managers Employees

Internal context	External context
Competitive strategy and HR strategy Strength of the HR system Leadership and HR focus	External stakeholders: • government and government agencies • legislation and compliance agencies • customers and potential recruits • shareholders Market conditions Market context (e.g. international focus)

appraisals or to treat them as a bureaucratic ritual. In other words, they can choose how seriously to take the appraisal process and whether to conform to intended practice. Each step in this process depends for its effectiveness on the previous stages; it would therefore be limiting to consider line management implementation and its impact without taking account of the nature and quality of the HR practices they are expected to implement. Within this sequence of implementation, the first two steps are typically seen as the responsibility of the HR function, often working in collaboration with senior management, while the third and fourth steps are the responsibility of line managers, sometimes influenced by signals from senior management and monitoring pressures from the HR department. Effective implementation is likely to depend to a considerable extent on features of the wider organizational context. We can examine each of the four stages in a little more detail.

The first stage concerns the decision to adopt specific HR practices. All organizations have to undertake a number of activities such as selecting staff, issuing contracts of employment, allocating roles and rewarding staff. There are choices about how to do these and about what sort of HR practices to adopt: for example, many organizations use interviews as a core selection practice; some go further and use psychometric tests and, perhaps, realistic job previews. Contextual factors such as organizational size and degree of formalization and centralization, as well as any corporate and HR strategy, are likely to influence the degree of sophistication of practices (Boxall & Purcell, 2011). Furthermore, Paauwe (2004) has argued that in most European countries, institutional factors (reflected in European-wide and national legislation and collective agreements) require organizations to have a range of HR practices in place. European research that explores whether a practice is present will therefore find that almost all organizations have a number in place while some, in line with their strategic aims, will have considerably more.

The second stage concerns the quality of the practices. Legislation may require organizations to avoid discrimination in selection, to undertake certain training and to ensure equal opportunities. As a result, organizations will invariably report that relevant practices are in place. In doing so, they may meet the minimum requirements to comply with legislation, but with no concern to ensure that they have a positive impact in the organization. Alternatively, practices may be carefully developed to assist the organization in achieving strategic goals, including outcomes such as high commitment or high performance. The presence of practices can differ from the effectiveness of practices in other ways. For example, firms may use psychometric tests but choose tests with poor predictive validity. We therefore need to look beyond the reported presence of a practice to determine its quality and likely effectiveness.

The third stage concerns the actual implementation of practices by line managers. Senior managers may endorse HR policies and practices, and the HR function may take steps to ensure their quality; but it is line managers who invariably have the responsibility for implementation on the ground. In doing so, they may be left to their own devices or they may be closely monitored, and their own values and priorities – and indeed those of their business unit – may be more or less aligned with the HR values implied in the practices. For example, the HR department may have developed a sophisticated system for local mentoring newly appointed staff: line managers may choose to ignore mentoring either because it is squeezed out by what they consider to be more important activities or because they perceive it as an irrelevant bureaucratic ritual.

The fourth and final stage addresses the quality of line management implementation. For example, using appraisals again as an illustration, line managers may complete appraisals but only as a ritual. In other words, even where there is the potential for effective implementation of a high-quality appraisal process, line managers choose not to utilize the system except to be able to report minimum compliance with central requirements. Also, line managers may differ in their motivation to implement HR practices as fully as possible and in their ability to do so (Nehles et al., 2006). For example, they may find it difficult to address interpersonal problems, take up disciplinary cases or introduce flexible working arrangements.

It can be argued that each stage is a necessary requirement for those that follow. Without an appraisal system, there can be no formal appraisal. Without a system of at least reasonable quality, there can be no effective implementation by line management. And if line managers chose not to implement the appraisal scheme, the question of the quality of their implementation becomes irrelevant. As already noted, this model highlights analytic distinctions that may become blurred in practice; for example, the decision to introduce a new practice and decisions about design and quality may overlap. Similarly, there may be a fine line between a decision to implement a practice and the quality of implementation. However, we believe these analytic distinctions are conceptually important if we are to advance our understanding of HRM implementation and its impact on the HRM–performance relationship.

Responsibility for implementation

The second dimension in the analytic framework concerns responsibility for HR implementation. A range of actors may have a stake in the process, including senior executives, HR specialists, line managers and, on some occasions, employees and their trade unions or representative bodies within the organization. Government and its agencies, clients and occasionally shareholders and customers outside the organization can also claim a stake. Consultancy organizations may sometimes have a role to play in the introduction and evaluation of HR practices. The first two stages – the introduction and quality assurance of HR practices – might typically be viewed as a primary responsibility of the HR function. Most of the research on HRM and performance is conducted in large organizations (although see Chapter 10 by de Winne and Sels on HRM in small businesses), where there is an established HR function with HR professionals who, through their expert knowledge, might be expected to press for the introduction of appropriate HR practices and ensure their quality and hence their potential effectiveness. When decisions are taken about the introduction of new HR practices, which can often reflect underlying policy initiatives, the chief executive and other senior executives outside the HR function may have a significant influence on the decisions.

On a day-to-day basis, line managers at senior, middle and supervisory levels will have a primary role to play in ensuring effective implementation of the HR practices in place. This analysis implies a top-down and centre-periphery perspective where the support and level of commitment of senior executives in ensuring effective implementation is likely to be important. There may also be an influential role for the HR function in monitoring implementation and in operating an HR information system that can identify variations in HR practice and in relevant outcomes such as labour turnover, absence, training activity and disciplinary cases. It is, of course, possible that in some organizations there are local initiatives to introduce HR practices that are not found elsewhere in the organization. This is particularly likely to occur where there are clearly separated internal labour markets (Lepak & Snell, 2002), where there are international operations that allow the influence of local national factors to come into play (Farndale & Paauwe, 2007), or where there is a highly decentralized and devolved organization structure.

External organizations can play a significant role in ensuring implementation of certain HR practices. Government legislation places obligations on organizations that can be monitored through various national agencies. Public sector organizations can be encouraged to engage in specific practices to support national policy. Potential purchasers of services can require evidence of quality standards and ethical practices relating to HR to be in place. Research on the 'war for talent' has revealed that graduates that an organization may wish to attract are likely to be influenced by the branding of the organization. An important element of the branding is likely to be the set of HR practices that graduates will experience, including promotion policies, development opportunities and scope for challenging work (Fulmer et al., 2003; Edwards, 2010).

Evaluation of implementation

The third element in the analytic framework addresses who judges the effective implementation of HR practices. Tsui (1987) has called for the use of multiple stakeholders. Importantly, she also noted (Tsui, 1990) that different stakeholders use different criteria to judge effectiveness. Those who promote HR, those who enact it and those employees affected by it may arrive at different judgements about implementation effectiveness. Wright et al. (2001b), adopting what is essentially a political perspective, argue that the views of senior executives matter most, since they determine the allocation of resources to HR and other activities.

It is also important to recognize that the evaluations made by the actors responsible for implementation will have implications for ongoing and future behaviour that can affect the HRM–performance relationship. Senior executives may be unwilling to continue to invest in HR practices they perceive as providing no identifiable benefit and line managers are unlikely to persist in devoting their time to implementing practices they perceive to have no impact.

The context of HRM implementation

The analytic framework in Table 5.1 is intended to suggest that the internal and external contexts of the organization will help to determine the priority attached to the introduction and implementation of HR practices. This is in line with the Harvard model presented by Beer et al. (1984). Much has been written, for example, about the way in which transnational corporations transfer HR and other practices from the host country to others in which they operate (Edwards & Kurvilla, 2005). Competitive strategy can affect the priority given to service quality and the role of HR implementation in achieving this. The work of Bowen and Ostroff (2004) has been influential in making the case for what they term a 'strong' HR system and culture to ensure more effective implementation of HR practices; and Schein (1986), among others, has written about the role of organizational leaders and the importance of what they pay attention to as a basis for shaping and focusing organizational cultures. Turning to the external context, in expanding and profitable economic circumstances, organizations may be more willing to invest in human resources. As already noted, institutional factors such as legislation and the role of trade unions can also influence the presence and implementation of HR practices.

Having outlined the analytic framework – including four stages of implementation, the key actors involved in HR implementation, the role and importance of the various stakeholders in the evaluation of implementation, and the contexts within which implementation occurs – we next explore evidence about the impact of implementation at each of the four stages on organizational performance.

Effectiveness of the decision to introduce HRM practices

Most of the early research on HRM and performance collected information about the presence of HR practices. In other words, it explored what practices had been introduced and were currently in place. These studies typically revealed quite large variations in the number of practices in place across organizations. There may be greater homogeneity in countries such as The Netherlands, where the institutional influences are strong (Paauwe, 2004). Data from the UK Workplace Employment Relations Surveys (Kersley et al., 2006) reveals that the spread in the number of practices is greater in the private than in the public sector. Reasons for this might include the persistence of forms of centralized collective bargaining in parts of the public sector and government exerting a homogenizing influence on practice.

We know surprisingly little about why some organizations report more practices in place than others, or about how decisions are arrived at to introduce new or improved practices. We might expect the presence of an HR specialist, and more particularly a specialist with professional qualifications, to influence this process. However, analysis of successive UK Workplace Employment Relations Surveys indicates that – at least in the UK – this is not the case (Guest & Bryson, 2009). This leaves open the question: if not the HR specialists, who? We have no good information on this. We might expect the top management to play a part and perhaps also consultants.

One way to explore this issue is to investigate what happens in greenfield sites where the organization has an opportunity for a fresh start. A study comparing practices in US, German, Japanese and European owned sites being opened in the UK revealed that past practice and experience from the host country often had a major influence on the HR practices applied in the UK (Guest & Hoque, 1996). This tendency either to follow instructions from the parent or to stick with what you know tends to militate against innovation. Yet there is some evidence that over the past 20 years the use of 'high-commitment' HR practices has tended to increase (Kersley et al., 2006). Given the ambiguities and uncertainties identified in the HR function (Legge, 1978), we might expect a high level of isomorphism and a tendency to follow fads and fashions (Abrahamson, 1991), and we can see some evidence for this in the phases of enthusiasm for particular practices. In the past these have included briefing groups and quality circles; more recently it has extended to incentive schemes for senior executives and employee engagement (Gibson & Tesone, 2001). But this does not tell us who shaped the decision to follow fashion and implement these practices. Some insight on this can be gained from the work of Mirvis (1997), who explored innovations in HRM and, specifically, the introduction of new HR practices in the US private sector. He reported an association with general firm strategy on innovation. A minority of firms wanted to be at the leading edge of innovation in HRM, a majority wanted to follow either closely or some way behind the leaders, while a further minority deliberately lagged behind waiting for clear evidence of positive impact.

The factors determining the introduction of HR practices in parts of the public sector may be rather different. In some countries, there has been a tradition for public sector organizations to act as exemplars of good practice, sometimes described as model employers (Bach et al., 2009). This has meant that they have to demonstrate that they have policies and practices in place to ensure (for example) equal opportunities and fairness of treatment. They are also more susceptible to government influence. Therefore, the government may wish to impose a specific payment system to ensure that practices designed to enhance performance management are in place or to require that regular staff attitude surveys are conducted.

Most research on HRM and performance has explored the relationship between the number of HR practices currently in place and organizational performance, generally confirming an association (Combs et al., 2006). The presence of a practice tells us it has been introduced. It often tells us little about its quality or how it is implemented; it is therefore a limited indicator of effective HRM. Furthermore, it has been noted that there is scope for error in the reporting of both the presence of practices and performance (Gerhart et al., 2000b) that might hide, and indeed underplay, the true association. Studies have consistently shown that HR managers will report more practices in place than the number reported by employees (e.g. Liao et al., 2009; Guest et al., 2010). While this may reflect differences in levels of awareness of practices, it is more likely to reflect differences between the presence of a practice, as reported by the HR managers, and the experience of the practice when implemented, as reported by the employee. Both may be providing reliable information, but they are reporting about different stages in the implementation process. There is very little research that compares the perceptions of different management groups about the presence of HR practices as opposed to their effectiveness, and this is clearly a gap in our research knowledge. The presence of HR practices has served as the dominant proxy for the implementation of HRM in most research on HRM and performance. Our analysis indicates that this is insufficient. HR practices must be both present and of a quality to be potentially effective. We now turn to this issue.

The quality and effectiveness of HR practices

A number of studies have explored perceptions of the quality and effectiveness of HR practices. However, there is often a lack of specificity in the questioning about what the respondents are being asked to judge. While the study may therefore appear to be concerned with the quality of the HR practices, in reality respondents may be offering a more global judgement about their quality but also about whether they are being implemented and are having any impact – in other words, they are being asked to judge their effectiveness. Indeed, it may be difficult to separate the quality of a practice from some consideration of its intended consequences. There is a need for more specific questioning in future studies. Whatever the specific focus of questioning, most observers agree with Tsui (1987) that it is sensible to adopt a stakeholder perspective in arriving at what are essentially subjective assessments. By involving at least two of the interested parties, it may be possible to arrive at a more reliable assessment (Gerhart et al., 2000; Datta et al., 2005).

In one of the early studies, Huselid et al. (1995) asked HR managers and a smaller number of line managers about the effectiveness of what they described as technical or traditional HR practices and strategic or high-performance HR practices. They found an association between the rated effectiveness of the latter (but not the former) and firm performance, suggesting that it is not just the effectiveness of practices *per se* but the effectiveness of specific practices that has the impact. Wright et al. (2001b) collected data from senior HR managers and senior line managers and found that HR managers took a consistently more positive view of effectiveness than line managers; they implied that line managers may have the more realistic view. Tsui (1990) found that senior executives tended to judge effectiveness (in this case of HR departments) in terms of strategy while more junior executives gave more emphasis to implementation. Perhaps more surprisingly, she found that senior executives had a more positive view of the HR function effectiveness than those in the HR function. Guest and Conway (2011) found no difference in perceived levels of effectiveness of HR practices between chief executives and HR directors. Finally, Bondarouk et al. (2009) compared the frames of reference used by HR managers and line managers in judging HR innovation and found differences in understanding and expectations. Overall, therefore, while it appears that HR managers and others may use different criteria to judge HR effectiveness, we cannot conclude that HR managers provide more generous ratings.

The comparison of ratings of effectiveness raises the question of levels of agreement between raters. This has not always been reported in studies among management groups. However, Guest and Conway (2011) found rather low levels of agreement between chief executives and HR directors, implying either that they use different criteria or that there are high levels of ignorance or uncertainty about effectiveness of HR practices.

Several of the studies of effectiveness have explored the association between effectiveness of HR practices or the HR function and performance. As we have noted, Huselid et al. (1995) reported an association between effectiveness of what they termed strategic or developmental HR practices and business performance. Richard and Johnson (2001, 2004) found an association between effectiveness of high-performance HR practices and firm performance. Guest and Conway (2011) explored the relative importance of the presence of HR practices and the rated effectiveness of these practices. They found that both had an independent and positive effect on a range of performance indicators and that effectiveness of practices, rather than the presence of practices, generally had the stronger effect. Richard and Johnson (2004) also explore this comparison and report similar findings. This is in line with our model, which assumes that the presence of a practice is unlikely to be as powerful as the presence of what are judged to be effective or high-quality practices, and confirms the assumption that studies exploring the association between the presence of practices and performance may understate the true association. However, there is always a risk that assessments of the effectiveness of HR practices may be influenced by knowledge of performance outcomes, resulting in a form of reverse attribution.

Line managers' decision to implement HR practices

Once high-quality HR policies and practices have been formulated and designed, they need to be translated into action. As several researchers have noted, line managers have the prime responsibility for implementation of HR practices at the operational level (Child & Partridge, 1982; Marchington, 2001; Gratton & Truss, 2003). They may even cover any shortcomings of organizational policies and top management decisions (Maertz et al., 2007). This is why Hutchinson and Purcell (2010) believe that 'the behaviour of front-line managers, particularly in discharging their HRM responsibilities, is too important to be ignored' (p. 359). Therefore, while the HR department can design a high-quality appraisal system or mentoring scheme, line managers must decide whether to utilize them. However, line managers are subject to a range of pressures and need to establish their priorities. As Brewster and Larsen (1992) note, they are expected to create a synergy between human, financial and physical resources.

Devolving HR implementation to line managers may appear attractive to HR managers, since it can allow them to focus on more strategic issues. However, it creates a new challenge with the need to monitor whether implementation has taken place and, as we discuss in the next section, whether it is effective implementation.

Line managers may feel more comfortable enacting some elements of their role and prefer to neglect others. In the case of implementing HR practices, much may depend on line managers' commitment towards and capability regarding their HR role (den Hartog et al., 2004; Purcell & Hutchinson, 2007). Khilji and Wang (2006), in their study of HR implementation in Pakistani banks, noted a gap between intended and implemented practices, with some line managers choosing not to implement the practices. This is by no means an isolated case. For example, Woodrow and Guest (2011) have shown how sophisticated policies and practices to reduce bullying and harassment of staff in hospitals were ignored by some line managers, who chose to give priority to other aspects of their jobs rather than deal with this challenging issue. The evidence therefore indicates that line managers can fail to implement HR practices for a variety of reasons and, as a result, limit the association between HRM and performance.

The quality of the line managers' implementation of HRM

The quality of implementation may vary because some line managers are unclear about how best to implement HR practices. The quality may also be poor because line managers choose not to implement HR practices effectively. This can happen for a number of reasons: one will be time pressures and competing priorities;

another will be a lack of commitment to, and belief in, the likelihood that devoting time and energy to quality implementation will result in any obvious pay-offs. In this context, the HR department has sometimes been perceived as a purveyor of systems that line managers consider to be unnecessary and unhelpful bureaucracy (Guest & King, 2004). We must also consider the possibility that some line managers may not be capable of implementing HR practices effectively.

Judgements about the quality of HR implementation can come from a variety of sources, including internal HR 'customers' such as line managers, employees and trade union representatives and also senior management (Delmotte, 2008), all of whom may evaluate HR implementation at the operational level differently. Indeed, what is perceived by employees to be high-quality implementation at the operational level may be viewed very differently at the corporate level (Tsui, 1987, p. 37). Therefore, in implementing HR practices, line managers may not be able to satisfy multiple constituencies simultaneously (Tsui, 1990) because they have different expectations and use different criteria for assessing effective implementation (Tsui, 1984). According to Tsui and Milkovich (1987), each constituency is concerned primarily with pursuing the 'fulfilment of its self-interests' (p. 522), and line managers may have to make some difficult choices in deciding which HR practices to give most attention and which to ensure they implement more or less effectively, bearing in mind the likely reactions of the differing constituencies.

Managers and employees, the most important constituencies at the operational unit level (Tsui, 1990), can often have divergent needs and expectations because line managers are implementers whereas employees are consumers of HR practices. Perhaps because of this, line managers have been found to evaluate the quality of HRM implementation as significantly higher than employees do (Geare et al., 2006). Nevertheless, there have been persistent claims that line managers may not give priority to ensuring high-quality HR implementation (a point we return to below), which may limit the strength of any HRM–performance relationship.

Having considered the evidence and issues concerning the stages of HR implementation, we now turn to explore in more detail the roles of three key classes of actor in the implementation process: top management, line managers and HR managers.

The role of top management in the implementation of HRM

One of the roles of senior management in an organization is to set the culture or climate for human resource management (Schein, 1986). This can be achieved by influencing the content of HR policies, by their own actions in implementing them (thereby demonstrating how seriously they regard them) and through the manner in which these policies and their underlying values are communicated. According to Bowen and Ostroff (2004), top management can help to improve the implementation of HR policy and practice if the message about HR practices is distinctive and communicated clearly, unambiguously and consistently throughout the organization.

Nishii et al. (2008) explored HR implementation from an employee perspective, finding that employees make different HR attributions regarding the goals underlying HR practices. They are likely to respond positively to those HR practices to which employees denote positive attributions about management aims concerning their impact on employees. Conversely, when employees perceive that the intended goals of HR practices are cost-driven, control-focused and unlikely to enhance employee well-being, lower levels of satisfaction and commitment result. These findings reinforce the importance of the way in which top management communicate the purpose behind HR practices. Lack of clarity and consistency is likely to result in varying attributions and responses, regardless of the intended and actual HR strategy pursued by management.

According to Maxwell and Farquharson (2008), understanding the view of top management is important because 'the attitude of the organization's CEO or managing director towards the HR function is critical to determining HR membership of main boards and their sub-committees' (p. 306). In other words, the involvement of the HR function in strategic decisions is dependent on what the dominant coalition in the organization allows or invites it to do. This view is reinforced by Brandl and Pohler (2010), who outline three conditions that need to be met in order for HR managers to get involved in more than traditional HR roles. CEOs need to have:

- A wide scope for action regarding HRM policies and practices themselves.
- Willingness to share responsibility for HRM with others.
- To choose the HR department to take over this responsibility.

It will become difficult for the HR department to provide a significant contribution to strategic decision-making when any of these conditions is missing. This highlights the key role of chief executives in shaping HR policy, practice and implementation in organizations.

We noted earlier that the ability to implement strategies can become a source of competitive advantage (Barney, 2001) and that this could include HR implementation (Becker & Huselid, 2006). If this is the case, we might expect top managers to take HRM seriously. Guest and King (2004) found, in their investigation of 48 senior executives from 16 British organizations, that 'better HR depended not so much on better procedures but better implementation and ownership of implementation by line managers' (p. 421). This implies that top managers need to pay serious attention both to the development of HR strategy and to its implementation as steps towards improving organizational performance.

In summary, top managers can play an important role in HR implementation. They can influence the content of HR practices by aligning the HRM strategy with the business strategy (see Chapter 4) and defining the core competencies required to gain competitive advantage. They can communicate the policies and values of HRM throughout the organization, and lead by example with their own implementation of HR practices. Finally, they can help to create a strong HR system by communicating the HRM priorities – and the importance of implementing HRM effectively – clearly, unambiguously and consistently. Despite the importance of top managers in implementing HRM, it has not been extensively researched and represents an important gap in our understanding of the influences on the link between HRM and performance.

The role of line managers as key implementers of HRM

Although line management is identified as responsible for operational HR implementation (Brewster & Larsen, 2000), many researchers believe that line managers have failed in this role (McGovern et al., 1997; Hope Hailey et al., 2005). In particular, they are viewed as reluctant to implement HR practices effectively (Hall & Torrington, 1998; Harris et al., 2002) although it is acknowledged that certain constraints can result in line managers not being able to complete their HR responsibilities and perform the required HR practices well (Cunningham & Hyman, 1999; Larsen & Brewster, 2003; Whittaker & Marchington, 2003).

Several observers have set out the conditions necessary for effective line management implementation of HRM, linked to their analyses and explanations for why they do not do it. There are five main factors:

- Line managers do not have the *desire* to perform HR responsibilities (Cunningham & Hyman, 1995; Harris et al., 2002). It is generally agreed that a significant number of line managers do not want to become engaged in HRM and are not motivated to perform their HR role (Brewster & Larsen, 2000; Kulik & Bainbridge, 2006). Because they lack the willingness to implement HRM, line managers will prioritize operational issues over HR issues (McGovern et al., 1997; Harris et al., 2002; Whittaker & Marchington, 2003).
- They do not have sufficient *capacity* to spend time on both operational and personnel responsibilities (McGovern et al., 1997; McConville, 2006; Hutchinson & Purcell, 2010). The heavy and increasing requirement to attend to operational issues squeezes out time to address HR issues (Brewster & Larsen, 2000; Whittaker & Marchington, 2003).
- They lack sufficient HR-related *competences* (McGovern, 1999; Renwick, 2000). Line managers often lack specialist knowledge on HRM, for example on legal requirements and agreed practices (Lowe, 1992; Hall & Torrington, 1998), and have limited people management skills (McGovern et al., 1997).
- They need but do not always receive *support* and advice from HR managers to perform their HR role effectively (Bond & Wise, 2003; Whittaker & Marchington, 2003). Line managers need content-related advice and coaching from HR specialists on how to perform HR activities (Hope Hailey et al., 1997; Hall & Torrington, 1998); however, HR professionals do not always provide line managers with the services they need (Bond & Wise, 2003), partly because they are reluctant to abandon their hold over HR responsibilities and play a new organizational role in supporting line managers (Gennard & Kelly, 1997). Ulrich's advocacy of a business partner role provides one means towards addressing this constraint (Ulrich, 1997).

- They require clear *policies and procedures* concerning their HR responsibilities and how to apply them (Brewster & Larsen, 2000; Bowen & Ostroff, 2004; McConville, 2006). HR departments tend to worry that line managers might manage people in an inconsistent way (Harris, 2001; Bond & Wise, 2003), so they try to prevent line managers from interpreting, adjusting and fine-tuning HR practices to address what they perceive to be local requirements.

Bond and Wise (2003) and Bos-Nehles (2010) concur that the devolution literature tends to identify the same five reasons why devolution 'does not work'. However, these reasons are mainly based on HR managers' views rather than on line management accounts. When line managers' views on the implementation of HRM are considered, the results look different. Some scholars found that line managers are enthusiastic about their involvement in HRM (Renwick, 2003; McConville, 2006; Nehles et al., 2006), rejecting the view that line managers lack motivation to implement their HR responsibilities. They also found that line managers reported a need for a clear overall HR policy and for clarity about which practices they should use and *how* they should do so at the operational level. They also reported line management perceptions that their roles and responsibilities are often not transparent and well communicated (Lowe, 1992; Nehles et al., 2006), leading to their belief that managing people is HR's responsibility (McGovern et al., 1997).

Bos-Nehles (2010) investigated which of the five reasons outlined earlier are perceived by line managers as constraining their effective implementation of HR practices and how these practices are actually implemented on the work floor. She found that line managers reported that they have the desire and competence to implement HR and that they get valuable support from HR managers, as well as clear policies and procedures to execute HR practices at the operational level. Only the capacity to spend sufficient time on their HR responsibilities when set against other operational responsibilities needed improvement in order to give HRM full attention. Furthermore, her findings reveal that their subordinates perceive the way line managers implement HR practices as effective. Thus, these line managers perceive themselves as effective HRM implementers because they perceive few constraints in performing their HR role and employees who work under their supervision also perceive them as effective in implementing HR practices. This research presents a much more positive view of how line managers implement HRM and shows that in the right circumstances, line managers will accept their HR responsibilities and implement HR effectively.

It seems likely that the effectiveness of HRM implementation by line managers is not evaluated in the same way by different stakeholders. Much of the research derives from a focus on HR managers and arrives at a generally negative assessment of the performance of line managers as implementers. This contrasts with the positive findings reported by Bos-Nehles (2010). It is important to note that there may be features of national systems that affect HR implementation and the results from continental Europe tend to be more positive than those from North America or the UK. At present, we lack research that systematically explores perceptions of line management's role in HR implementation from multiple stakeholders including line managers, HR managers, top management and employees, so that differences can be better understood and potentially reconciled.

The role of the HR function in the implementation of HRM

Most research on HRM and performance has ignored the role of the HR function. Yet we have argued that it has – or should have – a central role in the introduction and quality assurance of HR practices. HR professionals can claim some distinctive expertise in knowledge about best HR practices and should therefore be in a strong position to influence the introduction of such practices and to ensure their quality. However, the HR function has always had a somewhat ambiguous and potentially marginal role in organizations (Legge, 1978) and has been castigated, for example by Skinner (1981), for its inability to deliver high performance. Ulrich (1997) famously offered to save the function and provided templates to guide its focus, roles and structure so that HR professionals could become 'HR champions'. HR departments grasped at this promise and many functions were reorganized along the lines advocated by Ulrich. It seems to have made little difference. Lawler and Mohrmann (2003) found that in the period between 1995 and 2001, there was no growth in the involvement of HR departments in the USA in strategic decision-making. Kochan (2007), also writing about the USA experience, suggests that '[t] he human resource management profession faces a crisis of trust and a loss of legitimacy in the eyes of its major stakeholders. The two-decade effort to develop a "new strategic human resource management" role in organizations has failed to realize its promised potential' (p. 599).

One indication of the influence of the HR function in strategic HR decision-making is board representation. The UK evidence shows no increase over a number of years in HR directors who are board members (Kersley et al., 2006). As noted earlier, Guest and Bryson (2009) found no evidence that the presence of a qualified HR specialist is associated with greater innovation in the use of HR practices. While they found an association between HR practices and performance, there was no association between the presence of an HR specialist and performance.

It is unclear how far the limited impact of the HR function is due to the inherent problems in the role and how far it can be attributed to the kind of people who choose to work in the function. Whatever the explanation, it is a potentially serious issue in the context of our analysis of the role of effective implementation in understanding the HRM–performance link. This is based on the assumption, which can be challenged, that the HR function has an important role to play in developing a coherent high-commitment or high-performance HR strategy, in introducing and ensuring the quality of practices designed to pursue that strategy and in convincing line managers to take their implementation seriously providing them with support to do so. As our analysis (and that of Bowen and Ostroff, 2004) has indicated, this may well need to be reinforced by a strong HR climate backed by the chief executive and other senior executives. The risk is that, based on experience, line managers come to attribute to any HR initiatives a concern for bureaucratic monitoring and control, and therefore do not engage with them in any whole-hearted way. Where this is the case, it can count against effective implementation of HRM by line managers. Guest and King (2004), in their study of senior managers' perceptions of the HR function, highlight a number of examples of exasperated managers who offer clear explanations why they give low priority to initiatives emanating from the HR department, including their bureaucratic requirements and their transience as fads.

Some research has addressed the effectiveness of the HR function as opposed to HR practices. Much of the potentially relevant research concerns the roles adopted by HR professionals. For example, Caldwell (2001) reports on HR managers' perceptions of their roles in a UK sample and finds that they prioritize and believe they add value through their adviser and change agent roles. In a Belgian study, Buyens and de Vos (2001), using a sample consisting of HR managers, senior executives and line managers, found that role descriptions fitted the four categories identified by Ulrich (1997) fairly evenly. However, line managers believed that the HR function added value mainly through its management of infrastructure, delivering functional services; top executives highlighted management of transformation and change; while HR managers believed their main added value lay in their management of the employee contribution. The strategic HR role received rather lower priority from each of the three management groups. In a study of HR roles in The Netherlands, Paauwe and Farndale (2008) found only three roles, which they described as 'strategic and change partner', 'administrative delivery' and 'trade union/employee partner'. The latter role could be subdivided to provide a specific focus on trade union partnership and a rather less well-defined employee partner role. The study highlights the importance of the institutional context in shaping HR roles and in particular the strong Dutch tradition of working closely with trade unions. The key conclusion from this is that while the four roles identified by Ulrich (1997) are all recognized by a variety of managers, there is no consensus about the role that will be most effective in adding value.

Graham and Tarbell (2006) investigate the credibility of the HR function from a multiple-stakeholder approach. They find that employees, line management and top management define the credibility of the HR function differently. While employees emphasize trust, line managers emphasize expertise and effective relationships, and senior managers emphasize achievement of results. Guest et al. (2000) explore perceptions among 237 matched pairs of CEOs and senior HR managers about the effectiveness of HR department processes. The function was judged to be most effective in conventional and administrative activities such as 'maintaining up-to-date workforce information' and 'matching staff to jobs', and less effective in more proactive and strategic activities such as 'progressing HR projects and initiatives' and 'implementing HR aspects of the business plan'. There were no consistent or marked differences in the ratings of the CEO and the HR manager. These findings imply that HR staff continue to find it easier to address the traditional administrative elements of their role than those requiring them to be more proactive in providing a clear contribution to organizational performance.

Data on the role of the HR function in promoting high performance is sparse. Guest and Bryson (2009) found no evidence of any association; in a study of the

HR function in UK universities, Guest and Clinton (2007) found no evidence that any feature of HR structure or practice was associated with any of the numerous university performance indicators. Findings of this sort once again raise the question of where the responsibility lies for promoting and implementing high-commitment or high-performance HRM. Given the evidence from Guest and Bryson (2009) that, at least in the UK, the HR function makes little contribution to HR innovation, we need a better understanding of how HR innovation comes about. For example, is it best to bypass the HR function and focus on the role of senior managers, consultants and those in line management – those Kanter (1983) once identified as 'change masters' – to provide the innovation? The evidence to date suggests that we cannot look with confidence to the HR function to provide a lead in HR innovation and in ensuring effective HR implementation.

Future research

Research on HR implementation is much less developed than that on HRM and performance, and in this chapter we have signalled a number of research priorities. One of the aims of the chapter has been to present an analytic framework within which a relevant research agenda can emerge. We summarize some of the key priorities next.

One of the seriously under-researched topics concerns the process whereby new HR practices are introduced. We need histories of HR innovation with an analysis of the influences and the key actors. We therefore need to learn more about who takes the initiative and under what circumstances. Building on research such as that reported by Mirvis (1997), we need to know more about the role of external factors such as the competitive environment, government activity and the role of consultants and fashion. There is a suspicion that HR initiatives are subject to fads and fashion, and in this context we need to explore the role of mimetic isomorphism (DiMaggio & Powell, 1983). In an analysis of this issue, Paauwe and Boselie (2005a) developed a framework to analyse adoption of new HR practices, building on the new institutionalism of DiMaggio and Powell and on aspects of strategic management.

There is widespread evidence of differences in perceptions of both the presence and the effectiveness of HR practices. While there are some consistent patterns – such as a propensity for HR managers to report more in place than those reported by employees – other findings are less consistent. For example, some studies report that top managers provide a more negative assessment of effectiveness than HR managers, while others find no differences. Still other studies find that different criteria are used to judge effectiveness. We need further studies that explore judgements of the various elements in HR effectiveness from multiple constituencies that at the same time explore the criteria that are used to determine effectiveness. One aim would be to identify the circumstances under which consensus could be achieved. A way of progressing this, which is attracting research attention, is to test the propositions in the Bowen and Ostroff (2004) model.

Line managers clearly have a major role to play in day-to-day implementation of HRM. The evidence presented in this chapter has challenged the popular assumption that line managers are generally either unwilling or unable to implement HRM effectively. We need more evidence from different organizational and national contexts to determine how robust this finding is. At the same time, we need to explore the most effective relationship between line managers and the HR function. Despite the advocacy by Ulrich (1997) of the 'business partner' role, we still know too little about how this relationship can best be managed.

The core argument informing this chapter has been that too much attention has been paid to the presence of HR practices rather than their effectiveness. More research is needed to separate the presence of practices, the quality of practices (their fitness for purpose) and the effectiveness of their implementation. Rather like the standard model of training evaluation (Kirkpatrick, 1959/1960), unless we can trace each stage in the processes, we will remain uncertain about why, how and whether HRM and performance are linked. With this in mind, we also need to build a body of research that explores the presence of HR practices alongside appropriate measures of their effectiveness. This adds further complexity to the study of HRM and performance, but it will be a necessary step if we are to advance our understanding of this relationship.

6

STRATEGIC HRM AND ORGANIZATIONAL BEHAVIOUR: INTEGRATING MULTIPLE LEVELS OF ANALYSIS

PATRICK M. WRIGHT
AND LISA H. NISHII

A few trends have emerged in the field of strategic human resource management (SHRM) over the recent years. First, and most obviously, has been the extensive effort to demonstrate a link between HRM practices and firm performance (Becker & Gerhart, 1996). Researchers such as Huselid (1995), MacDuffie (1995), Delery and Doty (1996), and Guthrie (2000) have published empirical studies showing a statistically significant linkage between HRM practices and some measures of organizational performance.

A second trend has been to try to understand the mechanisms through which this relationship takes place. Authors such as Dyer and Reeves (1995), Becker and Gerhart (1996), Guest (1997), and Wright and Gardner (2003a) have all called for research that uncovers some of the mediating relationships that must exist between the HRM practices and organizational performance.

A final trend has been the interest in taking a multi-level approach to understanding SHRM. Wright and Boswell (2002) reviewed the SHRM literature and categorized this research as being differentiated along one dimension representing whether the focus was on single or multiple practices, and along a second dimension dealing with the unit of analysis – specifically, the individual versus the group or organization. Ostroff and Bowen (2000), and more recently Bowen and Ostroff (2004), have developed the most extensive multi-level model of SHRM to date. Their theoretical approach argues that HR practices serve as communications mechanisms signalling employees to engage in certain behaviours; relying on communications theory, they contend that different aspects of HRM systems impede or facilitate this communication process.

The purpose of this paper is related to these last two trends: we conceptually examine some of the mediating processes that might occur in the HRM–performance relationship and try to make explicit their multi-level nature. In order to accomplish this, we will first explore the concept of variance, which is crucial to the analysis of any phenomena across multiple levels. We will show how virtually all existing SHRM research focuses on variance at one level of analysis while assuming constancy at other levels. We will next discuss the process through which HRM practices must act, and identify some of the relevant variables that have heretofore been virtually ignored in the empirical SHRM literature, specifically focusing on variance at different (unit versus individual) levels of analysis. Finally, we will present some implications for theorizing and research in this area.

Variance as a scientific concept

The concept of variation, or variance, is central to all scientific endeavours. Virtually all scientific efforts assume that variation exists in some phenomena, and the research process aims at understanding and/or explaining this variation (Kerlinger, 1973). In fact, Nunnaly and Bernstein (1994) state that '[o]ne might say that scientific issues are posed only to the extent that they vary with respect to particular attributes. . . . The purpose of a scientific theory is to explain as much variation of interrelated variables as possible' (p. 116). In the context of SHRM research, the basic proposition suggests that variance in performance exists across organizations, and variance also exists in HRM practices. (Note that less attention has been paid to variance within organizations.) The empirical effort to tie HRM practices to performance that has dominated SHRM research consists of attempting to show that the variance in HRM practices covaries with the variation in performance. However, successfully explaining as much variation as possible in the two classes of variables (HR practices and outcomes) requires a more in-depth consideration of the sources of variation that exist in and around those variables.

Specifically, understanding variance in this context requires partitioning variance into its various components. Begin with the assumption that any empirical study entails attributing scores to each unit of analysis on each variable, which we will call the observed score. For ease of argument, we will also assume that the observed scores on each variable are normally distributed.

At the most basic level, variance in observed scores consists of two types: true variance and error variance. True variance represents the variation in true scores on a relevant variable (in this case, either HRM practices or performance) in the absence of any measurement or other error component. It represents true differences across units or subjects on the relevant construct. Error variance represents the components of a score that are unrelated to the true score (i.e. the true differences across units or subjects) and is due to things such as measurement error. Error variance can be random (randomly distributed around the true score) or systematic (exhibiting a consistent upward or downward bias in the observed score).

Thinking about variance as being comprised of both true and error variance is important because it forces us to consider what exactly it is that we conceptually consider to be true versus error sources of variance. For example, what might be considered error variance at the unit or organizational level may represent true variance at the individual level of analysis. Consider also the possibility that observed variance across organizations on HR practices that is assumed to represent true variance may in fact be error variance if the HR practices being captured represent 'actual' HR practices in some organizations but 'intended' HR practices in others. A consideration of both the many sources of variance that may exist for HR practices and outcome variables – as well as for the variables that mediate between the two – and the multi-level nature of the relationships among the variables is important, because it can deepen our understanding of the HR practices to performance relationship of interest.

To date SHRM researchers have focused on examining true variance at the organizational level, with relatively less attention being paid to variance at other levels of analysis. The implications for the reliability and validity of our science – about which scholars continue to be highly concerned – are two-fold. With regard to validity, can we adequately capture the constructs of primary interest without first considering the variance that exists surrounding each construct? For instance, in the debate regarding the reliability of single rater measures of HR practices, Gerhart et al. (2000a) noted that reliability is a precondition to validity and that unreliable measures severely limit the validity of those measures.

With regard to reliability, unless we recognize the cross-level nature of these relationships and pay more attention to individual- and group-level responses (variance) within organizations, can we be confident about the reliability with which we are capturing these constructs in our research? Again, Gerhart et al. (2000) noted that there might be real true score variance that exists among respondents within an organization that cannot be captured by single rater measures across job groups.

Because reliability and validity are central to good science, these issues cannot be ignored. However, unreliability, especially inter-rater reliability, while indicating low validity when aggregating across all respondents (e.g. all employees in an organization), may reveal highly valid measures when aggregating across particular subgroups of respondents (e.g. work groups). It is the interdependence of measurement (reliability and validity), design (particularly levels of analysis) and theory that underlies this examination.

Variance and SHRM

As previously discussed, SHRM research has predominantly focused on inter-relating variance in HR practices across organizations with variance in performance. Huselid (1995) found that HR practices were significantly related to accounting profits and market values (Tobin's Q) of firms. Delery and Doty (1996) found that HR practices were related to accounting profits among a sample of banks. MacDuffie (1995) found that HR practices were related to operating performance (quality and productivity) among a sample of auto assembly plants. Guthrie (2000) found practices related to profitability of firms in New Zealand. Guest et al. (2003) found that HRM practices were related to both productivity and financial performance in a sample of UK companies. This realm of research is growing, and consistently demonstrates the relationship between HRM practices and measures of organizational performance.

While some of the methodological details vary, most often these studies share a common approach to examining the relationship. It usually entails acquiring an assessment of the HRM practices that exist in the focal unit (usually the firm or plant and usually across jobs within the unit, although some studies focus on a core job), as well as a measure of the focal unit's performance. These two sets of measures are examined in a multivariate statistical technique and they are shown to covary.

This approach has revealed consistent relationships between the two focal variables (HR practices and performance), but may not have contributed much to our theoretical understanding of how these two measures relate. For example, one of the more thorough models of SHRM was proposed by Becker and Huselid (1998), which suggested that the firm's strategy dictates the design of the HR system. The HR system impacts the employee skills and motivation, which, in turn, results in creativity, productivity and discretionary behaviour. Employees' behaviour influences the firm's operating performance, which leads to profitability, growth and market value.

Note that of all these variables, most research has only focused on HR practices and performance – two variables that are quite distant from one another in the causal chain. Note also that because the level of analysis is the firm (or plant), the model seems to assume uniformity or constancy with regard to each variable (i.e. there is no variation within firm in HR practices, no variation within firm in employee reactions, etc.). This is not to criticize the assumption, because such assumptions are always necessary with regard to one level of analysis. However, in order to increase our understanding of how HR practices impact performance, we might benefit greatly from approaching the issue in a multi-level framework. That is to say that we would benefit from examining the mediating factors more carefully, and to do so using multi-level frameworks that recognize the many levels of analysis at which the mediators may be operating. In the next section we will examine how the basic process must take place across levels, and tie the discussion to some of the theoretical frameworks and concepts that have guided research at these levels.

SHRM across levels of analysis

To begin, we propose the following rudimentary process that must take place in order for HRM practices to impact organizational performance. In proposing this model, we by no means argue that we have identified all of the relevant variables.

However, we propose the model to provide a framework that allows us to identify some of the relevant theoretical frameworks and research literatures that can shed light on the sub-processes through which HR practices impact organizational performance.

Before describing the model in detail, we note a few assumptions. First, we are focusing on HRM practices at the level of the job group. Lepak and Snell (1999) explicitly note that firms have different HR systems for different groups of employees depending upon the value and uniqueness of the skills of employees in particular job groups. In addition, researchers such as MacDuffie (1995) and Delery and Doty (1996) note the value of focusing assessment of HR practices on 'core' job groups in order to more accurately describe the practices that exist. Thus, we strongly agree with the idea that a variety of HRM systems will exist within a firm with regard to particular job groups; but for the ease of understanding the process through which HRM impacts performance, our discussion will assume that the practices are intended to be uniform and consistently applied to the focal job group.

Second, to a large extent we assume business strategy to be largely outside the purview of the model. This does not imply that business strategy is not relevant or does not play an important role in the development of the intended HRM practices; however, business strategy is treated as an exogenous variable.

Figure 6.1 depicts this model. We describe each of the components to this model in detail below and, in doing so, aim to highlight the variability that is likely to exist within each section of the model. Together, the components illustrate that the focal relationship of interest in SHRM research – the HRM–performance link – spans multiple levels of analysis, with important variance occurring at each of those levels.

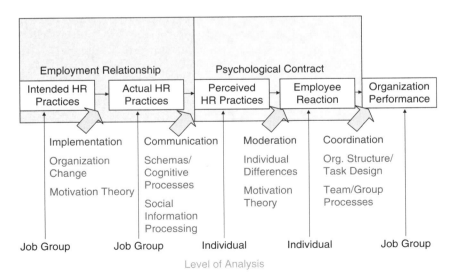

Figure 6.1   Process model of SHRM

Intended HRM practices

The first concept in Figure 6.1 is the intended HR practices. These practices represent the outcome of the development of an HR strategy that seeks to design an HRM system or practice that the firm's decision-makers believe will effectively elicit the employee responses desired. This may be tied directly to the business strategy or determined by some other extraneous influences. However, the important point to note is that the decision-makers have proactively analysed the situation and determined that a certain set of HR practices will best elicit the kind of affective, cognitive and behavioural responses from employees necessary for organizational success.

Actual HRM practices

Consistent with Truss and Gratton (1994) and Wright and Snell (1998), the next box is labeled 'Actual HR practices.' This recognizes that not all intended HR practices are actually implemented, and those that are may often be implemented in ways that differ from the initial intention.

Mintzberg (1978) noted the differences between the espoused strategy of an organization (what leaders say the strategy is) and the realized strategy (what it actually is). He noted that there is a disconnection due to a number of factors, be they political, institutional or rational. Bringing these concepts into the SHRM literature recognizes that while there may be a designed or intended HR system determined by the decision-makers, the system is rarely perfectly applied by those charged with its implementation.

Regarding this conceptual variable, one must understand that the basic level of analysis is the job group, but that some variance is likely to exist. This variance stems from the fact that the practices must usually be implemented by multiple individuals (supervisors, interviewers, trainers, etc.) who will not be uniform in their implementation efforts (Zohar, 2000). Consequently, one could begin to consider actual HR practices as varying across individual implementers (see Figure 6.2).

Perceived HRM practices

According to the model in Figure 6.1, the actual HR practices exist objectively, yet must be perceived and interpreted subjectively by each employee in the focal group. Consequently, the process then moves down to the level of the individual. Considerable variance can occur at this level due to both variation in the actual HR practices (which would likely cause valid variance in perceived HR practices) and variation in the schemas that individuals employ in perceiving and interpreting HR-related information.

Employee reactions

Employees will react in some way, based on the perceived HR practices. Each employee processes the information in a way that elicits some reactions, be they affective (attitudinal), cognitive (knowledge or skill) and/or behavioural. Affective

Job Group with Multiple Supervisors

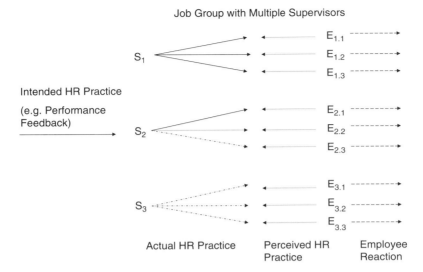

Figure 6.2   Job group with multiple supervisors

reactions include various aspects of job satisfaction and/or organizational commitment (often according to principles of social exchange theory). Cognitive reactions may include increased knowledge or skill. Behavioural reactions can be classified as reactions with regard to task, counterproductive and discretionary behaviour (Ones et al., 1993):

- Task behaviour describes the kind of behaviour prescribed as part of the job. Increasing job-focused behaviour aimed at being more productive or making fewer mistakes exemplifies task behaviour.
- Counterproductive behaviour describes negative behaviour aimed at either hurting the organization or at bettering one's own position at the expense of the organization. Theft of goods, sabotage or time theft (spending work time on personal activities) are examples of counterproductive behaviour.
- Discretionary behaviour consists of behaviour that is not prescribed by the organization but is aimed at benefiting the organization. Going beyond job duties to satisfy a customer or performing non-prescribed preventative maintenance on a machine would be examples of discretionary behaviour.

In theory, the goal of designing and implementing HR practices is to do so in a way that leads to positive attitudinal reactions, increased cognitive skills relevant to the job and/or organization, and increased productive task and contextual behaviours of employees. The question of interest, then, is whether HR practices successfully do so as intended, and to uncover the factors that explain the variance in the success with which they do so (i.e. the individual employee factors, organizational communication mechanisms, etc.).

Performance

Dyer and Reeves (1995) classified the types of performance outcomes examined in SHRM research into employee, organizational, financial and market value outcomes. Employee outcomes reflect such things as absenteeism and turnover. Organizational outcomes consist mostly of operational performance measures such as productivity, quality, and customer satisfaction. Financial outcomes deal with accounting measures of performance such as profits or return on assets (ROA). Finally, market value outcomes reflect measures of the value of a firm according to the equity markets.

In our model, in order for organizational-level outcomes to accrue, individuals' reactions must be consistent or complementary enough across one another in order to have a positive outcome at the level of the job group. Because the focus is on the job group, the performance outcomes most relevant are the employee and organizational outcomes. In some cases where employees within a job group have some level of interdependence (such as assembly line workers), the performance outcomes at the job group level are reasonably obvious and objective (productivity, quality, scrap, etc.). In other cases, where there is little interdependence among employees in the job group (such as clerical staff), the performance outcomes may be neither obvious nor easily quantified at the group level. In such cases, the performance outcomes expected should be increases in average individual performance.

Linkages as avenues for gaining increased understanding

The model proposed covers some of the basic processes that seemingly have to take place in order for the HR practices to impact performance. However, it is the linkages between the different processes that provide avenues for exploring relevant issues that may help to increase our theoretical and empirical understanding of the process by which HR impacts firm performance. Exploring these linkages elicits a number of questions unaddressed in the SHRM literature. However, many of these questions have been addressed in other literatures, thus providing a framework for integrating some common theories within the organizational behaviour literature into the SHRM literature. We explore these next.

Intended → actual HRM practices: implementation

Beginning with the assumption that decision-makers have designed an intended system of HRM practices that they believe will lead to positive organizational outcomes, the next challenge is to actually implement those practices in the organization. In some cases, this entails a massive transformation of systems/practices; in others it simply requires minor changes. In either case, the implementation challenge is not easily addressed, because obstacles exist at both the institutional and individual levels.

Many authors have noted that HR practices, once institutionalized, are notoriously intractable (Snell & Dean, 1994). The challenge is to implement a consistent set of processes in a consistent manner across what may be a large and diverse organization. It may require a coordination of communication, training, incentive and information technology systems across the firm, for it is the redundancy of mutually reinforcing HR practices that ultimately underlies the impact of HR systems on organizational performance.

At the individual level, the implementation of (new) HR systems is made difficult by the fact that those charged with the actual execution of practices (interviewers in a recruiting context, supervisors in a performance appraisal/ feedback context, etc.) develop a comfort that comes with familiarity of behaviour and results. New practices threaten that comfort because individuals must learn new, unfamiliar behaviours with unknown effectiveness, and consequently elicit resistance.

In some cases this may be a question of implementing organizational change, an area that has been addressed in the organizational behaviour literature for decades. Whether the change is massive or minor, theoretical frameworks such as force field analysis (Lewin, 1951), survey feedback (Bowers & Franklin, 1972), or other OD-type interventions provide frameworks and tools for implementing HR systems changes.

The ultimate goal in implementing HR practices, hopefully as intended, is to institutionalize the new employee behaviours into a regular routine. That is, HR practices play an important role in developing and maintaining organizational routines. These organizational routines are defined as 'recognizable patterns of interdependent actions, involving multiple actors' (Feldman & Pentland, 2003, p. 96). These routines help establish connections between employees that enable them to develop shared understandings about what actions to take; these shared understandings are ultimately what enable employees to coordinate their actions (Gersick & Hackman, 1990; Feldman & Rafaeli, 2002). In the aggregate, these coordinated behaviours contribute to organizational-level performance and may have the potential to provide a competitive advantage for organizations (Hitt & Ireland, 1985).

This distinction between intended and actual HR practices also raises an interesting measurement issue. Does the existing SHRM research base measure actual or intended HRM practices? The answer might depend on who is being surveyed: we may be more likely to measure intended HR practices when we survey single HR representatives, but we may be more likely to measure actual HR practices when employees and line managers are surveyed (Gerhart et al., 2000a).

Actual → perceived HR practices: communication

The linkage between the actual HR practices and the perceived HR practices represents the communication challenge. Bowen and Ostroff (2004) provide one of the most thorough multi-level frameworks for understanding the SHRM process, and their framework is based on communications theory. They argue that HR practices are organizational communication devices that aim to communicate certain messages to employees. They explore how different aspects of the HRM systems can either promote or impede the message.

While their analysis provides exciting avenues for exploring the SHRM process, other theories of OB have relevance as well. For instance, at the individual level, significant research attention has been devoted to understanding how individuals' schemas influence the information that they attend to, and how that information is processed. This research has demonstrated how individuals' past histories with similar phenomena can strongly influence their perceptions of a focal phenomenon. For example, in the psychological contracts literature, Rousseau (2001) argues that people's past experiences with HR practices influences the way that they perceive and interpret HR and other organizational practices in their current organization. Considering such information-processing differences among individuals may become even more important with increasing cultural diversity in the workforce, as people's cultural backgrounds also influence the way that they collect, process, store and use information from their environments (Shaw, 1990).

With regard to SHRM, this highlights the importance of the variation in individuals' schemas for influencing how they perceive any given practice or set of practices. For instance, individuals whose past history found them exploited by a company are highly likely to have different perceptions of a participative system than individuals whose history is one of a trusted relationship with their company.

The variance also may be exacerbated or reduced by the social context of the practices. For instance, Salancik and Pfeffer (1977) promoted a social information processing approach to understanding job characteristics: they argued that because individuals' realities are in part socially constructed, exploring job characteristics as objective realities apart from the social context misses important determinants of employee reactions. They hypothesized (and significant empirical research has supported them) that individuals' perceptions of job characteristics were determined, in part, by how co-workers described the characteristics.

A direct analogy can be applied from this approach to job characteristics (assumed to be objective, but found to be partially subjective) to the HR practice literature (again, assumed to be objective, but almost unarguably partially subjective). When new practices are introduced, there is likely to be a period of 'sense-making', during which employees seek to understand the goal of the new practices. During this phase, social information may play a significant role in how individuals perceive and interpret the practices.

Again, this linkage elicits a number of interesting questions about the SHRM process and illustrates the potential for integrating OB theories/literatures into the SHRM literature.

Perceived HR → employee reactions: moderation

Once individuals have processed the information regarding the HR practices, they will have to form some internal strategy for how they will react. In essence, this linkage explores the concept of moderation. In theory, moderated relationships posit that the impact of one variable (in this case, the HRM system) on another variable (in this case, the employee reactions) varies depending upon the level of a third variable (such as individual differences). This linkage actually begins to highlight the variation across individuals that exists, yet is assumed to be constant in research conducted at the unit level. This is variance that can provide a much deeper understanding of the phenomena we study.

At one level, much of the OB literature has addressed these issues in a variety of areas. Virtually all of the attitudinal, motivational and individual differences literatures have been aimed at understanding individual reactions to a variety of organizational stimuli. However, usually this research has been directed at examining the impact of one organizational stimulus (e.g. goal-setting or incentive pay) on individuals' attitudinal (goal commitment, satisfaction with pay) or behavioural (performance) reactions. One area where SHRM tends to differ from OB is the simultaneous consideration of a system of HR practices as opposed to one practice in isolation (Wright & Boswell, 2002).

One exception to this is the psychological contract literature (Rousseau, 2001). This literature has tried to explore how individuals develop their beliefs about the 'deal' they have made with the organization in terms of all of the benefits they receive from the organization for all of their inputs, and how they react when they perceive that this 'deal' has been broken. As Wright and Boswell (2002) noted, there are considerable contributions that can be made by empirically examining these issues, because this is currently the major literature that examines individuals' reactions to multiple HRM practices.

For example, Nishii et al. (2008) examined the relationship between employees' attributions for HR practices (the goals that they perceived as underlying certain HR practices), organizational commitment and satisfaction, OCBs, and ultimately customer satisfaction in a largely unionized sample where the HRM practices were quite uniform across units. At the unit level they found that considerable variance in unit-level customer satisfaction can be explained by differences in HR attributions across units. This suggests that variability in the interpretations and reactions to HR systems can, in fact, be related to organizational outcomes.

This does not preclude useful contributions coming from research arenas that examine more specific, individual issues. For instance, motivation theory provides a strong set of theoretical and empirical analyses to explore how a variety of HRM practices – pay, incentives, job design, empowerment/participation – influence individual motivation. In fact, much of the high-performance work systems (HPWSs) theorizing is based on individual motivation theory, albeit that the research efforts have been at the unit level.

In addition, the individual differences literature has frequently been tied to interventions as moderators of a particular intervention's impact. For example, early job design researchers (Hackman & Oldham, 1976, 1980; Oldham, 1976) hypothesized growth need strength as a moderator of the relationship between job characteristics and employee responses. In support of their theory, research has found that jobs with high motivating potential have a stronger positive effect on internal motivation, satisfaction and/or performance for individuals with strong growth needs (Hackman & Lawler, 1971; Oldham, 1976; Pierce et al., 1979). In addition, researchers have suggested that personality characteristics such as need for achievement, conscientiousness, openness to experience, and so on, might influence how individuals react to particular organizational practices and inter-ventions. For instance, individuals high in need for achievement are more attracted to organizations that reward performance as opposed to seniority (Turban & Keon, 1993), and exhibit higher organizational commitment in response to high job scope than individuals low on need for achievement (Steers & Spencer, 1977). Similarly, pay for performance is more strongly associated with motivation for individuals with a higher desire for control (Eisenberger et al., 1999). As for the Big Five personality factors, a wide range of research focusing on the relationship between employee personality and reactions to organizational practices has been conducted. Examples include research that shows that extroversion and agree-ableness interact with job autonomy in predicting contextual performance (Gellatly & Irving, 2001), and that extraversion and conscientiousness are posi-tively associated with self-efficacy for operating successfully in self-managed work groups (Thoms et al., 1996). Together, this body of research clearly suggests that there is within-organization variance in the way that employees react to perceived HR practices, and that this represents true variance – that, when examined explicitly, can enrich SHRM research.

Employee reactions → performance: coordination

Finally, the linkage between employee reactions and unit performance makes another jump across levels of analysis from individual to organizational. Indivi-duals may behave differently as a result of their perceived HR practices, but whether or not the behavioural differences positively impact organizational per-formance may depend on the level of coordination across them. This leads into exploring the areas of organizational structure/design and team/group processes.

In terms of organizational design, the concept of interdependence clearly has a strong effect on the extent to which positive individual behaviours result in increased aggregated outcomes. Thompson (1967) noted that three types of interdependence exist in firms: pooled, sequential and reciprocal.

- Pooled interdependence means that each individual's performance is under his or her control, and that the aggregated outcome is simply the sum of the individual outcomes. Such interdependence requires little coordination across individuals.
- Under sequential interdependence, the outputs of one individual become the inputs for the next. Consequently, the second individual's performance is limited by the first's, and the aggregated outcome is constrained by the lowest performer. Such interdependence is often coordinated by scheduling.
- Finally, under reciprocal interdependence, each individual's outputs become the inputs for the others. Such coordination is accomplished through mutual adjustment.

This illustrates that the unit performance outcomes stemming from increased individual performance may depend upon the type of interdependence that exists among the members. When pooled interdependence exists, higher average unit performance will result from any increased individual performance. However, under sequential or reciprocal interdependence, increasing individual performance does not necessarily translate into increased unit performance. Also, the level and nature of interdependence will influence group sense-making (James et al., 1988; Kozlowski & Hattrup, 1992; Weick, 1995; Kozlowski & Klein, 2000).

Finally, the teams and/or group process literatures (see Kozlowski & Bell, 2003 for a review) may also provide insight into the processes through which SHRM impacts performance. What the organization design literature discusses with regard to the task context, the teams/groups literature explores with regard to the social context. Group norms regarding appropriate behaviour (Barsade & Gibson, 1998) and productivity may negate or impede the effect of HRM practices. This may be why a significant body of research is evolving within the SHRM literature examining the concept of climate, or shared perceptions regarding the behaviours that are expected and rewarded by HRM practices within an organization, as a predictor of organizational performance (Schneider et al., 2003). In addition to the potential role of shared climate perceptions, group cohesion (Zaccaro & McCoy, 1988) and a shared understanding of the task, team, equipment and situation influence the extent to which team members coordinate their actions toward the attainment of positive outcomes (Cannon-Bowers et al., 1993).

Summary and conclusions

This paper has argued that existing theory and research in SHRM has ignored (via assumption) the individual variance and processes that are necessary in order for HR practices to impact organizational performance. It has suggested a multi-level framework for examining these issues as a means for increasing our understanding of the phenomena we seek to explain. Such an analysis suggests two important future directions for SHRM research. These are discussed next.

Develop multi-level theories of SHRM

As previously discussed, Bowen and Ostroff's (2004) multi-level approach to SHRM currently provides the most comprehensive attempt to integrate organizational and individual processes. However, additional theoretical contributions can be made.

One approach would be to develop comprehensive theories that integrate across levels of analysis. Such a theory would attempt to link organizational concepts to individual concepts back to other organizational concepts. While such an all-encompassing theory would be desirable, it may not be feasible.

Alternatively, one could attempt to develop more specific cross-level theories that explain smaller aspects of the linkage between organizational and individual phenomena. Bowen and Ostroff's (2004) attempt to link HR practices to employee reactions via communications theory illustrates this approach. Some of the theories and literatures discussed earlier might be likely candidates for providing a deeper understanding of the SHRM process.

Conduct multi-level research

Multi-level research has been historically constrained by two issues: a lack of willingness on the part of organizations to gather and/or share individual and organizational data, and a lack of data analytic techniques able to synthesize the data. Regarding the former issue, an increasing number of studies have appeared over the years that demonstrate that organizations are more willing to share internal data such as climate and performance with researchers who seek to increase knowledge (Gerhart et al., 2000a; Purcell et al., 2003; Guest et al., 2003; Wright et al., 2003). These studies seem to imply that HR professionals within firms are seeking to be more analytical in their decision-making processes and are reaching out to the academic community to help them. This bodes well for the future.

Regarding the latter constraint, as Wright and Boswell (2002) noted, previous attempts at multi-level research were limited by a lack of statistical techniques to analyse the data. However, recent developments such as within and between analysis (WABA) (Yammarino & Markham, 1992) and hierarchical linear modelling (Hoffman et al., 2000) provide the statistical data analytic tools necessary to empirically assess organizational and individual phenomena simultaneously. Consequently, we seem to be entering an era where data is plentiful, and we finally possess the tools necessary to harvest it. Our belief is that the intersection of these two trends will result in an exponential increase in our understanding of just how HRM practices influence organizational performance.

7

MEASURING HUMAN CAPITAL: A STRATEGIC HUMAN RESOURCE MANAGEMENT PERSPECTIVE

GARY C. MCMAHAN
AND CHRISTOPHER M. HARRIS

An organization's human resources have been recognized as an important element in the success of organizations (e.g. Wright et al., 1994; Wright et al., 1995b; Carmeli & Schaubroeck, 2005; Lopez-Cabrales et al., 2006; Takeuchi et al., 2007). According to the resource-based view of the firm, resources that are valuable, rare, inimitable and non-substitutable create a competitive advantage for organizations (Barney, 1991). Therefore, performance differences across organizations can be attributed to variance in organizations' resources (Hitt et al., 2001). Organizations employ both tangible (e.g. physical and financial resources) and intangible resources (e.g. human capital) (Barney, 1991; Ployhart et al., 2009). While tangible resources are important to the success of organizations, intangible resources such as human capital have greater potential to provide a competitive advantage (Barney, 1991; Wright et al., 1994; McMahan et al., 1999). Thus, variance in the human resource capital of each organization creates performance differences across organizations.

With human capital important to the success of organizations, it becomes increasingly important to consider the manner in which human capital is measured. The level of analysis is an important consideration in the measurement of human capital. Previous human capital research (under the rubric of individual differences) has been conducted at the individual level (e.g. Hunter & Hunter, 1984; O'Reilly & Chatman, 1994; Ree et al., 1994; Martocchio & Judge, 1997; Phillips & Gully, 1997; Ellis et al., 2005) the team level (e.g. Barry & Stewart, 1997; Barrick et al., 1998; Bell, 2007) and unit/organization level (e.g. Wright et al., 1995b, Carmeli & Schaubroeck, 2005; Lopez-Cabrales et al., 2006; Takeuchi et al., 2007). The nature of human capital provides opportunities for human capital to be aggregated from the individual level of analysis to the team, department, job, unit, organization and/or firm level. Therefore, a multi-level approach becomes important when considering the measurement of human capital (Koslowski & Klein, 2000; Ployhart et al., 2006; Ployhart et al., 2009) beyond the individual level of analysis. Another way to consider the measurement of human capital is whether the measure is general or specific in nature (Becker, 1964). Accordingly, Becker's human capital theory states that general and specific human capital is important to the success of firms (Becker, 1964). General human capital increases the marginal productivity of labour across organizations and specific human capital increases the productivity of labour at a specific organization (Becker, 1964).

The purpose of this chapter is to review how human capital has been measured and to provide suggestions for its measurement in future research. First, the importance of human capital to the development of a competitive advantage is discussed. Second, human capital has been measured at a variety of levels, which has led to a lack of clarity in its measurement. Therefore, a critical review of individual-, team- and organization-level measures of human capital is conducted. Third, with the multi-level nature of human capital, a review of studies that have taken a multi-level approach to human capital are reviewed. Fourth, a review of general and specific measures of human capital is provided. Finally, some considerations for the future measurement of human capital are suggested.

Human capital and competitive advantage

The resource-based view of the firm differs from the traditional strategy viewpoint in that it examines resources within firms (Barney, 1991). Under the resource-based view of the firm, the resources are the source of competitive advantage. Competitive advantage is defined as an organization 'implementing a value creating strategy not simultaneously being implemented by any current or potential competitors' (Barney, 1991, p. 102). Human resources, which comprise the pool of human capital under a firm's control in direct employment relationships, are internal to a firm and may assist a firm in achieving a competitive advantage (Wright et al., 1994).

As previously stated, according to the resource-based view of the firm, resources that are valuable, rare, inimitable and non-substitutable create competitive advantages for organizations (Barney, 1991). Resources are valuable when they enable a firm to implement strategies that improve its efficiency and effectiveness. Resources are rare when they cannot be possessed by a large number of competing firms. Firm resources can be inimitable for one or a combination of three reasons: unique historical conditions, causal ambiguity and social complexity. The last requirement for a resource to provide a competitive advantage is non-substitutability. Barney (1991) stated in order for a resource to be non-substitutable, 'there must be no strategically equivalent valuable resources that are themselves either not rare or imitable' (p. 111).

Human capital has been recognized as a critical resource in most firms (Pfeffer, 1994; Wright et al., 1994). It is an intangible asset – best thought of as a stock of knowledge comprising education, information and productive and innovative skills – that is formed through investments in education, training, health and informal knowledge transfers (Becker, 1962). Additionally, human capital can be defined as the full range of knowledge, skills and abilities that an individual can use to produce a given set of outcomes (Hitt et al., 2001). Recently, Wright and McMahan (2011) defined human capital as the 'knowledge, skills, abilities and other characteristics (including health, ethics, personality, etc.) possessed by an employee or potential employee of the firm that can yield positive outcomes'.

Wright et al. (1994) applied the concepts of the resource-based view of the firm to human resources to provide circumstances under which human resources may be a source of sustained competitive advantage for organizations. Human resources may provide added value to a firm because the supply of labour is heterogeneous; thus, people possess different levels of knowledge, skills and abilities. Also, the demand for labour is heterogeneous, which means that different jobs require different knowledge, skills and abilities (Steffy & Mauer, 1988). Based on the levels of knowledge, skills and abilities needed for a certain job, individuals with different types and levels of knowledge, skills, and abilities may perform differently in similar jobs. Thus, individuals' contributions to firms may differ, which argues that human resources may create value for firms (Wright et al., 1994).

Human resources are rare when jobs require knowledge, skills and abilities that allow for differences in individual contributions. Under these conditions, knowledge, skills and abilities should be normally distributed in the population and high quality human resources would be rare (Wright et al., 1994). Wright et al. (1994) used firm cognitive ability as an example of how human resources could be rare. Cognitive ability has been shown to have a strong positive relationship with individual job performance (Hunter & Hunter, 1984). If cognitive ability is normally distributed in the population, there would be fewer individuals with higher levels of cognitive ability – thus making higher levels of cognitive ability rare. If organizations are able to acquire human resources with higher levels of cognitive ability then they would have a resource that is rare.

In order for human resources to be a source of sustained competitive advantage they must also be inimitable. The unique history of an organization such as its culture and norms may make human resources inimitable (Wright et al., 1994). The path that an organization has taken through time may influence the human capital that the organization acquires and develops. Also, the unique history of an organization (which includes a firm's culture and norms) may influence how people work together in the organization, which would be difficult for other organizations to imitate. Human resources may also be a source of causal ambiguity. Team production can present causal ambiguity, because with teams the whole is greater than the sum of its parts (Wright et al., 1994). Thus it is difficult to determine what exactly it is about a team that leads it to perform at a higher level. Social complexity may arise from the communications across different departments in organizations, from employees' contact with customers and many other situations. Complex social situations may constitute a competitive advantage for an organization because social situations cannot be easily recreated (Wright et al., 1994).

Lastly, for a human resource pool to be a source of a sustained competitive advantage, it must not have substitutes. Wright et al. (1994) used an example of whether resources such as technology have the potential to offset advantages gained through human capital. In this situation human resources would be able to be transferred across technologies. Thus, in the short term, human resources may have substitutes; however in the long term, if an organization has human resources with higher levels of human capital then the human resources would not easily be substituted (Wright et al., 1994).

The following section reviews how human capital has been measured at different levels of analysis. One of the difficulties in human capital literature is that research on human capital has been conducted at many levels, thus leading to a lack of clarity in its measurement. The different levels of analysis in which human capital has been studied has provided a variety of conceptualizations and measurements of human capital. To demonstrate the difficulties and challenges of human capital research, the next section critically reviews the measurement of human capital at the individual-, team-, organization- and multi-level of analyses.

Human capital measurement at different levels of analysis

Individual-level human capital

Knowingly or unknowingly, human capital has been measured in a multitide of ways and has been related to an array of individual outcomes. Individual-level studies of human capital have tended to take place within the field of psychology. Judge et al. (1995) measured human capital at an individual level as education level, quality, prestige and degree type. Each of these measures of human capital was positively related to financial success in one's career (Judge et al., 1995). Similarly, in a meta-analysis of individual career success, Ng et al. (2005) assessed human capital as number of hours worked, work centrality, job tenure, organizational tenure, work experience, willingness to transfer, international work experience, education level, career planning, political knowledge and skills, and social capital. In the meta-analysis, each of these measures of human capital was positively related to career success and salary.

Another aspect of human capital is general cognitive ability. Individuals' general cognitive ability and its relationship with performance outcomes across a variety of tasks has been widely studied (e.g. Hunter & Hunter, 1984; Ree et al., 1994; Wright et al., 1995b; Martocchio & Judge, 1997; Phillips & Gully, 1997). O'Reilly and Chatman (1994) defined general cognitive ability as 'representative of the general population and refers to individual differences in tasks or pursuits that demand mental effort, such as abstraction, rule, inference, generalization, and manipulating or transforming problems' (p. 603). General cognitive ability has been measured in a variety of ways including GMAT scores (O'Reilly & Chatman, 1994), Wonderlick (Barrick et al., 1998), EIMP Battery and Miller's Analogies Test (Dreher & Bretz, 1991), among others. In a study of airmen in 82 different jobs, Ree and Earles (1991) found that general cognitive ability was the best predictor of job performance. Similarly, McHenry et al. (1990) found general cognitive ability to be the best predictor of an Army job performance measure. General cognitive ability has also been found to be related to greater career success (Dreher & Bretz, 1991; O'Reilly & Chatman, 1994).

How general cognitive ability can produce improved job performance and career success has also been studied. Hunter (1986) found that higher levels of general cognitive ability enable individuals to acquire job knowledge and that this increased knowledge is related to greater job performance. Theories of knowledge acquisition predict that cognitive ability affects job performance because it accounts for the pace and completeness with which individuals acquire information (Dreher & Bretz, 1991). It is recognized that cognitive ability predicts performance because it captures the ability of individuals to set priorities and be innovative in novel situations (Hunter, 1986). Therefore, it is important to examine not only cognitive ability but also processes or mechanisms through which it impacts performance.

In a recent longitudinal study, Judge et al. (2010) examined individuals' general mental ability. They found that over time, the careers of individuals with higher levels of general mental ability advanced more quickly in terms of income and occupational prestige. General mental ability was measured with the Armed Forces Qualifying Test, which consists of four sections: maths, reasoning, word knowledge and paragraph comprehension. The authors also found that high general mental ability individuals attained more education, completed more training and were in more complex jobs. These factors had a positive influence on the extrinsic career success of high general mental ability individuals. Therefore, individuals with higher levels of general mental ability perform at higher levels and achieve greater career success.

While general cognitive ability is an important predictor of job performance, it is not specific to a task or situation. Different jobs require different profiles of knowledge, skills and abilities; consequently, different people may complement jobs differently (Wise et al., 1990). Typically a job analysis is used to determine the knowledge, skills and abilities necessary for a specific job. Job analysis provides a foundation for human resource practices, including, recruitment, selection, training and performance appraisal (van Iddekinge et al., 2005). The knowledge, skills and abilities that are identified through a job analysis for a specific job may be used by firms as criteria for selection. Along these lines, Neuman and Wright (1999) conducted a job analysis to determine the task-specific knowledge, skills and abilities needed for a human resource position, and found that individuals with greater levels of task specific knowledge, skills and abilities performed at a higher level. Therefore, individuals that possess the required knowledge, skills and abilities for a job tend to perform better than individuals that do not (Edwards, 1991; O'Reilly et al., 1991).

As can be seen from the studies described above, human capital at the individual level has been conceptualized and measured in a variety of ways. This variety of measures adds to the confusion and difficulties in human capital research, because the focus is not on an individual's choice to develop aspects of his/her human capital; instead it has most frequently focused on the practices, policies and programmes that organizations via human resource departments impose on people (i.e. training, performance feedback, etc.) that might develop human capital in individuals (Bell & Kozlowski, 2008; Wright & McMahan, in press).

Team-level human capital

Studies of human capital at the team level have tended to focus on personality traits and general cognitive ability. Barry and Stewart (1997) reported that the team mean level of conscientiousness was not related to team performance, task focus or team cohesion. The team mean level of extraversion was negatively related to team task focus, but teams with a moderate proportion of extraverted members performed better than teams with a greater or lesser proportion of extraverted members (Barry & Stewart, 1997). On the other hand, Barrick et al. (1998) reported the mean team level of team conscientiousness was positively related to team performance. Additionally, in a meta-analysis, Bell (2007) found that the team-level personality traits of conscientiousness, agreeableness, extraversion, emotional stability and openness to experience had little to no relationship with team performance in lab studies. However, in field studies, team-level measures of conscientiousness, agreeableness and openness to experience were related to team performance (Bell, 2007). These inconsistent findings with personality traits at the team level make it difficult to draw any conclusions regarding the relationship between team-level personality traits and performance.

Team-level general cognitive ability and its relationship with team performance has also been examined. Hill (1982) found that higher team member cognitive ability was positively related to performance of teams of systems analysts. Similarly, Tziner and Eden (1995) found that crews with higher ability soldiers exhibited higher performance, and Williams and Sternberg (1988) found team mean level of intelligence to be positively related to team performance. Barrick et al. (1998) examined team-level general cognitive ability and found that it was positively related to team performance and team viability. Meta-analyses have found results similar to the studies listed earlier with regard to the relationship between team-level general cognitive ability and team performance. In a meta-analysis, Stewart (2006) found that team-level general cognitive ability to be positively related to team performance. Also in a meta-analysis, Bell (2007) found a positive relationship between team-level general cognitive ability and team performance. While the positive relationship between team-level cognitive ability and team performance has been established, little research has been conducted on team-level task-specific abilities and team performance.

Neuman and Wright (1999) conducted a job analysis in a human resources department of a firm to determine the task-specific knowledge, skills and abilities needed to perform the job. After determining these, they aggregated individuals' scores in 79 teams on the task-specific knowledge, skills and abilities to the team level. Neuman and Wright (1999) determined that the tasks that the human resources teams were performing were conjunctive in nature; thus, according to Steiner's (1972) typology, they used the lowest score of each member in each group on the task specific knowledge, skills and abilities measure as the group score. They found teams with higher scores for their lowest-scoring member exhibited higher performance (Neuman & Wright, 1999).

More recently, Harris et al. (2009) examined the relationship between team human capital, behaviours and team performance in a sample of NCAA basketball teams. A third-party recruiting firm assessed and provided ratings of the human capital of each basketball player in playing basketball. The individual human capital scores were aggregated to the team level. The authors found a higher level of team human capital was related to greater team coordination and team performance.

In comparison to individual-level assessments of human capital, fewer measures of human capital have been employed at the team level. The primary focus of human capital studies at the team level has tended to only consider general measures of human capital, such as cognitive ability and personality traits. While fewer studies at the team level have considered more context-specific measures of human capital, as mentioned previously, Neuman and Wright (1999) and Harris et al. (2009) have attempted to move beyond general measures of human capital to more context-specific measures, with the goal of identifying the critical human capital that is needed by specific organizations to succeed.

Organization-level human capital

Recently, human capital research has taken place at the organizational level and its influence on organizational performance has been examined. Organizational-level research has tended to use more general measures of human capital (e.g. Carmeli & Schaubroeck, 2005; Lopez-Cabrales et al., 2006; Takeuchi et al., 2007), with only a few using more context-specific measures (e.g. Wright et al., 1995b; Hitt et al., 2001).

Within a strategic human resource framework, Carmeli and Schaubroeck (2005) examined human capital and the distinctive value of human capital and their relationships with organization performance. They measured human capital by having the CEO or a top manager at each organization assess the organization's perceived human capital and the organization's perceived distinctive value of its human capital. Human capital was measured as a perception of the levels of education, training, work experience and skills of the entire organization. The four items were:

- 'our employees have a suitable education for accomplishing their job successfully'
- 'our employees are well-trained to accomplish their jobs successfully'
- 'our employees hold suitable work experience for accomplishing their jobs successfully'
- 'our employees are well-skilled professionally to accomplish their jobs successfully'.

Distinctive value of an organization's human capital was assessed with a four-item scale (Carmeli & Schaubroeck, 2005). The items asked respondents to assess:

- 'the value of human capital (i.e. how much it contributes to organizational success)'

- 'the rarity of human capital (how rare and unique is the firm's human capital)'
- 'the degree to which the human capital is inimitable'
- 'the degree to which the human capital is non-substituable (i.e. how many competing firms already have strategically equivalent human capital)'.

Thus, only perceptions of human capital and perceptions of the value of human capital were measured; not actual human capital, nor the actual value of human capital. Additionally, the CEO or top manager at each firm rated the firm's performance in terms of overall financial performance, return on equity, quality of the organization's products and customer satisfaction. The scale for these items had anchors of 'much worse than competitors' to 'much better than competitors'. Carmeli and Schaubroeck (2005) found a significant interaction between perceptions of human capital and perceptions of human capital value in predicting organization performance. Thus, higher levels of perceived human capital, along with higher levels of perceived value of human capital, resulted in greater organization performance than when perceived human capital and perceived value of human capital were low. These results are not surprising, since the CEO or a top manager at each firm assessed both human capital and performance. It is unlikely that a CEO or top manager would rate their capital as low; therefore, the positive relationship between human capital and performance was expected.

Similarly, core employees have been found to have a positive influence on organizations; specifically, organizations that utilize the most valuable and unique core employees have higher capability (Lopez-Cabrales et al., 2006). Core employees were defined in the study as full-time employees engaged in the firm's core activity. The value and uniqueness of core employees was assessed by the HR manager in each firm. The items used to assess the value and uniqueness were adopted from Lepak and Snell (2002). In another study, Lopez-Cabrales et al. (2009) also employed measures of the value and uniqueness of human capital based on items developed by Lepak and Snell (2002). It was found that unique human capital positively influenced innovative activity. Additionally, unique human capital mediated the relationship between collaborative HR practices and innovative activity.

Carmeli and Tishler (2004a) examined human capital and performance in a sample of local government authorities in Israel. The top management of the local authority received a survey that asked them to assess, among other things, the human capital of the local authority. The human capital scale was made up of items to assess education, work experience and the competence of the local authorities' members. Four items assessed education and work experience and eight items assessed competence. Therefore, based on this study design, a single individual in the organization assessed the human capital of the entire organization. Performance measures used in the study were collected from archival sources. Human capital was found to be a predictor of self-income ratio, collecting efficiency ratio, employment rate and municipal development of the local government authorities. Carmeli and Tishler (2004b) employed the same human capital measure as mentioned above and tested its relationship with a variety of performance measures among a sample of Israeli industrial firms. The authors found that human capital was significantly related to the performance measures of return on equity, market share and customer satisfaction; however, human capital had little to no effect on return on sales.

A critical issue with both of the organizational-level studies of human capital described here is that a single individual rated the human capital for the entire organization; it is highly unlikely that one individual could accurately assess the human capital of an entire organization. Therefore, it is desirable to have more than one rater of human capital or to measure human capital at the individual level and aggregate to a higher level of analysis, in order to get a more accurate assessment of the organization's human capital.

More recently, Takeuchi et al. (2007) examined the mediating role that human capital plays between the high-performance work system and organization performance relationship. The high-performance work system was based on the work of Lepak and Snell (2002) and included measures of staffing, training and development, compensation, and performance management. Takeuchi et al. (2007) surveyed managers and employees of Japanese organizations to gauge the usage of high-performance work practices. In order to assess organizational human capital, managers completed a human capital scale that assessed general human capital such as employee skill level, creativity and propensity to develop new ideas. Takeuchi et al. (2007) assessed the collective human capital of a sample of Japanese establishments by asking multiple managers at each establishment to rate the extent to which all of their employees 'are highly skilled', 'are widely considered to be the best in our industry', 'are creative and bright', 'are experts in their particular jobs and functions' and 'develop new ideas and knowledge.' This human capital scale was adopted from Subramaniam and Youndt (2005) and Youndt et al. (2004). Additionally, managers provided a subjective rating of establishment performance. Delaney and Huselid's (1996) eight-item organization performance scale was employed. An item from the scale is: 'How would you compare the establishment's performance of the past three years to those of other establishments that do the same kind of work?' Takecuchi et al. (2007) found that this measure of collective human capital was positively related to organization performance, and that collective human capital mediated the relationship between high-performance work systems and organization performance.

Subramaniam and Youndt (2005) examined various aspects of intellectual capital, including human, social and organizational capital. The two highest-ranking executives (CEO and president), along with the vice president of HR for each organization, received a survey to assess the human, social and organizational capital of the organization. The items assessing human capital tended to be more general in nature and have been listed previously. The innovative capability of each organization was assessed by the vice president of marketing and the vice president of R&D in each organization. Contrary to their hypothesis, Subramaniam and Youndt (2005) found that human capital was negatively related to innovative capability. Additionally, it was found that human capital and social capital interacted to positively predict innovative capability. Under conditions of high human and social capital, organizations tended to have higher innovative capabilities. The studies reviewed up to this point employed measures that assessed general human capital at the organization level. It is also important for research to examine more specific measures of human capital that are congruent with the strategy or context of organizations in order to align the organization's human capital with organization strategy to achieve competitive advantage.

Moving towards more context-specific examinations of human capital, Lepak and Snell (1999) placed an emphasis on human capital and theorized a human resource architecture of four different employment modes: internal development, acquisition, contracting and alliance.

- The internal development mode is characterized by human resources that have firm specific skills, are highly unique and have high value.
- In the acquisition mode, organizations acquire human resources that do not require further investment. Here, human capital has low uniqueness and high value.
- The contracting employment mode is utilized when organizations contract work with individuals outside of the organization or outsource functions. In this case, the human capital has low uniqueness and value.
- Lastly, the alliance mode is used when organizations form alliances with other organizations to utilize human capital. With the alliance mode, human capital is highly unique and has low value.

The framework proposed by Lepak and Snell (1999) provides a way to study different employment arrangements used by organizations to allocate work. These are important considerations when an organization seeks to assess the human capital that is specifically needed for the organization.

Lepak and Snell (2002) empirically tested their human resource architecture. In the study, the internal development mode was renamed 'knowledge-based employment' and the acquisition mode was renamed 'job-based employment'. Lepak and Snell received surveys from 206 senior executives, senior human resource managers or line managers representing 148 firms. On each survey, they defined each of the four employment modes and asked each respondent to complete the survey for only one employment mode, as specified by Lepak and Snell. The authors found that human capital value was highest for knowledge-based and job-based employment, next highest for alliances and lowest for contract work. Also, the uniqueness of knowledge-based employees was significantly higher than the uniqueness of contract workers and job-based employees. The findings by Lepak and Snell (2002) clearly demonstrate the differences in human capital that can be attained through the different employment modes that an organization may choose to employ.

Wright et al. (1995b) used NCAA men's basketball teams to study human capital in a strategic human resource management framework. They examined three different basketball strategies (finesse, power and speed), along with 16 different basketball skills. It was found that the importance placed on different skills when recruiting players was based on coaches' preferred strategies. Similarly, the strategy that a firm employs influences the types of knowledge, skills and abilities sought by an organization. Wright et al. (1995b) also found that when a team implemented a strategy that was inconsistent with its coach's preferred strategy, the team exhibited lower performance than when it implemented a strategy that was consistent with the coach's preferred strategy. A team may implement a strategy that is inconsistent with its coach's preferred strategy because the players on the team may not have the knowledge, skills and abilities needed to implement the coach's strategy; this may particularly be the case when a team hires a new coach. In this situation, it may take time for the coach to recruit players to the team with the knowledge, skills and abilities needed for the coach's strategy, or for the coach to develop players that are currently on the team. As the coach recruits and develops players that are consistent with the coach's strategy, the team may perform at a higher level. Lastly, Wright et al. (1995b) found strategy moderated the relationship between human resource capabilities and team performance. Thus, when a team has players with knowledge, skills and abilities that are consistent with the team's strategy, the team performs at a higher level than if the knowledge, skills and abilities of the players are inconsistent with the team's strategy. Wright et al. (1995b) demonstrated the importance of human resources to firm performance and the importance of consistency between the knowledge, skills and abilities of the human capital pool and a firm's strategy.

While findings from sports team may not be completely transferable to business organizations, they do provide information that is useful for business organizations. For example, Wright et al. (1995b) shows the importance of human capital matching strategy among basketball teams. This finding can easily be applied to business organizations as they seek to recruit, select and retain individuals with the human capital necessary to execute the business strategy. Additionally, the study shows that when there is a change in strategy, performance may decrease because the basketball team does not have the requisite human capital. Once again, this is important to business organizations, because if they change strategies then they may have to search for different types of human capital in order to execute the strategy and perform at a higher level.

In a more context-specific study, Hitt et al. (2001) examined human capital in law firms. Human capital was measured as the quality of the law school attended by partners and the experience as partners in the current law firm. A U-shaped relationship was found between human capital and firm performance such that the relationship between human capital and firm performance was initially negative, but turned positive with higher levels of human capital (Hitt et al., 2001). This suggests that early investments in human capital may not produce enough benefits to offset the costs; however, over time, as employees gain experience, these investments may result in large benefits to the organization (Hitt et al., 2001). Hitt et al. (2006) also examined law firms and employed a human capital measure similar to that used by Hitt et al. (2001). The measure of human capital employed in the 2006 study included the quality of law school attended by partners, the average experience of the partners in the focal firm and the total partner experience in the legal field averaged across the partners in the focal firm. This measure of human capital had a marginally significant relationship with internationalization. These studies demonstrate the importance of context-specific human capital to organization performance. While proxy measures of human capital were employed, these measures are an attempt to measure human capital that is actually needed for law firms, rather than simply assessing general human capital as was done in previous studies. Context-specific measures of human capital provide greater insight into the human capital that is actually needed for organizations to execute their strategies and perform at higher levels.

Hatch and Dyer (2004) employed a variety of proxy measures of human capital and examined their relationships with learning and performance. The authors conceptualized human capital selection as education requirements and the use of pre-employment screening tests. This measure of selection was found to improve learning by doing, which in turn improved performance. Additionally, human capital development in terms of training received and human capital deployment were found to improve learning by doing, which in turn improved performance. It was also found that acquiring human capital with prior industry experience from outside sources reduced learning performance. Finally, the authors found firms with higher turnover significantly underperformed their competitors. These findings point to the importance of firm-specific human capital because when firms have higher turnover, they lose their firm-specific human capital – which may have detrimental effects on their performance.

Within the strategic human resource management literature, the organizational-level studies have had the greatest impact in drawing additional interest to the concept of human capital. This interest has brought to the forefront the need to integrate or understand the human capital concept at multiple levels of analysis.

Multi-level human capital

The previous sections reviewed the measurement of human capital at the individual, team, and organizational levels. This leads to the inherently multi-level nature of human capital. With human capital being measured at these different levels of analysis and the interest in the relationship that human capital has with performance at different levels of analysis, research has begun to take a multi-level approach to the study of human capital.

In a multi-level study of teacher human capital and performance, Pil and Leana (2009) employed both general and specific measures of human capital. This multi-level study was conducted at the individual and group levels of analysis. The measures of teachers' general human capital were the level of education that they had achieved and the years they had taught at a particular grade level. The task-specific measure of teachers' human capital assessed teachers' ability to teach mathematics. At the individual level, the authors found teacher experience at a grade level and maths teaching ability were positively and significantly related to growth in students' achievement in maths. Additionally, as predicted, a significant relationship was not found between formal education and student attainment. To aggregate to the team level, Pil and Leana (2009) used the average of individuals' education, experience and ability to teach maths. Therefore, teams that were better educated, more experienced and had higher abilities in teaching maths had higher human capital scores. The authors found that at the team level, the average educational attainment was significantly and positively related to growth in student performance. However, there was not a significant relationship between either team experience or ability to teach maths and student achievement growth.

Ployhart et al. (2009) also conducted a multi-level study of human capital in retail organizations. Their study consisted of 114,198 individual-level assessments of service orientation that were aggregated to the unit level to produce a unit-level sample size of 1255. The human capital (unit service orientation) and performance of each unit was tracked over a three-quarter period of time. Service orientation was conceptualized as human capital. The measure of service orientation included items that assessed emotional stability, agreeableness, conscientiousness, educational success and situational judgment. To aggregate individual service orientation to the unit level, the unit-level mean of aggregate individual-level service orientation scores was used. Unit performance was assessed with three measures: sales per employee, profit and same-store sales. A positive relationship between unit service orientation and performance was found. However, over time, the positive relationship began to decrease. Additionally, units that maintained a flow of higher levels of unit service orientation outperformed units that had a flow of lower levels of unit service orientation.

In another multi-level study, Ployhart et al. (2006) assessed human capital using personality traits. The authors collected individual-level personality trait data and aggregated to the job and organization levels to conduct their multi-level study. The personality traits of emotional stability, conscientiousness, agreeableness and extraversion were assessed. Two measures of performance were employed in the study: job satisfaction and job performance. At the individual, job and organization levels, mean emotional stability was significantly and positively related to job satisfaction and job performance. Additionally, mean conscientiousness at the individual, job and organization levels was significantly and positively related to job satisfaction and job performance. It was also found that only mean-level agreeableness at the individual and job level were significantly and positively related to job satisfaction and job performance. Additionally, job-level variance in agreeableness was negatively and significantly related to job satisfaction. The authors found that mean extraversion at the individual, job and organization levels was significantly and positively related to job satisfaction and job performance. Finally, the variance in extraversion at the job level was negatively and significantly related to job satisfaction, and was positively and significantly related to job performance.

The multi-level studies listed above point to the importance of assessing the human capital and performance relationship at multiple levels within organizations, including the individual level, team level, job level, unit level, and organization level (Ployhart & Moliterno, 2011; Wright & McMahan, 2011). Additionally, these studies have demonstrated the variety of ways that have been employed to measure human capital and highlight the need for future research to improve upon these early measures.

General and specific human capital

As mentioned previously, human capital theory states that general and specific human capital are important to the success of organizations (Becker, 1964). General human capital increases the marginal productivity of labour across organizations and specific human capital increases the productivity of labour at a specific unit (Becker, 1964). Based on this review, general human capital measures have received most of the attention in human capital research, while specific measures of human capital have received little attention. At the individual level of analysis, many different measures of general human capital have been employed, such as cognitive ability, education level, quality of education and experience to name a few (e.g. Hunter & Hunter, 1984; O'Reilly & Chatman, 1994; Judge et al., 1995; Martocchio & Judge, 1997; Ng et al., 2005). Additionally, at the team level, the general human capital measures of cognitive ability and personality traits are the primary measures (e.g. Tziner & Eden, 1985; Barrick et al., 1998; Stewart, 2006; Bell, 2007). Measures of general human capital have also been employed at the organization level. Organization-level studies of human capital have tended to use a scale of items to assess general human capital (e.g. Carmeli & Tishler, 2004a, 2004b; Youndt et al., 2004; Carmeli & Schaubroeck, 2005; Subramaniam & Youndt, 2005; Lopez-Cabrales et al., 2006; Takeuchi et al., 2007). While these studies have generally found a positive relationship between general human capital and organization performance, they do not consider the specific context or strategy of organizations. The human capital needed for specific contexts and organizational strategies is important to the success of organizations.

Following the logic of the resource-based view, human capital that is more specific to a context will assist an organization in creating a competitive advantage. This occurs because specific human capital is not easily transferrable among organizations, while general human capital is. The few studies that have examined human capital that is more specific to an organization's context and strategy have tended to find a positive relationship between human capital and performance (e.g. Wright et al., 1995b; Neuman & Wright, 1999; Hitt et al., 2001; Pil & Leana, 2009; Ployhart et al., 2009).

The studies listed above demonstrate how the dimensions of general versus specific human capital relate to organization performance. While general human capital is important, it is also important to consider the specific human capital that an organization needs in order to execute its strategy and create a competitive advantage.

Critical issues for human capital measurement

The previous sections reviewed research on human capital and performance at the individual, team, organization and multiple levels of analysis. Additionally, we have discussed both general and specific human capital. This review outlined a multitude of ways in which human capital has been measured. Based on the studies reviewed here and the measures of human capital employed, it is easy to see that there is little agreement on the measurement of human capital. In this section, issues to consider in the future measurement of human capital are discussed, including general and specific measures of human capital, single rater measures of human capital, and aggregation and multi-level issues.

General and specific measures of human capital

As mentioned previously, both general and specific human capital are important to the success of organizations. Previous research has tended to use measures of general human capital at the individual and team levels of analysis and a scale of items to assess general human capital at the organization level. While these measures appear to be accepted in research, they do not provide insight into the human capital that is needed for specific contexts. Therefore, measuring human capital that is more specific becomes increasingly important. The measurement of specific human capital poses challenges, such as differentiating between what is general human capital and what is specific human capital. For example, Ployhart et al. (2009) assessed service orientation as human capital. While service orientation may be considered general human capital, the organizations in which this measure was employed were in the retail sector; therefore, service orientation becomes specific to that context. This example demonstrates the importance of considering the strategy of the organization when measuring human capital. The strategy of the organization helps determine the human capital that an organization will need in order to execute the strategy and perform at a high level (Wright & McMahan, 1992). Taking the strategy of an organization into account will lead to a better measurement of the specific human capital needed by the organization.

Wright et al. (1995b) considered the strategy that basketball teams employed and its influence on the human capital of the team. Based on strategy employed by the team, different types of human capital were sought. Additionally, Hitt et al., (2001) assessed the strategy of law firms and the role it played in the human capital–performance relationship. Therefore, strategy is a contextual factor that should be taken into consideration in future human capital research. The strategy of a firm dictates the type of human capital acquired by an organization (Wright & McMahan, 1992); therefore, considering the strategy of an organization along with the human capital of an organization helps to develop a clearer picture of the relationship between human capital and organizational performance.

Another item to consider in future human capital research is the use of third-party raters of human capital. Previous research has employed third-party ratings of human capital as measures of context-specific human capital. In their studies of law firms, Hitt et al. (2001) and Hitt et al. (2006) assessed the quality of the law school attended by partners. In these studies, the quality of the law school was taken from an outside third party's assessment of the quality of each law school. Similar to these studies, Harris et al. (2009) employed a third-party rating of basketball players' human capital. The measure of basketball players' human capital came from a third-party recruiting firm that assessed basketball players and, based on that assessment, provided a rating of each player's human capital. The use of an outside third party to assess human capital may provide for a more objective assessment of human capital than someone inside an organization would supply. Additionally, third-party ratings of stock analysts have been used to determine 'star' analysts (e.g. Groysberg et al., 2008). These third-party ratings provide context-specific measures of human capital. Unlike an insider, the outside third party may not have a vested interest in the human capital of an organization; therefore, a third party rating of human capital would be desirable for use in future research.

Additionally, future human capital research should measure – or at least recognize the existence of – both general and specific human capital. Pil and Leana (2009) did this by measuring general human capital as education level and experience of teaching, and by measuring specific human capital as the ability to teach maths. It is desirable for future research to consider both general and specific human capital in the same study, so that researchers can test to see if specific human capital significantly contributes to performance above and beyond the contribution of general human capital.

Single rater assessments of human capital

Previous research at the organization level (e.g. Wright et al., 1995b; Carmeli & Tishler, 2004a, 2004b; Carmeli & Schaubroeck, 2005; Lopez-Cabrales et al., 2006) has tended to rely on a single rater in an organization to assess the human capital of the entire organization. Typically, the individual assessing the human capital of the organization in these studies is the CEO, other top manager or the vice president of human resources. Few organization-level studies of human capital have employed the use of multiple raters of human capital (e.g. Subramaniam & Youndt, 2005; Takeuchi et al., 2007). Issues have been raised with the use of single raters in strategic human resource management research (Gerhart et al., 2000b; Huselid & Becker, 2000): a significant problem with these measures is that they are based on the perceptions of a single respondent and so common method bias, rater bias and/ or inaccuracy of reporting might be present (Gerhart et al., 2000b). Such responses may also have inconsistencies or low reliabilities (Gerhart et al., 2000a; Wright & McMahan, in press).

It is difficult for a single individual to accurately assess the human capital of an entire organization, since human capital may vary by location, employee and business unit. Additionally, the size of organizations makes it difficult for one individual to know what is going on in all aspects of the organization. Finally, the individual may have a potential bias due to their vested interest in the organization (Seidler, 1974). Due to these issues, the use of a single respondent can generate significant levels of error measurement (Gerhart et al., 2000a).

As mentioned previously, human capital research at the organization level has tended to rely on a single scale to assess the human capital of an entire organization. The use of a single scale to evaluate the human capital of an entire organization is not desirable; nor does it provide an accurate assessment of the human capital of an organization. These issues are further enhanced by the use of single respondents. Therefore, if a single scale must be used to evaluate human capital, it is desirable to have multiple raters within organizations complete the scale, which may provide for a more accurate assessment of organization level human capital.

Aggregation and multi-level issues

This review of human capital measurement at the individual, team and organization levels points to the inherently multi-level nature of human capital. Human capital and resource-based view theories predict that the unit aggregate of individual knowledge, skills and abilities that lead to unit performance (Wright et al., 1995b; Wright & McMahan, in press). With this in mind, studies (e.g. Ployhart et al., 2006; Pil & Leana, 2009; Ployhart et al., 2009) have taken a multi-level approach to the study of human capital. In these studies, individual-level measures of human capital have been aggregated to the team, job, unit and organization levels. By aggregating from the individual level, it allows for more fine-grained measures of human capital to be employed. Measuring human capital at the individual level and then aggregating to higher levels of analysis may provide a clearer picture of the emergence human capital of an organization (Ployhart et al., 2009; Ployhart & Moliterno, 2011) than assessing the human capital of an entire organization with a single scale. Multi-level analysis also provides an opportunity for longitudinal human capital research to be conducted (e.g. Ployhart et al., 2009). Assessing human capital and performance over time will allow researchers to examine how performance changes with changes in human capital. Therefore, the use of more fine-grained measures of human capital and longitudinal studies is suggested for future research.

With multi-level research comes the issue of determining how to aggregate data. As mentioned previously, prior research has tended to aggregate individual-level measures of human capital to higher levels of analysis (e.g. team, job, unit and organization). Previous studies (Pil & Leana, 2009; Ployhart et al., 2009) have used the mean of individual-level scores as the score for the higher level of analysis. Additionally, it has been suggested that the nature of the task that individuals are engaged in should be considered in order to properly account for the influence that certain individual traits have on performance (Steiner, 1972). For additive tasks, such that each team member contributes to performance in proportion to their ability, the mean of the variable being examined can be taken. For disjunctive tasks, where a team can perform as well as its best member, a maximum score of the individual member scores can be used as the team measure. When the task is conjunctive – that is, when the performance of a team depends on the team's weakest member – a minimum score of the individual member scores can be used as the team/firm measure (Steiner, 1972). Therefore, the tasks that individuals are engaged in should be considered when aggregating data to perform a multi-level analysis.

Multi-level research presents many opportunities for human capital to be studied at multiple levels and longitudinally. With these opportunities come challenges of developing individual-level measures of human capital that can be aggregated to higher levels of analysis. Additionally, the manner in which human capital is aggregated can have an impact on its relationship with performance. The process by which human capital emerges or combines at higher levels of analysis is important to consider, because the emergence of human capital influences performance at higher levels of analysis (Kozlowski & Klein, 2000; Ployhart & Moliterno, 2011).

This section highlighted some of the critical issues in the measurement of human capital such as general and specific measures of human capital, single rater assessments of human capital, and multi-level human capital research. Each of these issues presents challenges for the measurement of human capital. Along with these issues, suggestions for how to address these issues in future research were given.

Conclusion

Human capital is a resource that can provide a competitive advantage for organizations (Wright et al., 1994). Therefore, the measurement of human capital and its associated influence on performance are important to consider. Previous research has measured human capital and examined its relationship with performance at the individual, team and organization levels. More recently, multi-level research on human capital has begun to take place.

This review of the literature describes how human capital has been measured in a variety of manners. A consistent finding is that higher levels of human capital tend to be associated with higher levels of performance. Because human capital has been operationalized in a variety of ways, future considerations for the measurement of human capital were offered – these included examining general and specific human capital. Next, it was specifically recommended to take context into consideration when measuring human capital, in order to develop and employ measures of human capital that align with the context being studied. Additionally, the use of third-party assessors of human capital was suggested. Third parties may not have a vested interest in the human capital of the organizations that they are assessing; therefore, they may provide an unbiased assessment of human capital. Issues to consider when using single respondents to assess the human capital of an entire organization were also discussed. Finally, where appropriate, continued multi-level human capital research and methodology was suggested. Additionally, multi-level analysis facilitates longitudinal human capital research and allows for the performance effects of changes in human capital to be examined.

Overall, the measurement of human capital and its associated influence on performance are important for researchers and organizations to consider as organizations seek to gain or maintain a strategic human capital advantage.

8

MEASUREMENT OF HUMAN RESOURCE PRACTICES: ISSUES REGARDING SCALE, SCOPE, SOURCE AND SUBSTANTIVE CONTENT

ANGELA LANGEVIN HEAVEY, SUSANNE BEIJER,
JESSICA FEDERMAN, MICHEL HERMANS,
FELICE KLEIN, ELIZABETH MCCLEAN
AND BRIAN MARTINSON

Introduction

The relationship between HR practices and various measures of firm performance has been established through empirical studies across industries (Huselid, 1995; Guthrie, 2001), within a variety of industries (MacDuffie, 1995; Delery & Doty, 1996), across business units within companies (Wright et al., 2005), and in a variety of country settings (Takeuchi et al., 2007; Gong et al., 2009). Recent meta-analyses of this relationship have revealed reasonably consistent effect sizes for this relationship (Combs et al., 2006; Subramony, 2009).

Given the increasing volume of research in this area, researchers have begun to critically examine the methodological approaches used in studies on the HR–performance relationship. Empirical studies have examined the inter-rater reliability of reports of HR practices (Gerhart et al., 2000b), as well as the causal order (Wright et al., 2005). In addition, Gerhart (2007a) has conceptually explored the impact of the statistical modelling issues with regard to the HR–performance relationship. Finally, Becker and Gerhart (1996) noted that little agreement existed with regard to which HR practices should be included in HR practice scales, and this issue still remains largely unresolved (Lepak et al., 2004).

While these rigorous explorations of this literature have been helpful for revealing methodological improvements that can guide future research, a number of issues remain relatively unexplored. For instance, studies have varied from using a Likert scale of 'extent of use', dichotomous yes/no reports, or reports of the percentage of employees covered by a practice. Second, some studies have asked respondents to report the practices for all employees, for all managerial, professional or all hourly employees, or for employees in a particular job group. Third, the source of gaining the HR practice information has varied from HR managers or line managers to employees. Finally, there is little agreement concerning the substantive content or functional categories of HR practices that should be assessed (i.e. which HR practices to assess). The purpose of this chapter is to examine the various operationalizations of HR practices relative to the scale, scope, source and substantive content, and to provide guidance for the trade-offs regarding the different operationalization choices that future researchers must make in the design of their studies.

Rating scale issues

When confronted with the issue of HR practice measurement, much attention is placed on the construction of the actual items used in the survey or interview. The preponderance of pilot surveys, reliability tests and the like speak to our desire as researchers to ask the 'right' questions. While the question of what to ask is a vitally important aspect of the data collection process, the question of *how* to ask our questions is an equally important – yet far less discussed – topic. One largely unexplored issue concerns the type of response scale used by researchers. A review of the strategic human resources literature reveals that a variety of rating scales have been used. While some variety is to be expected, it is also clear that there is inconsistency in the types of rating scales used to measure the same (or very similar) HR practices. This issue is problematic as it has been found that even identically worded items may yield differing information from respondents depending on the rating scales used by the researcher (Schwarz & Hippler, 1991; Schwarz, 1996). This issue should be of concern to researchers, as the use of inappropriate ratings scales may influence scale reliability, contributing unnecessary measurement error (Wright et al., 2001a). The following section discusses this issue in greater depth, discussing the types of rating scales employed in the HR literature, as well as the advantages and disadvantages of each scale type.

Types of rating scales

At the broadest level, rating scales used in the human resources literature can be classified as either objective or subjective in nature. As the name implies, objective response formats request information from respondents that is considered factual. Objective response scales are often dichotomous, asking for a 'yes/no' response (e.g. 'Do you offer training to existing employees?'). An objective rating scale may also request specific information, such as a percentage or number: for instance, a question using an objective rating scale might ask for the number of training hours provided per week or the percentage of employees who receive training in a given year. Another type of objective rating scale is the 'check all that apply' approach, which asks respondents to check all HR practices used in their organization.

One issue regarding the use of objective rating scales concerns the quality and accuracy of information obtained. Because objective ratings scales ask for specific information, respondents must have adequate knowledge in order to provide accurate answers. This creates methodological challenges because it requires researchers to identify the most appropriate person from whom to solicit information. This issue will be discussed in a later section.

In contrast to objective rating scales, subjective response formats allow for more personal interpretation on the part of the respondent. This is because they often use a Likert format, which provides respondents with a response continuum. These responses often range from 'strongly disagree' to 'strongly agree' and ask respondents to rate their agreement with statements concerning human resource practices in their organization. Consider the previous example involving training; rather than asking for a dichotomous 'yes/no' response, a subjective response format might involve a five-point Likert scale that asks the respondent to rate their agreement with a statement such as 'My organization offers training to existing employees'. This type of format provides the respondent with a wider range of possible answers, as well as more flexibility in choosing their response. One argument in support of this type of rating scale is that it gives researchers access to the 'actual' practices in an organization rather than just those that are espoused (e.g. Khilji & Wang, 2006), as respondents are able to go beyond a simple yes/no or numerical answer. Providing multiple response options prevents a respondent from facing the dilemma of choosing between two options that do not fit, and can help to reduce non-response bias.

As Wright et al. (2001a) note, there is no clear consensus about which type of rating scale is most appropriate for the measurement of human resource practices. Cases can be made for the merits or drawbacks of both objective and subjective rating scales, and there is no clear agreement regarding the 'best' rating scale type. In a study comparing subjective and objective ratings of company performance, the authors found convergent validity between the two types, suggesting that they reap similar results (Wall et al., 2004). While this study focused on measures used to assess company performance rather than HR practices, the results are pertinent to HR practices measures because they suggest that both objective and subjective rating scales can be useful in research.

While both objective and subjective rating scales may be effective, given the debate regarding the measurement of HR practices (Gerhart et al., 2000a; Gerhart et al., 2000b; Huselid & Becker, 2000), it is important to consider the potential measurement error involved with different types of rating scales. As Wright et al. (2001a) point out, rating scales may influence the reliability of survey instruments in a positive or negative way. Using a rating scale that is inappropriate for the question at hand may have an adverse impact on scale reliability, as it may involve more measurement error than another rating format. By examining the impact of rating scales on reliability, researchers may be able to learn better ways to measure HR practices.

Review of rating scale use in recent literature

While there is a lack of consensus regarding which type of rating scale is most appropriate for measuring HR practices, it is possible to gain an understanding of which rating scales are most frequently used by reviewing the recent literature. Accordingly, 30 papers published between 1992 and 2007 were examined to determine which types of rating scales were used. Recognizing that authors may incorporate multiple types of rating scales depending on the items being used, the review was conducted at the item level, examining the specific rating scales used for individual items in each study. Even if a rating scale was only utilized for one item, it was considered used in the study for the purposes of this review. It should be noted that in some cases, authors did not denote the specific rating scale being used. This most often occurred in cases where an established instrument (or an adapted version) was employed. In such cases, we used the rating scale utilized in the original version of the instrument.

Overall, the review revealed that Likert scales were the predominant response format, as they were utilized in more than 75 per cent of the studies. While the number of anchor points ranged from three (e.g. Delaney & Huselid, 1996) to eight (e.g. Tsui et al., 1997) across studies, the most frequently used format was a five- or seven-point Likert scale. Generally, these scales assessed a respondent's level of agreement or disagreement with the item statement, although in some studies respondents were asked about their level of control over HR practices (e.g. Batt, 2002), the extent to which an HR practice was used (e.g. Tsui et al., 1997; Fey & Bjorkman, 2001), or the effectiveness of a particular practice (e.g. Delaney & Huselid, 1996).

The second most common rating scale was the 'yes/no' format, which was utilized in more than 30 per cent of the studies in the sample. This type of rating scale was mainly used to assess whether a particular human resource practice was present in the organization. Two other prevalent rating scale formats consisted of open-ended questions that asked respondents to provide a number or percentage. Most commonly, these items requested information concerning the number or proportion of employees covered by a particular HR practice. Finally, one study (van den Berg et al. 1999) utilized a 'check all that apply' approach, which provided a list of options that respondents could choose from. One advantage of the 'check all that apply' approach is that respondents are provided with choices that appear to be equal in social desirability or equal in favourability. However, while this type of forced-choice scale offers some benefits, a disadvantage is that confined lists reduce the likelihood that respondents report the use of practices that may not be on the list (Schwarz et al., 1999). Such omissions may result in a mis-specification of the HR practices construct.

Overall, the review of the recent literature indicates that subjective Likert scales are the most commonly used rating scale method, although the use of objective 'yes/no' responses and percentages are also frequently used. It should also be noted that although many studies consistently used only one rating form, eight of the reviewed studies incorporated at least two different types of rating scales. The fact that one-third of the studies used at least two different rating scale types is encouraging, as this shows that researchers recognize the need to incorporate different rating formats for different questions. As Wall et al. (2004) noted, using both subjective and objective rating scales is useful, as each type has its own associated measurement error. Using both types in combination may help to alleviate this problem, as the shortcomings of one type are made up for by the advantages of the other.

Recommendations for rating scale use

As mentioned earlier, it has been noted that rating scales may potentially influence the reliability of scales measuring HR practices (Wright et al., 2001a). While this issue has received less attention than other measurement issues, such as the use of single versus multiple raters (Gerhart et al., 2000a; Gerhart et al., 2000b; Huselid & Becker, 2000), it deserves attention. Depending on the scale item, as well as what the research question is asking, various rating scales may be more or less appropriate in different situations. In basic terms, the context of the research study becomes important when considering which type of response format to use. For example, using an objective 'yes/no' format may be useful when a researcher is only interested in whether a certain HR practice exists *at all* in an organization, or if the item is asking about a specific aspect of an HR practice (such as 'Does your organization use web-based training for any of its employees?'). However, this type of response format is inappropriate when the *amount* of training offered is important to the research question. In this case, a Likert format that provides respondents with a range of response options is more suitable. By providing respondents with an opportunity to choose from a range of response options, the scale is capturing variance that could be of potential importance to the research question at hand. For example, while a 'yes/no' question will only allow a researcher to say that the presence of any amount of training influences firm performance, responses based on a Likert format would allow the researcher to see how different amounts of training may influence firm performance.

While the above example is rather simplistic, it illustrates how using an unsuitable rating format may adversely impact a researcher's ability to infer results. Simply put, using inadequate rating scales could negatively affect an author's ability to find meaningful relationships among variables of interest. In addition, these rating scales may be negatively influencing scale reliability, which then affects construct validity. Such issues pose a challenge to authors who must justify the legitimacy of their findings. As Wright et al. (2001a) suggest, one potential way of enhancing the reliability of HR practice scales is to try different rating scales to see which are most appropriate. While initially time-consuming, such investigation could be hugely beneficial to the human resources field.

Overall, it appears that researchers are utilizing a variety of different rating scales in their assessment of HR practices. Among these methods are subjective Likert scales, which supply respondents with a range of response options, as well as objective rating scales such as dichotomous 'yes/no' formats and open-ended responses that ask for numbers or percentages. While Likert scales were the most commonly used method (appearing in 75 per cent of the studies in the sample), approximately one-third of the authors incorporated at least two of the rating scale types in their studies.

While there is no consensus on the 'best' type of rating scale (Wright et al., 2001a), it is important that authors take into consideration which response formats are most appropriate for the question at hand. By choosing suitable rating scales, researchers may be able to increase the reliability of their measures. Because it is not always clear which rating scales are most appropriate, this might require researchers to try different response formats to see what works best. Just because an established scale uses a particular rating scale does not mean that another response format may not be a better choice; as Wright et al. (2001a) note, exploring alternative rating scales may reveal ways to decrease measurement error by increasing scale reliability. Not only would this help individual researchers to measure HR practices more effectively, it would also potentially advance the field as researchers would have access to more reliable measures that are better suited to revealing the effects of HR practices.

Scope issues

Just as it is important to consider issues revolving around ratings scales used to measure human resource practices, it is also vital to consider another largely ignored measurement issue: measurement scope. In general, measurement scope refers to the level at which HR practices are measured. Most commonly, HR practices have been measured at the job, business unit or firm level. Just as the use of different rating scales may influence the type of data collected, research scope may also have methodological implications. Because HR practices may be different at different levels, a study researching the use of HR practices at the firm level will likely have very different results than a project examining HR practices at the job level. If the impact of scope on results is not considered, inaccurate inferences may be drawn about the impact of HR practices on firm performance. As we discuss in the following section, adequate consideration of scope issues, as well as proper scope operationalization, is vital to a methodologically sound investigation.

Review of scope in recent literature

To investigate the use of scope in the SHRM literature, we reviewed 30 studies examining the HR–performance relationship. This was the same sample used to examine rating scale use discussed earlier. The review revealed that, in general, studies used an aggregate measure of HR practices or a set of HR practices for all employees within a firm or business unit. For example, Huselid (1995) collected data on exempt and non-exempt employees, but ultimately aggregated these to create a firm-level measure of HR practices. Across all 30 studies, approximately 48 per cent used a firm-level measure of HR practices.

A few researchers assessed the relationship between HR and performance at the business unit level. For example, Sun et al. (2007) used a sample of business units across 12 hotel organizations in China. The use of business units as a source is similar to using the firm level, because the HR measure is for all employees within each unit. Similarly, Arthur (1994) assessed the impact of a control and commitment system of HR practices on a plant-level performance measure and turnover rate. Across all 30 studies, approximately 25 per cent used a business unit-level measure of HR practices.

Other authors used a narrower, job-level scope to measure HR practices. For example, Batt (2002) measured HR practices for the core workforce, which in this case were the customer service and sales representatives within call centres. Similarly, Delery and Doty (1996) measured HR practices for the core workforce of bank loan officers. Tsui et al. (1997) measured HR for 36 different jobs in order to create four employee–organization relationship approaches. However, these studies are an exception, because few used the job as the level of analysis for HR practices. Across all 30 studies, approximately 27 per cent used a job-level measure of HR practices. Finally, while few researchers in SHRM have measured HR practices at the employment mode or group level, two studies examined HR practices using this narrower scope. Lepak and Snell (2002) found that HR strategies varied across employee groups and Tsui et al. (1997) found that different employment relationships existed across job groups.

As evidenced by the studies outlined above, researchers have primarily examined HR practices at the firm, business unit, and job levels. While the majority of studies have used a broad, firm-level scope to examine the HR–performance relationship, some research has been undertaken that examines HR practices at lower levels. The following section outlines our scope-related recommendations for future research in this area.

Recommendations for scope use

Based on our review of the pertinent SHRM literature, we suggest that the use of a narrow, job or employment mode scope is preferable, given that firms typically use different employment modes across employee groups. Employment modes within an organization may differ based on the job definition, rules concerning how employees move from job to job within an organization as well as, security and wage rules (Osterman, 1987). From a psychological contract perspective, employment modes within organizations vary such that there is an organization-focused and a job-focused contract; each differs on the scope of HR investments based on the contribution of certain employee groups to the firm (Tsui et al., 1995).

Given that internal labour markets exist within organizations for various reasons, logically, it would follow that certain HR practices might be standardized for all employees, but others may vary to match the specific requirements of particular employee groups (Miles & Snow, 1984). Using the theoretical perspectives above, organizations may use different HR practices (i.e. commitment) with certain employee groups that do not need monitoring and others (i.e. control) for those that do. Thus, variation in HR practices may exist at the job or employment mode level. To fully capture this variation, requires that HR practices be measured at these lower levels. While firm-level HR practices may be informative, they simply may not reflect the actual practices that are (or are not) influencing performance.

This prompts a question: if the variation in HR practices may exist at a lower level than the firm level, why have researchers continuously focused on firm-level HR practices? The primary reason is likely to be that it is easier to study HR at the firm level. As many have noted, typically the top HR manager in a firm is the source of information on HR practices at the firm level (Gerhart et al., 2000b; Wright et al., 2001a). Collecting data from one person is much easier than surveying multiple respondents, which would be necessary to get at the variation across employee groups. The unit or HR manager for an employee group would be the most knowledgeable person regarding the employee groups they manage. Surveying multiple units or HR managers not only requires more resources, but the requisite inter-rater reliability can be difficult to achieve (Gerhart et al., 2000a).

Additionally, defining the HR and performance constructs becomes more difficult when using the employment mode or job group as a unit of variation. For example, the HR construct can be measured at the policy or practice level. Typically, a broader approach is taken to measuring HR practices at the policy level; but if the HR practices are to be measured at the job group level, then a practice level construct might be used. Additionally, when using a job group level of analysis, decisions regarding the firm performance construct are important. For example, if variation in HR practices exists at the job level, is overall firm financial performance the appropriate measure to use or would a more proximal measure of performance be better? These are questions that the research community must ask if we wish to improve our methodological approaches.

It should be stressed that we do not seek to invalidate past findings on the HR–performance relationship. In fact, we argue that these findings allow us to conclude that HR impacts firm performance, but we cannot conclude by how much, in what cases, or for whom. Future researchers should focus on where the variation actually exists – whether it is truly at the firm, business unit or job level. Such focus would help us to explain a larger amount of variance in performance because the two variables will be more proximally related. This argument implies a multi-level approach such that it may be important to look at the job level within the business unit within the firm. Wright and Nishii (Chapter 6) argue that explaining as much variation as possible in HR practices and outcomes requires a more detailed consideration of the sources of variation that exist in and around those variables. We have a theoretical and practical rationale for studying HR at a narrower scope.

Source issues

Along with issues relating to scale and scope, researchers interested in studying the HR–performance relationship must also consider another important methodological issue: source. In general, the SHRM literature is mainly composed of studies surveying a single HR representative for data on HR practices and other company information (Gerhart et al., 2000a). Yet research has shown that this may not be the most reliable method to gain information on human resource practices. Gerhart et al. (2000a) found that HR measures may suffer from significant measurement error due to low reliability and consistency when a single source is used to gather information: 'raters are likely an important source of measurement error and . . . corrections for measurement error will result in substantial changes to substantive estimates of the HR–firm performance relationship' (p. 870). Therefore, the source of information could greatly affect the findings in the SHRM literature.

Two factors appear most relevant when determining the correct source of information to assess HR practices: who within the organization to ask and how many people to ask. A number of different organizational respondents have been used to obtain information on HR practices within SHRM research, from a single HR manager or multiple employees to a single supervisor, and so on. In general, source choice appears to be largely based on research practicality, as researchers are constrained by the degree of access they have to organizational members. Generally, surveying a single HR representative appears to be the most common method (Gerhart et al., 2000). This propensity to survey HR managers is most likely to be due to a belief that these individuals hold the most knowledge of their organization's HR practices. In addition, it is normally far easier to contact a single HR manager within an organization to collect data.

Although issues of practicality are a concern, it is also necessary to consider how choosing sources based solely on ease of access may be influencing our research findings. While it is understood that researchers may not always have access to the most ideal respondents, it is important to understand how the source choice impacts the data that is collected. For instance, while HR managers may be most knowledgeable about the general existence of certain HR practices within their organization (HR policy), they may be less able to provide accurate information concerning their actual implementation or use (actual HR practice). Thus, source choice may depend largely on the research question at hand – is the researcher interested in learning which HR practices exist or which are actually used (e.g. Becker & Gerhart, 1996; Khilji & Wang, 2006)? The following section discusses these issues in greater depth, outlining the different sources used in the literature, as well as considerations for each source type. In addition, we provide a discussion of the policy versus practice debate, and how this discourse impacts source choice.

Review of source use in recent literature

Researchers interested in gathering HR practice data have several options in terms of who to survey within an organization. While the most common source for this data is HR managers, this information can also be obtained from line managers, employees or a combination of sources. The following section considers the advantages and disadvantages of each source type, taking into account factors related to research design and practical feasibility.

HR managers

The HR practices construct has typically been operationalized in terms of the extent to which particular practices are applied in a focal organization (e.g. Arthur, 1994), or the share of an organization's total number of employees to which practices apply (e.g. Huselid, 1995). Because this operationalization ostensibly requires the respondent to have knowledge of HR practices, researchers have typically collected data from HR managers. Huselid and Becker (2000) justified this approach by arguing that, unlike measures of constructs based on perceptions such as organizational culture or climate, measures of the HR practices construct require respondents be informed. Since HR managers are more knowledgeable with regard to the attributes of an organization's HR practices than line managers or employees in general, Huselid and Becker (2000) suggested that HR practices obtained from randomly selected raters do not have equal validity to those obtained from HR managers. Data collection from HR managers may be supported by the focus of research and the level of analysis as well. Regarding focus, researchers increasingly distinguish between HR principles, policies, strategies, practices and product (e.g. Wright & Sherman, 1999; Colbert, 2004). Since HR managers are most actively involved in the definition of HR principles, policies, strategies and practices, they can provide more accurate data regarding intended effects of HR than line mangers or employees.

Concerning level of analysis, researchers have proposed to study HR–performance linkages at the corporate (Huselid & Becker, 1996, 1998), business unit (Rogers & Wright, 1998), establishment (Batt, 2002), job group (Osterman, 1994), strategic business process (Becker & Huselid, 2006), and individual (Wright & Boswell, 2002) levels of analysis. Since HR managers' responsibilities typically imply an organizational or cross-departmental perspective, they are better positioned to provide data on organization-wide HRM practices compared to line managers or employees who work in a particular functional area (Huselid & Becker, 2000).

Finally, researchers may choose to collect data from HR managers because of practical considerations. In a review of SHRM studies, Becker and Huselid (1998) found that response rates ranged from 6–28 per cent, with an average of 17.4 percent. Given the possibility of non randomness in decisions to refrain from responding to a survey, low response rates imply a risk of biased research findings. Because SHRM research caters mainly to the interests of HR managers, this group is most likely to respond to surveys that serve research purposes only.

While the predominant approach among SHRM researchers has been to obtain data from HR managers, several observations have been made regarding the reliability and validity of data collected. First, Gerhart et al. (2000a) observed that most SHRM research is based on single respondent designs, in which an HR manager assesses to what extent an organization has adopted certain HR practices. They argued that the reliability of these measurements may be low as a result of the size and complexity of organizations, and because of HR managers' potential vested interest in HR practices. Drawing upon multiple samples, Gerhart et al. (2000a) and Wright et al. (2001a) found that single-respondent measures of HRM practices contained considerable amounts of measurement error and suggested that researchers use measures based on aggregated data obtained from multiple raters.

Second, Gerhart et al. (2000a) and Wright et al. (2001b) reported limited convergent validity of measures of the effectiveness of the HR function, as rated by HR managers and line managers. They found that HR managers rated HR effectiveness consistently higher than line managers did, although HR managers' perceptions of the relative effectiveness of services provided and roles fulfilled by the HR department were similar to that of line managers. Explanations for differences in ratings may vary across firms and range from line managers' unwillingness to recognize the HR function's contributions to organizational success, to HR's creation of excessive expectations with regard to the impact of HR services. As a result, research that is based exclusively on ratings obtained from HR managers, irrespective of the number of raters per organization, may be biased due to implicit theories or social desirability.

Third, Huselid et al. (1997) found that professional capabilities of HR staff (such as financial, leadership and communicative skills) had a significant effect on the perceived effectiveness of HR management. Since the perceived effectiveness of HRM – in particular of HR activities that support business needs – was significantly associated with indicators of business performance, the authors concluded that the professional skills and abilities of HR staff members are an important factor in the implementation of HR practices. As HR managers are likely to assume that eventually HR practices will be implemented according to design, measures of HR practices obtained from HR managers will not reflect potential shortcomings in their staff's skills and abilities. Consequently, ratings will be upwardly biased.

Notwithstanding these limitations, HR managers remain an important source of information. In particular, researchers who are interested in measures of intended HR practices and who require detailed information about specific HRM practices, or need a large sample size, may choose to survey multiple HR managers per organization. Furthermore, the reliability of measures obtained from HR managers may be improved through triangulation. For example, Batt (2002) verified data obtained through her survey among HR managers by contrasting responses with data contained in the Dun & Bradstreet listing, and examining union contracts to verify wage rates and job titles. Likewise, Ichniowski et al. (1997) complemented the archival data on HRM practices they had obtained from HR managers by conducting on-site interviews with labour relations managers, union representatives, steel mill operations managers and production workers.

Line managers
Becker and Gerhart (1996) argued that research on HR–performance linkages should consider the actual effects of HR practices as compared to HR practices as reflected in policies. In a similar vein, Khilji and Wang (2006) distinguished between 'intended HRM' (which referred to HR practices formulated by policy-makers) and 'implemented HRM' (which referred to HR practices as operationalized in organizations). These authors acknowledge that the HR practices functioning throughout the organization may differ from the HR practices that were designed by the HR department. Moreover, in many organizations line managers are actively involved in the implementation of HR practices, which allows for further differences between actual and intended HR practices.

Notwithstanding rationales for obtaining data from line managers, researchers have only modestly done so. For example, Capelli and Neumark (2001) drew on the National Employers Survey, which targeted the plant manager in the manufacturing sector since 'the goal was to measure how work is actually done in the facility, not the policies that might exist in employee handbooks' (p. 745). Curiously, their study was among the few that did not find a positive effect of HRM practices on labour efficiency. Collins and Clark (2003) collected data on HR practices from the CEOs of 73 high technology companies in order to test to what extent the relationship between network-enhancing HR practices and indicators of firm performance such as sales growth and stock performance was mediated by internal and external social networks of top management teams. They considered CEOs to be the best source of information about practices used to manage top executives, since CEOs typically negotiate decisions regarding hiring, compensation and training with the firm's board of directors.

While line managers are well positioned to provide information concerning HR practices as implemented in their sphere of responsibility, researchers who ask line managers to rate HR practices as implemented throughout the organization may obtain biased results. Extrapolation of personal experiences with HR practices to the organization in general, and potential lack of detailed information about specific HR practices, may lead to measurement error. Furthermore, data collected from single raters in line management functions are likely to be as unreliable as data obtained from single raters representing the HR department. Researchers may address this issue by surveying multiple line mangers, preferably from different functions, in order to minimize bias.

Employees
SHRM researchers may also defer to employees as a potential source for data collection. Researchers argue that the use of employee samples may reduce measurement error because of employees' exposure to HR practices as implemented, and the possibility to obtain ratings from multiple employees. For example, Wright et al. (2001a) presented a study based on employee ratings of implemented HRM practices, in which the authors attempted 'to control for as many extraneous sources of variance possible and to provide best-case estimates of inter-rater reliability' (p. 886). While Wright et al. (2001a) considered HR practices to be 'an objective characteristic of the organization' (p. 896), they were surprised to find a lack of agreement among raters and proposed that raters may perceive HR practices differently due to individual information processing capabilities.

Instead of conceptualizing HR practices as an objective organizational characteristic, and building on advances in micro HR research (Wright & Boswell, 2002), SHRM researchers increasingly acknowledge the importance of employee reactions to implemented HRM practices. Bowen and Ostroff (2004) explained variance due to employee perceptions in terms of communications theory, interpreting HRM practices as communication mechanisms through which the organization sends signals to its employees that allow them to understand the desired and appropriate responses and form a collective sense of what is expected. To the extent that an organization develops a strong climate, in which employees share a common interpretation of what is important and what behaviours are rewarded, Bowen and Ostroff (2004) proposed that organizational performance will be enhanced as the result of collective employee behaviours that are consistent with organizational strategic goals. Likewise, Wright and Nishii (Chapter 6) argued that HR practices are perceived and interpreted subjectively by each employee in a focal group, which causes variation in the behavioural responses that ultimately lead to performance.

Purcell and Hutchinson (2007) illustrated the role of employee perceptions in the causal chain between HR practices and organizational performance assessing the effects of front-line managers' leadership behaviour and employee satisfaction with enacted HR practices on employee outcomes. Employee perceptions of leadership behaviour explained up to 20 per cent of the variance in employee outcomes such as commitment, satisfaction, sense of achievement and job challenge. Additionally, enacted HR practices explained up to another 14 per cent of the variance in employee outcomes. Since perceptions of leadership behaviour and employee satisfaction with HR practices were strongly correlated ($r = 0.569$), Purcell and Hutchinson (2007) concluded that the quality of HRM practices per se cannot explain performance outcomes. Employees' perceptions of front-line manager leadership behaviour and perceptions of how HRM practices are applied may condition HRM–performance linkages to a large extent.

Nishii and colleagues (2008) have also shed light on the role of employee perceptions of HR practices via their work on HR attributions, which are defined as the "causal explanations that employees make regarding management's motivations for using particular HR practices" (p. 507). In addition to finding that employees ascribe different attributions for the same HR practices, they found evidence that these attributions affect individual attitudes, which in turn influenced unit-level performance outcomes. In particular, their results indicated that HR attributions related to the enhancement of quality and employee well-being had a positive effect on employees' individual-level commitment and satisfaction, while attributions relating to cost-reduction and employee exploitation had negative effects. Thus, Nishii and colleagues work illustrates not only variation that may exist across employee perceptions of HR practices, but also the role of these perceptions in the HR-performance relationship.

Thus while data collection from employees allows for a better approximation of the real effects of HR practices, researchers cannot escape from tapping individual perceptions that may vary widely. While researchers have begun to explore the role of employee perceptions in the HR–performance relationship, it is clear that further research in this area is necessary. While HR practice data gathered from employees may be immensely useful for understanding HR practices, we must also be cognizant of the methodological challenges associated with collecting data from this source.

Recommendations for source use

Multi-source approaches
In recognition of concerns about the measurement of HR practices (e.g. Becker & Gerhart, 1996; Gerhart et al., 2000a; Gerhart et al., 2000b; Wright et al., 2001a) and building on theoretical claims regarding possible variance at multiple levels

(Bowen & Ostroff, 2004; Wright & Nishii, Chapter 6), researchers are increasingly obtaining measures of HR practices from multiple sources. Takeuchi and colleagues (2007) used two measures of high-performance work systems (HPWS) to assess whether collective human capital and social exchange mediated the effects of HPWSs on performance. The first measure was aggregated from employee responses and the second was based on managerial responses. The aggregation statistics indicated high inter-rater agreement in both the employee and manager group, although manager ratings of HR practices demonstrated more agreement than employee ratings.

In a multi-level study of the effects of HR practices on individual employee performance, Liao et al. (2009) found that aggregate managerial ratings of HR practices correlated significantly with group average employee ratings of the same HR practices ($r = 0.39$). Notwithstanding this relationship, management ratings for each of three categories of employees at each of 91 branches were significantly more positive than employee ratings. Managerial ratings were based on an average of three managers per branch. The median rwg value was 0.97 for ratings targeted toward Group 1 employees, 0.98 targeted toward Group 2 employees and 0.97 targeted toward Group 3 employees. Furthermore, ICC(1) values were 0.16, 0.11 and 0.17, respectively, while ICC(2) values were 0.38, 0.28 and 0.34 respectively. Liao et al. (2009) attributed the latter finding to the low ICC(1) values and the low number of managerial raters per branch. The authors also found significant differences in employee perspectives of HPWSs among employees who differed in employment status and among employees of the same status.

These studies provide empirical evidence for theoretical claims regarding the existence of variance in measures of different aspects of HRM practices as proposed by Wright and Nishii (Chapter 6). However, whereas ICC(1) values indicate considerable variance at the individual level, the generally low ICC(2) values suggest limited reliability of average ratings of HR practices aggregated at the organizational unit level of analysis. While reliability may be enhanced statistically by increasing the number of raters, the impact of individual-level variance in perceptions of and reactions to HR practices on the linkage with unit-level performance will vary across organizational units. For example, an individual may be a key team member or possess critical skills, thus having a larger impact on performance outcomes than other individuals in the same organizational unit. In order to further reduce measurement error, researchers will need to account for these differences.

While consideration of different facets of the HR practices construct allows for a more complete understanding of how HR practices affect firm performance, samples typically comprise numerous sub-units of one particular firm. Thus, the generalization of obtained results is limited at best. Further research is needed in which similar multi-level designs are applied across multiple organizations with different activities. However, because such research increases the required commitment of participating organizations, researchers may face difficulties finding organizations that are willing to collaborate voluntarily. This may limit the feasibility of more generalizable large-scale research.

Policy versus practice

While it is important to consider the advantages and disadvantages of the different sources discussed above, it is equally crucial to consider how the research question influences source choice. The choice of source may ultimately depend on whether the researcher is interested in HR policy or HR practice (Wright & Nishii, Chapter 6). There is general agreement among researchers that policy and practice are two distinct constructs (Gerhart et al., 2000a; Huselid & Becker, 2000). Wright and Nishii (Chapter 6) discuss policy, titled 'intended', as what decision-makers design to elicit certain employee behaviour: it is the outcome of the development of an HR strategy. In contrast, practice is described by Wright and Nishii (Chapter 6) in terms of what actually gets implemented. Because different people are responsible for implementing practices within organizations, managers may implement HR practices in very different ways. Further the way a manager implements a practice could be very different than what was initially intended by the organization.

Indeed Khilji and Wang (2006) argue that there are inconclusive findings in the HR–performance literature because of the failure of researchers to distinguish between intended and implemented HRM. By examining reports from managers and non-managers inside and outside HR departments in 12 Pakistan banking organizations, these authors found a substantial distinction between intended and implemented practices. Recognizing the policy-practice issue Gerhart (2007a) argues that the field of SHRM needs to decide whether to focus its efforts on HR practices or on higher levels of analysis, such as policy and principles.

If a researcher is interested in policies ('intended'), it has been recommended that the best person to ask is the organization's HR executive. However, if the researcher is interested in actual HR practices, it may be best to survey employees or managers. Gerhart et al. (2000b) argue that while an HR executive may be knowledgeable of HR policies, they are less confident in the ability of the HR executive to gather and accurately report on actual HR practices due to the diversity of practices that are likely to be implemented across units. For practices, they believe that employees or line supervisors will provide the most accurate information. This is because employees and managers are in a better position to see what actually gets implemented (Purcell & Hutchinson, 2007) and are less likely than HR managers to be excessively optimistic in their assessments (Wright et al., 2001b).

As researchers have increasingly shifted their focus towards unravelling the mechanisms through which HR practices affect firm performance, different dimensions of the HR practices construct have been identified, necessitating a discussion of whether HR managers are always an ideal source of HR information. Wright and Nishii (Chapter 6) distinguished between intended, actual and perceived HR practices, and employee reactions to HR practices. Since each of these dimensions of the HR practices construct has been found to account individually for variance (e.g. Purcell & Hutchinson, 2007; Nishii et al., 2008; Liao et al., 2009), researchers need to decide from which source to obtain data. In general, HR managers should be most knowledgeable regarding intended HR practices. Likewise, line managers are best positioned to provide information on HR practices as implemented in the organization. Finally, employees can provide first-hand information concerning their perceptions of implemented HR practices. While each of these sources has its share of advantages and disadvantages, each is useful in different research situations, and researchers must consider which is most appropriate given their research question.

Overall, there are many source-related issues that researchers must consider when choosing from whom to gather their data. In general, this discussion suggests that researchers need to design their data collection methods according to the research question at hand. While studies that seek to explore the more general effects of HR practices at the organizational level may gather data from knowledgeable HR managers, studies that aim to unravel the specific mechanisms at play in the HR–performance linkage should draw on different types of sources (e.g. employees, line managers, etc.) to tap the true source of variance. While there are numerous methodological challenges associated with gathering data from multiple sources within an organization, such data has the potential to better inform our understanding of the HR–performance relationship.

Substantive content issues

In addition to the crucial issues discussed regarding who to ask about HR practices (source), how to ask these questions (scale) and at what level (scope), another vital issue concerns the substantive content of HR practice items. The substantive content of items refers to the functional category of HR activities that is captured through the item (e.g. training, compensation).

Several authors have argued that no consensus exists on the functional categories that should be part of HR practice scales (e.g. Wright & Gardner, 2003a, 2003b, Purcell & Kinnie, 2007). While common themes can be identified, no single agreed upon list of HR practices exists (Paauwe, 2009) and considerable variation exists across studies in the range of practices included (Boselie et al., 2005). Although this issue is frequently mentioned, few (explicit) debates have taken place in the literature regarding potential criteria for the selection of functional categories (Purcell & Kinnie, 2007). One of the explanations for these inconsistencies could lie in how HR practices are defined. A distinction has for example been made between practices aimed at the management of the work domain (work practices) and practices used for the management of people who do the work in question (employment practices) (Boxall & Macky, 2009). One could argue that the more narrow range of employment practices (including recruitment and selection, training and development, compensation, and performance appraisal) is commonly included in HR practice scales, but much more variation exists in the inclusion of work practices (Boselie et al., 2005; Purcell & Kinnie, 2007).

Review of substantive content in recent literature

To address this topic, an analysis of 25 key studies was performed to gain an insight into the HR practice items used in extant research. Each item was provided a label that indicated the functional HR practice assessed (e.g. performance-related pay, the use of a share option scheme), and these practices were subsequently aggregated into broader functional categories of HR practices (e.g. compensation).

In total, 36, functional categories of HR practices were identified (see Table 8.1). The majority of items assess one of six main functional categories of HR practices (these categories are assessed in approximately 56 per cent of all items). These six functional categories are compensation (represented in 17 per cent of all items and included in 23 out of 25 studies), training (13 per cent, and included in 24 out of 25 studies), selection (9 per cent, and included in 15 out of 25 studies), performance appraisal (9 per cent, and included in 17 out of 25 studies), communication (5 per cent, and included in 11 out of 25 studies), and organizational structure (4 per cent, and included in 6 out of 25 studies).

The functional category compensation includes a wide range of items on various fixed and variable compensation practices (such as performance-related pay and pay level) – see Table 8.1 for an overview of functional categories and two examples of functional practices for each category. Items assessing training are more similar, since these mainly assess (formal) training programmes. Selection focuses on the extent to which extensive selection procedures are in place. While the use of selection tests occurs frequently, Items are also included to assess whether specific selection criteria are used in selection procedures (e.g. selection for problem-solving skills). Performance appraisal is assessed through the use of appraisal, and items focus on the performance review process and the assessment criteria used. Communication concerns the use of formal information-sharing programmes and the use of briefings. The functional category organizational structure includes items concerning the position and role of the HR function in the organization (e.g. decision-making in the HR function, and the nature and position of the HR function).

The remaining 30 functional categories are each represented in less than 4 per cent of all items. These categories for example include career development, teamwork, autonomy, and job control. One remarkable finding is that no study included all six of the major functional categories of HR practices.

In addition to examining of the range of functional categories across all items, the average number and range of functional categories covered in individual studies is also examined. The mean number of categories covered in individual studies is ten, ranging from three functional categories (Collins & Clark, 2003; Gelade & Ivery, 2003) to 16 (Guest et al., 2003).

The number of items used to cover a functional category also differs across studies. For example, when examining the functional category training, an average of 2.7 items were used but the number of items this ranged from one to six across studies. The number of items used to assess different functional categories within a study was also sometimes found to be unbalanced. This poses an issue in cases where HR practice scale scores are computed by averaging all scores on the items without first calculating a score for each functional category, as a functional category assessed by many items is more strongly reflected in the HR practice scale score (Guest, 2001).

Recommendations for substantive content

While it is clear that very little agreement exists on the functional categories of HR practices that should be part of HR practice measures, it is debatable whether an agreed upon list of functional categories would actually be desirable. On the one

Table 8.1   Overview of functional categories of HR practices and examples of functional HR practices

Functional categories of HR practices	Examples of functional HR practices
Compensation	Performance-related pay, pay level
Training	(Formal) training programme, on- or off-the-job training
Selection	Selection tests, selection criteria
Performance appraisal	Performance review process, assessment criteria in performance appraisal
Communication	Information-sharing (programme), briefings
Organizational structure	Decision-making in HR function, nature of the HR function
Participation	Decentralized decision-making, consultation of employees
Job security	Extent of job security
Internal labour market	Fill vacancies from within, career paths within the organization
Staffing	Staffing levels, staff composition
Job description	Availability of up-to-date job description
Recruitment	Active recruitment, job preview
Career development	Career paths, career planning
Development	Employee development plans, emphasis on development
Job design	Broad/small jobs, connection with skills/abilities
Climate	Atmosphere, commitment to the organization
Equality	Single status, harmonized terms and conditions
Job control	Employee influence over work (conditions)
Organizational strategy	Vision concerning organizational strategy and HRM
Performance management	Performance targets, performance vision
Teamwork	Teamwork, self-managed teams
Autonomy	Decision-making by employees, degree of influence
Grievance	Formal grievance procedures, resolving disputes
Quality	Problem-solving groups, quality circles
Survey	Attitude survey
Monitoring	(Electronic) monitoring of employees
Redundancy	Termination of employment
Discipline	Formal discipline policy, punishment of violation of rules
Drug, violence and sexual harassment policy	Policy on drug use, violence and sexual harassment
Job rotation	Rotate across jobs or tasks
Responsibility	Employee responsibility for certain goals

Table 8.1. Continued

Functional categories of HR practices	Examples of functional HR practices
Job analysis	Formal job analysis, job classification system
Union	Involvement and collaboration with unions
Work hours	Overtime
Work/life balance	Support for balancing work and personal lives
Justice	Formal procedures to ensure fair treatment

hand, agreement would benefit knowledge accumulation as studies would become more comparable; on the other, using tailor-made measures allows the selection of functional categories to be adapted to the context.

The finding that not one functional category of practices is included in all reviewed studies suggests that fundamental differences exist concerning what should be counted as an HR practice. For example, whereas some studies include both employment practices and work practices in their definition of HR practices, others only include employment practices. Although these different views are valuable and deserve attention in future research, it would be beneficial if researchers explicitly stated their definition of HR practices. If studies adopting similar definitions of HR practices used similar measures of these practices, this would allow a better comparison study findings. One approach might be to adopt a constricted view of HR practices that would at a minimum include recruitment and selection, performance appraisal, compensation, and training and development. However, more research is needed to identify different views about the basis for determining relevant HR practices and the associated selection of functional categories of practices.

In addition to selecting functional categories based on the definition of practices adopted, contextual factors (such as organizational, sectoral and national context) can provide further guidance in making these choices. While more empirical research is needed to understand the distinct effects of HR practices in different contexts, such work would help us to identify the functional categories most appropriate for the research context at hand. For instance important contextual factor could concern the specific outcome measure that HR practices are expected to predict. Based on additional theorizing, functional categories of practices can be identified that predict the drivers of this specific outcome measure, perhaps resulting in a more theoretically informed selection of functional categories (see Chapter 2). For example, based on the job demands–resources model, functional categories of HR practices that impact job demands and resources would be expected to predict levels of work engagement (Bakker & Demerouti, 2008; Peccei et al., Chapter 2). By empirically testing such the selection of functional practices, empirically driven theory refinement could take place (Guest, 2001).

Summary

The relationship between HR practices and firm performance has been documented across a variety of studies. While researchers in the field generally agree that a significant HR–performance relationship exists, we continue to explore ways to improve upon the methodological approaches used in this body of research. In line with previous discussions of issues relating to inter-rater reliability (Gerhart et al., 2000), causal order (Wright et al., 2005), and scale items (Becker & Gerhart, 1996), the goal of this chapter was to shed light on four relatively unexplored issues relating to the operationalization of HR practices: scale, scope, source and substantive content. As researchers continue to explore the HR–performance relationship, we recommend that attention be paid to not only the intended scope of the investigation, but also to the types of rating scales used to measure HR practices, and the sources from which this data is gathered. While practical feasibility is always a concern, we urge researchers to resist the temptation to collect 'easy' data, and to consider which scale types, sources, scope and functional categories of practices best fit the research question at hand. Improving our methodological approaches may ultimately help us to reduce measurement error, moving us closer to a better understanding of the HR–performance relationship.

9

RESEARCH ON HUMAN RESOURCES AND EFFECTIVENESS: SOME METHODOLOGICAL CHALLENGES

BARRY GERHART

Introduction

Scientific progress, as well as the validity of any policy implications that may follow, depends not only on advances in theory but also empirical work that is relevant and conducted with sufficient methodological rigour. The conduct of science has been described as follows:

> Researchers collect and analyse data, develop hypotheses, replicate and extend earlier work, communicate their results with others, [and] review and critique the results of their peers. (Committee on Science, Engineering, and Public Policy, 1995).

Thus, data collection and analysis, replication and peer 'review and critique' are each as central as theory to the scientific process. However, in the field of management, there is some concern that this balance may be out of kilter. Pfeffer (2007) argues that there has been 'an excessive preoccupation with theory over facts' (p. 1338). Likewise, Hambrick (2007) speaks of a 'theory fetish' (p. 1346) in management, arguing that 'if we aspire to develop a reliable body of knowledge that managers can use for "evidence-based" decisions, as called for by Pfeffer and Sutton (2006) and Rousseau (2006), we must allow an accumulation of evidence' (p. 1350). In contrast to that objective, Hambrick (2007) describes the current situation as follows: 'We in management, however, are so riveted on new and revised theories, and so dismissive of simple generation of facts and evidence, that our revealed ethos is that we care much more about what's fresh and novel than about what's right' (p. 1350).

Although few would argue that the study of human resource (HR) management and performance has been 'riveted on new and revised theories', there is nevertheless a need to establish 'what's right' using the best empirical evidence and methodology possible. In this regard, for example, Guest et al.'s (2003, p. 295) summary of the research literature on HR and business performance suggests that there is a need for more attention to methodological issues in the HR and performance literature:

> Despite the positive thrust of most published empirical findings, Wood (1999) among others has noted that the quality of the research base supporting the relationship between HR and performance is relatively weak. . . . [Q]uestions remain about the measurement of both HR and performance, and about the weight and relevance of tests of association and causation.

In this paper, my purpose is to help researchers accumulate empirical evidence to use in testing, evaluating, revising and formulating theories in the area of human resource (HR) management and business performance. In particular, my focus is on the importance of using appropriate methodologies and of the 'review and critique' of existing results and their implications for theory. The present paper continues and updates my discussion of such issues found in Gerhart (2007a) and Weller and Gerhart (2012).[1]

Errors of inference in empirical work can take two general forms. Research may incorrectly deem an effective HR system as ineffective or an ineffective HR system as effective. Incorrect research inferences of the former type may stifle research in a fruitful area, while those of the latter type may help foster a line of research that will ultimately turn out to have been unhelpful and a poor use of resources. If, as we hope, research has some effect on managerial policy and practice, these errors of inference could likewise lead to errors in the adoption or retention of HR systems in organizations. My goal in this paper is to provide readers with information that will help them better evaluate the contribution and relevance of published research on HR and performance, and also help them design and conduct their own research in the area in a way that reduces the likelihood that methodological issues provide an alternative explanation for their observed results.

A simple model of HR and performance

The typical approach in HRM and effectiveness/performance[2] is to use a model like the following:

$$\text{Perf} = \beta_0 + \beta_{\text{perfhr}}\text{hr} + \varepsilon$$

where population parameters are: β_0, the intercept, β_{perfhr}, an unstandardized regression coefficient representing the performance–HR relationship, and ε, the error or disturbance term, which captures all unspecified causes of Perf. This is the classical linear regression model. Estimation using sample data, by ordinary least squares (OLS), for example, yields:

$$Perf = b_0 + b_{perfhr}hr + e$$

Under standard assumptions, the OLS/classical regression estimator is unbiased and efficient among the class of linear estimators (the Gauss-Markov theorem). 'Unbiased' means that the mean (or expected value) of the distribution of b across repeated samples is equal to the population parameter, β. Efficient (or best) means that b has minimum variance (relative to other estimators in the class) across the distribution of repeated samples.[3] Adding the assumption that the disturbance term is normally distributed turns the model into the classical normal regression model, which facilitates hypothesis-testing and formation of confidence intervals (e.g. Greene, 1993, Chapter 10). In empirical work on HR and performance, this basic model can and should, of course, be expanded to include other determinants of performance.

'Significance' and effect sizes

The term 'significant' is used in one of two ways in the social science and management literatures (Gerhart, 2009). First, it is used to refer to statistical significance, typically using an alpha level of $p < 0.05$. In the equation presented above, the statistical significance of the b_{perfhr} coefficient would be of interest. Most frequently, the significance test is of the null hypothesis: whether the parameter (here, a regression coefficient) is different from zero.

However, Tukey observed that 'because the null hypothesis is always false, a decision to reject it simply indicates that the research design had adequate power to detect a true state of affairs, which may or may not be a large effect or even a useful effect' (p. 100). Likewise, Kerlinger (1973) stated that 'tests of statistical significance like t and F unfortunately do not reveal to the research scientist the magnitude or the strength of the relations [they are] studying' (p. 227). In other words, statistical significance tests alone tell us whether our statistical estimates meet some minimum level of precision, which is important, but it is only a binary index. Knowing that a relationship is non-zero is, by itself, not terribly interesting. With a sufficiently large sample size, even relationships that are so small as to be trivial with respect to practical relevance can be statistically significant.

In studies of HR–performance, where large sample sizes are difficult to obtain, given the unit or firm level of analysis, the opposite problem – that practically important relationships may be missed because of inadequate statistical power – is more common. Standard practice in statistical significance testing is to fix the Type I error rate (usually at $p = 0.05$), thus forcing an increase in Type II error (i.e. a decrease in statistical power) rates as sample size decreases. Rosnow and Rosenthal (1989) show that in the case of a population $r = 0.10$ (a reasonable estimate for the HR-performance correlation)[4] and using a significance level of $p = 0.05$, the ratio of Type II to Type I error is 2 with $N = 1000$, 10 with $N = 400$ and 17 with $N = 100$.

Likewise, Cohen (1992) shows that with a population $r = 0.10$ and $p = 0.05$, to have a 0.80 probability of detecting the effect (i.e. statistical power) would require $N = 783$, a sample size much larger than typically used in the HR–performance literature.

Thus statistical significance testing is not enough. In an effort to avoid this limited definition of significance, a second way to define 'significant' is in terms of practical significance, which relies on estimating some effect size indicator (Cohen, 1994; Kirk, 1996; Schmidt, 1996).[5] However, not until 1994, for example, did the American Psychological Association (APA) Publication Manual begin to emphasize the importance of effect size reporting – and even then it was 'encouraged', not required.

What we really need in an area like HR and performance, which aspires to have practical implications, is (a) a meaningful index of effect size (Becker & Gerhart, 1996), typically an unstandardized regression coefficient – as in the simple model introduced above – if the dependent variable is measured on a ratio scale (e.g. profitability, shareholder return, turnover, uptime), and (b) a confidence interval placed around the effect size that conveys the precision of the estimate. Both are important, because investing in an HR system having a mean effect that is smaller but less variable/uncertain could, for example, be preferred to investing in an HR system having a larger mean, but also a higher variance, effect (Gerhart et al., 1996). Smaller variance (i.e. the standard error of the regression coefficient) is achieved as the sample size and R^2 for the performance equation increases and as the collinearity of HR with other independent variables decreases (e.g. Cohen & Cohen, 1983, p. 109).[6]

When effect sizes are expressed in unstandardized regression coefficient terms and the variables are in ratio scale form (e.g. dollars), it changes the discussion of research findings and the discussion of implications from what it is when a binary test of statistical significance is the focus (Becker & Gerhart, 1996). Indeed, many of the issues I discuss here may not matter a great deal if the inference goal is to simply make a binary statistical significance decision. In contrast, when one begins to estimate and report policy-relevant effect sizes such as 'firms using HR system A have 20 per cent higher profits than firms using HR system B' (e.g. Huselid, 1995 – see below), one finds that conclusions can change significantly depending on methodological issues such as the level of reliability (which in turn depends on estimating reliability correctly). Therefore, once one interprets point-estimate effects of HR-related variables on natural metric outcomes such as profits and total shareholder return, one is forced to a much greater degree to think about whether the effect sizes are plausible or not.

There are other advantages as well to using unstandardized regression coefficients rather than standardized regression coefficients. First, whereas unreliability in the dependent variable biases the standardized regression coefficient, it does not bias the unstandardized regression coefficient. (Unreliability in the independent variable biases both types of regression coefficients and unreliability in either the independent or dependent variable also leads to downward bias in R^2). Second, range restriction in the independent variable (variance in the sample is less than its variance in the population) biases the standardized regression coefficient toward zero, but does not bias the unstandardized regression coefficient (Cain & Watts, 1970; Cohen & Cohen, 1983; Darlington, 1990).[7] This bias in the standardized coefficient is a major drawback, and as Cain and Watts (1970) observe, stems from this effect size estimate being 'dependent upon the particular policies pursued when the data were collected' – and if these polices have restricted variance, using the standardized coefficient 'runs the risk of declaring a policy feeble simply because historically it was not vigorously applied' (p. 236). (Range restriction in the independent variable does lead to downward bias in R^2. Range restriction in y biases both standardized and unstandardized regression coefficients. See also Gerhart's (2007a) discussion of sample selection bias.)

Not surprisingly then, guidelines for statistical methods (even) in psychology journals now advise researchers that:

> If the units of measurement are meaningful on a practical level . . . then we usually prefer an unstandardized measure (regression coefficient or mean difference) to a standardized measure (r or d) [and that] it helps to add brief comments that place these effect sizes in a practical and theoretical context (Wilkinson and the Task Force on Statistical Inference, 1999, p. 599).

Likewise, a later article on meta-analysis (Bond et al., 2003) calls for cumulating effect sizes in terms of 'raw mean differences' whenever meaningful, rather than using standard deviation units or other standardized effect sizes (e.g. d or r). Of course, the latter are appropriate when the variables of interest are not measured on a ratio scale. For example, standardized effect sizes are useful when estimating the effect size of country on individual cultural values (e.g. Gerhart & Fang, 2005). However, as discussed next, the fact that the literature on HR and business performance seeks to provide policy implications means that whenever possible, ratio level (e.g. total shareholder return, productivity) firm/unit performance measures are preferred and non-ratio measures of firm/unit performance (e.g. subjective assessments of firm performance) are of limited practical relevance, unless their relationship with ratio measures is specifically documented.[8]

Challenges in inferring causality and potential solutions

Cook and Campbell (1979), drawing on John Stuart Mill, give three necessary conditions for inferring causality: (a) covariance between cause and effect (i.e. a non-zero effect size), (b) time precedence (cause occurs in time before the effect), and (c) 'rule out alternative interpretations for a possible cause and effect connection' (p. 31). It is useful to keep in mind, however, the following points:

- Effect size estimation and ruling out alternative causal models is often not separable. The wrong causal model (e.g. omitting variables, ignoring reciprocal causation) often results in biased effect size estimates. As another example, a statistically significant and credible causal relationship may be of trivial magnitude.

- The requirement to 'rule out' alternative models may have the unfortunate effect of leading researchers to believe that they must choose between two models rather than combining elements of both. This is especially a problem with reciprocal causation, where researchers sometimes seem determined to show that causation runs one way or another, but not in both directions. I return to this point later.

In a previous paper (Gerhart, 2007a), I addressed three specific issues that arise from the violation of one assumption of the earlier-described classical regression/OLS model (Duncan, 1975; Wooldridge, 2002, pp. 50–51): that the independent variable (HR here) and e are independent, or $cov(HR,e) = 0$.[9] These three issues were measurement error ('errors in variables'), specification error (usually referring to omitted variables) and simultaneity (i.e. reciprocal or nonrecursive causation).[10] Sample selection bias can be viewed as a form of the omitted variable problem (Heckman, 1979) and, as such, was discussed in that context.

When the $cov(HR,e) = 0$ assumption is violated, OLS is no longer unbiased and a search for alternative estimators may be undertaken. While other estimators, in theory, are capable of providing less biased (or in large samples, more consistent) estimates,[11] it is important to remember that these estimators make their own assumptions that – if not sufficiently met – can lead to no better, or even worse estimates than provided by OLS. For a discussion of the pros and cons of these estimators, see Gerhart (2007a). Gerhart also discussed the application of propensity scores (Rosenbaum & Rubin, 1983) to the literature on HR and business performance.

Measurement error and construct validity

Random measurement error
The standard paradigm for studying HR and performance has been to define and measure HR in terms of HR practice use by either asking the percentage of employees covered by a practice or by using a Likert-type rating scale that asks the degree to which a practice is used, important, and so on. The strength of implementation of practices has not generally received much attention (Bowen & Ostroff, 2004), nor have employee descriptions of practices been used. Rather, for better or worse, a single managerial respondent typically provides the HR practice use information.

For some reason, the HR and business performance literature has been fixated on internal consistency (e.g. Cronbach's alpha) reliability, which provides an estimate of how much error in responses stems from the sampling of items from the universe of items in a particular construct domain, given the traditional reflective measurement model. Although this aspect of reliability is important, recent evidence indicates that the far more serious source of measurement error in measuring HR is the sampling of raters. This fact has either been ignored or mistakenly addressed using an index, r_{wg}, that is not a reliability and gives an overly optimistic view of measurement error (Gerhart, 1999). Gerhart et al. (2000a, 2000b; Wright et al., 2001) have documented that measurement error due to raters in studies using the *firm* level of analysis is substantial. For example, Gerhart et al. (2000b) reported an inter-rater reliability of no more than 0.30 and probably more like 0.20.

What are the consequences? First, such low inter-rater reliabilities mean that the HR practice scores that a researcher obtains for a particular firm depends more on the particular person completing the survey than on what practices are actually used in the firm because the HR practice scores are idiosyncratic, rather than being consistent across different managerial respondents.

Second, the correction for attenuation in an unstandardized regression coefficient, though little discussed, differs from the correction for attenuation in a correlation (Gerhart, 1999; Gerhart et al., 2000a). The corrected regression coefficient is equal to the observed regression coefficient divided by the reliability of HR, whereas the corrected correlation is obtained by dividing by the square root of HR's reliability *and* performance's reliability. Therefore, unreliability in the independent variable, HR has a larger impact on the unstandardized regression coefficient than on the correlation.[12]

Thus, the 20 per cent effect of HR on firm performance (for an increase in 1 SD in HR practices) found by Huselid and others (see Gerhart, 1999), once corrected, becomes a 67 per cent (0.20/0.30) effect size using the 0.30 reliability estimate. That is the effect size compared to the mean. If comparing low (−1 SD) and high firms (+1 SD), the high firms are 167 per cent of the mean and the low firms are at 33 per cent of the mean, which implies that the high firms have 167/37 = 4.5 times higher performance. Is this effect size credible? (Keep in mind that other influences on firm performance, e.g. finance, marketing, operations, etc., are typically not included in obtaining such estimates.) If not, it may indicate a need to re-examine the entire approach. With a more positive assessment, it is still clear that methodology (reliability estimation in this example) matters a great deal in quantifying the impact of HR.[13]

To estimate inter-rater reliability, multiple raters must be used. However, Huselid and Becker (2000; Becker & Huselid, 2006) argue that requiring that multiple raters is not feasible because it leads to reduced sample sizes. It certainly is the case that placing greater demands on responding companies can result in fewer responses. On the other hand, it may not be necessary to exclude companies/plants having a single rater from the main substantive analyses, as long as *some* companies/plants provide multiple rater data. One can use the companies/plants for which there are two or more raters to estimate inter-rater reliability. If it is close to unity, all companies/plants (including those with a single respondent) can be used and nothing further needs to be done. On the other hand, to the degree that inter-rater reliability is considerably lower than unity, one should revisit the measure and/or correct for unreliability in the substantive analyses. In the latter case, it would again be unnecessary to drop any cases.

Also relevant to the feasibility issue is the existence of studies that have, in fact, successfully obtained and used data from multiple raters. For example, in a study of HR and performance in manufacturing plants, Youndt et al. (1996) obtained multiple rater data by collecting information on HR practice use from 160 general managers and 90 HR managers in 160 plants. Another study (Takeuchi et al., 2007) of 76 business establishments from 56 different companies located in Japan was able to obtain ratings of HR practices from 324 managers (i.e. 4.3 per establishment) and 525 non-managerial employees (i.e. 6.9 per establishment).

Another example is a study by Wall et al. (2004) of 80 single-site manufacturing companies. Indeed, Wall et al. introduced a measurement process for HR practices that may serve as a model for future research. It included the following steps:

- Three different people per company were interviewed.
- '[E]vidence from each interviewee was *cross-checked with that from others* [emphasis added], and with additional information from company documents and a tour of the manufacturing facility' (p. 101).
- Finally, 'based on this information, two researchers, unaware of company performance, independently rated the extent of use of each of the practices' (p. 101).

This is a very sophisticated and systematic measurement process that, in essence, relied on five raters per company. As a result, high inter-rater reliability was obtained in the final step.

Given that in research on HR and performance there are multiple sources of measurement error (both items and raters in the case here), reliability is best addressed by estimating a generalizability coefficient (Cronbach et al., 1972; Gerhart, 1999), which is equivalent to a reliability that recognizes multiple sources of error. Gerhart et al. (2000a) provide a tutorial and example. Corrections for unreliability can then be undertaken if the researcher decides such corrections make sense. In the multivariate case, LISREL is very useful for this purpose.[14]

In our own recent work (Fulmer et al., 2003), we have talked about employee relations as a source of competitive advantage, conceptualized and measured in terms of (multiple) employee (not a managerial informant's) views. A methodological advantage of this approach is that multiple responses from each organization are averaged, which, with enough responses, virtually eliminates measurement error due to sampling of raters. What employees perceive, think and feel about HR and employee relations may also have more theoretical credibility as a cause of business performance than what Purcell (1999) described as 'crude' measures of HR practices.

In summary, empirical evidence clearly shows that inter-rater reliability in measuring HR practices is far from unified, thus making it important to use multiple raters. Doing so helps improve measurement and allows estimation of inter-rater reliability, which is essential for assessing measurement validity and can also be used for correcting estimates for measurement error.

Non-random measurement error

Single-respondent reports of HR practices can cause additional problems, especially if the same respondent also serves as the source of performance data. This design may result in measurement errors in HR and performance being correlated. For example, a respondent may consistently have positive or negative response errors across scales – or firms having better performance may over-report levels of HR effectiveness or even use of practices thought to be desirable (Gerhart, 1999).

There has been much debate about whether this common method variance makes a difference in management research findings. While method variance may not make much difference in binary tests of statistical significance (Doty & Glick, 1998), it does influence effect size. Specifically, Doty and Glick's meta-analysis found that correlations between an array of measures used in organizational behaviour were on average 25 per cent higher when both measures were based on single-source self-reports than when they were not. They also found that this difference was larger still when the study design was cross-sectional.

Until recently, no evidence was available to tell us whether common method variance would be a similar problem in multi-level data. Multi-level data is likely to be a fruitful area for future research, given the logic of using it to measure employee relations (Fulmer et al., 2003) and/or HR system strength (Bowen & Ostroff, 2004). Fortunately, Ostroff et al. (2002) have addressed this situation. They used data from 8052 employees in 71 hotels, comparing correlations based on two methods: aggregating data by hotel on the independent and dependent variable, and a split-sample approach/correction where one-half of the employee sample data is aggregated to obtain the independent variable score for each hotel and the data from the other half of employees is aggregated to obtain the dependent variable score for each hotel. Their Table 3 provides a comparison of ten correlations (of climate and work environment perceptions with satisfaction) with and without this split-sample correction for method variance. The mean correlation without any correction was 0.391 versus 0.268 using the split-sample correction, indicating that common method variance resulted in 45 per cent higher correlations on average (i.e. without any correction).

Previous strategies for control of common methods variance include the use of the multitrait–multimethod matrix (Campbell & Fiske, 1959) to assess convergent and discriminant validity, with later approaches applying structural equation modelling (e.g. Alwin, 1974). In the absence of multiple methods (and thus the ability to identify and remove method variance this way), a more recent suggestion is to use a marker variable (Lindell & Whitney, 2001) that theory says should have no relationship with other constructs in the study. Any observed relationship is thus assumed to be due to common method variance only. This relationship is then partialled from the relationships of substantive interest. As discussed later, longitudinal data can also be used to remove person-specific, time-invariant omitted variables of this sort. Finally, when conducting aggregate (e.g. organization) level analyses, the method introduced by Ostroff et al. (2002) of using different employee subsamples to measure different constructs, eliminating within-person correlations, is highly recommended.

Construct validity

The empirical methods discussed above are important in assessing construct validity. However, construct validity cannot be established by empirical methods alone; rather, it must be interpreted in the context of a careful definition of the construct and its role in a nomological network (Schwab, 1980). Indeed, Schwab notes that '[s]ince the criterion in construct validity is conceptual, direct tests are not possible' (p. 34). Therefore, one must first decide whether the conceptual definition of the construct is adequate, then consider the empirical evidence.

One could argue that early studies of HR and performance did a reasonable job of defining the HR construct, but the correspondence of the chosen measures with the definition was not always what one might have liked. For example, Huselid (1995) essentially conceptualized HR as having an impact on ability, motivation and opportunity to contribute (AMO) (Bailey, 1993; Appelbaum et al., 2000; Boxall & Purcell, 2003). (I would add cost as a fourth mediating variable (Gerhart, 2007b).) However, his two HR scales were only indirectly related to these sub-constructs – or perhaps, more accurately, mediating variables. Consider, for example, that the two highest loading items on his first HR scale, 'employee skills and organization structures' were: 'What is the proportion of the workforce whose job has been subjected to formal job analysis?' and 'What is the proportion of the workforce who are included in a formal information-sharing program[me] (e.g. a newsletter)?' The question is whether these items are critical components of the HR domain, and are they the major drivers of ability, motivation, opportunity to contribute and cost?

This is part of a broader issue that the field is currently trying to address. The 'HR' in HR and business performance has been defined and measured in a variety of ways (Becker & Gerhart, 1996; Boxall & Purcell, 2003; Gerhart, 2007b). There is perhaps some convergence regarding AMO as a useful way to define the key dimensions or mediators through which HR practices influence business performance. However, there has been less convergence across studies in the HR practices measured (Boselie et al., 2005; Combs et al., 2006; Gerhart, 2007b).

Another construct validity issue has to do with the distinction between HR policy, HR practice use and HR practice implementation/execution/effectiveness. This is not a new issue. It has been addressed previously and also includes concepts such as HR architecture and HR principles (Becker & Gerhart, 1996; Huselid et al., 1997; Gerhart et al., 2000a; Bowen & Ostroff, 2004; Becker & Huselid, 2006; Khilji & Wang, 2006). The field needs to decide whether it wants to continue to focus its efforts on the concept and measurement of 'use' of HR practices (often measured as the percentage of employees covered by the practice) or does it feel that more attention should (also) be given to higher level of abstraction concepts such as principles and architecture, as well as the quality of the implementation of such practices? If the latter, it seems all the more necessary to include employees (not just managers) as respondents, because employees are arguably in a better position to report the degree to which intended policies have actually been implemented and how successfully. In addition, even when it comes to managerial respondents, there is some sentiment that less use (or less exclusive use) of HR department respondents and greater use of line manager respondents (e.g. Purcell & Hutchinson, 2007), who often have responsibility for actually implementing many HR policies, would be desirable.

There are also construct validity issues on the performance side of the equation. Business performance is one very important aspect of effectiveness, but there are, of course, other stakeholders beyond shareholders; and the relative importance of business performance, as well as the relevance of specific measures, varies from country to country (Brewster, 1999; Paauwe, 2004). However, in the long run, business performance – at least where market competition operates – is important not just to shareholders but also to employees, communities and customers.

How business performance is measured also depends on the level of analysis. At the firm level, total shareholder return, profitability and other financial measures have been used and are publicly available in the case of public firms in countries such as the USA. At the facility level, typical performance measures have included productivity, unit labour costs and quality measures (e.g. defects).

One issue has been the use of objective versus subjective measures of business performance. Objective measures are often archival (e.g. profitability, productivity), whereas subjective measures are often framed in relative terms and either ask for an estimate of archival measures (e.g. 'How profitable have you been relative to competitors?') or else ask about overall effectiveness ('How has your performance been relative to competitors?').

While both types of measures are subject to error, there are three issues that are potentially more of a concern with subjective measures:

- Subjective measures, especially when based on a single respondent, may suffer from modest or weak inter-rater reliability.
- If collected from the same respondent providing the data on HR practices, subjective measures may introduce common methods variance.
- Subjective measures are on an interval scale, whereas objective measures are often on a ratio scale – this last issue makes it more difficult to translate findings into terms that have direct policy relevance (Becker & Gerhart, 1996; Becker & Huselid, 2006).

There is evidence that subjective measures of performance show significant convergence with objective measures (Dess & Robinson, 1984). However, this convergence was obtained using multiple respondents (4.3 raters per company) and by asking for subjective reports of archival financial performance (sales and return on assets) measures. Presumably, respondents may have actually consulted these archival sources in arriving at their 'subjective' ratings of financial performance. In addition, Dess and Robinson (1984) cautioned that because their study was conducted within a single four-digit industry, 'subjective performance measures are probably most appropriate in examining relative performance *within* [emphasis added] an industry' (p. 271).

Wall et al. (2004) also examined the use of subjective versus objective measures of performance. In two studies, they show that subjective and objective measures of performance show highly similar patterns of correlations with a set of HR practices. This suggests their possible interchangeability. On the other hand, in their first study – where subjective performance was measured as 'What is your company's performance in comparison to your main competitors?' on a Likert scale – their Table 2 shows that the mean correlation of HR practices with the subjective measure is $r = 0.20$, whereas their mean correlation with the objective measure is $r = 0.10$. Thus, there is a difference in magnitude of 100 per cent. That difference would argue against the two types of measures being interchangeable.

Their Study 2, while using a different sample, obtained similar results in that the patterns of correlations of HR practices with the objective and subjective measures of performance were similar. In this instance, unlike Study 1, the mean of the correlations did not differ for the objective versus subjective performance measures. However, in Study 2, similar to the Dess and Robinson (1984) study, the subjective measures of performance asked about specific (available from archival data) performance measures: productivity and profitability. If the archival measures are readily available, perhaps the fact that 'subjective' ratings of these measures lead to similar findings is not surprising.[15]

The results of the studies by Dess and Robinson (1984) and Wall et al. (2004) suggest that, in some respects, the use of subjective measures of performance is not a major drawback, at least in terms of patterns of correlations and statistical significance. However, the drawbacks noted earlier (the challenge of translating results based on interval scales, the increased chance of common method variance if using the same rater to measure HR and performance) remain. Finally, if archival measures of financial performance are available (as in these two studies), it is not clear why subjective assessments of these variables would be used. Thus, it would seem that subjective measures of performance are most easily justified where relevant objective measures are simply unavailable. In such cases, however, with no specific and agreed upon performance referent (e.g. a specific dimensions of financial performance), one might anticipate greater subjectivity (i.e. lower reliability). Therefore, in this situation, it is strongly advised that multiple raters be used and that different raters are used as sources for HR and performance data.

Summary

To accurately describe the magnitude of the HR–performance relationship, one must report a practically meaningful effect size estimate, typically an unstandardized regression coefficient, as well as its precision (e.g. the confidence interval). Further, the definition and measurement of 'HR' (and performance, for that matter) can greatly influence observed effect size estimates. The use of subjective performance measures may not materially affect results in terms of statistical significance, but the magnitude of the effect obtained with such measures may be more subject to common methods variance (in a single-source design) and more difficult to put into meaningful policy terms.

Omitted variable bias

Many factors presumably influence performance, but most empirical studies include a short set of right-hand side variables beyond those related to HR. Huselid and Becker (2000) argued that omitted variable bias was likely to be the major statistical challenge in HR and performance research. They suggested, for example, that 'firms that understand the advantages of high performance HR are also good at other types of management (e.g. marketing, operations)' (p. 851). Another variable that must be included in research on HR and performance is industry, with narrower (a three- or four-digit SIC code) being preferable to more coarse categories (a one- or two-digit

SIC code). The use of 'industry studies' in automobile assembly plants (MacDuffie, 1995), telecommunications (Batt, 2002) and financial services (Hunter & Lafkas, 2003) uses single industry samples as a way to control omitted variables and to understand the industry-specific institutional workings of HR and performance. Recent evidence provides further support for the idea that this relationship may vary by industry (Datta et al., 2005). Becker and Huselid (2006) concur that work 'may benefit from a return to more narrowly drawn industry studies,' although they recommend that such studies go beyond the plant level of previous such work and focus on what they call 'strategic business processes' (p. 908).

To estimate the magnitude of bias from omitting a relevant variable (e.g. industry, management quality/expertise in non-HR areas), call it 'control,' take the fully (i.e. correctly) specified equation to be (Kmenta, 1971, pp. 392–3):

$$perf = b_0 + b_{perfhr.control}hr + b_{perfcontrol.hr}control + e,$$

but we omit control and estimate instead:

$$perf = a_0 + b_{perfhr}hr + e^*$$

Then the expected value of b_{perfhr} will equal not $b_{perfhr.control}$, but rather:

$$b_{perfhr} = b_{perfhr.control} + b_{perfcontrol.hr}d_{controlhr}$$

where $d_{controlhr}$ is the regression coefficient from the auxiliary regression of control on the included independent variables (hr only in this example):

$$control = d_0 + d_{controlhr}hr + residual.$$

The bias in estimating $b_{perfhr.control}$ grows more severe as $d_{controlhr}hr$ and $b_{perfcontrol.hr}$ become more different from 0.00. In this two variable example, $d_{controlhr}hr$ is a direct function of $\rho_{controlhr}$. However, with more independent variables, it would be mathematically possible for $\rho_{controlhr}$ to be 'large' but for $d_{controlhr}hr$ to be 'small' due to the inclusion of other independent variables. This then means that it is incorrect to say that omitted variable bias exists when the omitted variable 'is correlated with' the dependent variable and any of the included independent variables when there are three or more independent variables. Rather, it is the *partial* relationship of the omitted variable with the included variable that matters.

There are two traditional approaches to reducing omitted variable problems. The first is the randomized experiment, which has the major advantage, in sufficiently large samples, of achieving what Cook and Campbell (1979) refer to as equivalent groups. By definition, cov(hr,e) = 0 under successful random assignment. Moreover, this equivalence can be achieved without any knowledge whatsoever or statistical control of potential omitted variables. Although this is a unique advantage, a true field experiment is not something that has proven feasible to date in the HR and performance literature. Some evidence indicates, however, that non-experimental designs can produce results quite similar to experimental designs *if* the studies are similar in other design characteristics such as degree of attrition, type of control group, size of pretest differences between groups and degree of self-selection (Heinsman & Shadish, 1996).

A second approach is statistical control using regression analysis, or – when the treatment is a group variable – analysis of covariance (ANCOVA). A problem with ANCOVA, however, is that the researchers must not only be able to identify and include all variables that, if excluded, (significantly) bias the effect estimate, they must also measure them reliably because partialling unreliable control variables results in under-correction for group differences (e.g. Cohen & Cohen, 1983). In the multivariate case, the most practical way to correct for measurement error is to use a structural equation model (SEM) such as LISREL.

Three other approaches to omitted variable bias, propensity scores, selection bias correction and fixed effects are covered by Gerhart (2007a). I limit my discussion here to the use of fixed effects, given its central role in some studies of HR and performance.

Fixed effects

A fixed effects model can be considered where there is longitudinal data on both HR and performance, as well as sufficient variance in changes in HR and performance over time. This estimator is also known as the dummy variable, within-subjects or first difference (in the special case of two time periods only) estimator. To see the potential advantage, specify equations for the relationship between HR and performance for time t–1 and time t, respectively with $b_{t-1} = b_t$:

$$\text{perf}_t = \text{hr}_t b + e_t$$
$$\text{perf}_{t-1} = \text{hr}_{t-1} b + e_{t-1}$$

Decompose the residuals into a time-varying, v, and time-invariant, u, parts:

$$\text{perf}_t = \text{hr}_t b + v_t + u$$
$$\text{perf}_{t-1} = \text{hr}_{t-1} b + v_{t-1} + u$$

Subtract the second equation from the first:

$$(\text{perf}_t - \text{perf}_{t-1}) = (\text{hr}_t - \text{hr}_{t-1})b + (v_t - v_{t-1})$$

The key result is that u, the omitted, time-invariant (i.e. 'fixed') component, is eliminated. Thus, any bias due to time-invariant omitted variables is also eliminated. With more than two waves of data, it is mathematically equivalent to pool cross-sections and include dummy variables for each firm (in this example).

Huselid and Becker (1996) used a fixed effects model and reasoned that if this estimate for the HR–performance coefficient was similar to the estimate based on cross-sectional data, it would reduce any concern about omitted variable bias in studies that have used cross-sectional data. Recognizing that fixed effects estimates (operationalized as difference scores with two waves of data) are often smaller than the cross-sectional estimates because of more serious measurement error problems in the former,[16] Huselid and Becker (1996) wisely corrected for unreliability in their fixed effects estimates.

Unfortunately, however, Huselid and Becker (1996) did not correct their cross-sectional estimates for measurement error, resulting in an 'apples and oranges' comparison. To make the comparison more informative, both sets of estimates need to be corrected. Gerhart (1999) found that upon additionally correcting the coefficient derived from the cross-sectional data, it was nearly twice as large (0.240) as the comparable fixed effects coefficient of 0.125. This suggests that, in contrast to Huselid and Becker's conclusion, omitted variables may be a problem in cross-sectional studies, given that the fixed effects coefficient was only one-half the size of the cross-sectional estimate. By Huselid and Becker's logic, the difference in magnitude would be due to a substantial omitted variable problem with the cross-sectional estimate.

Cappelli and Neumark (2001) also used longitudinal data and a fixed effects model as a means of controlling for omitted variables. (They use the term 'heterogeneity'.) They conclude that the effect of high-performance work practices on profitability is unclear, although like Huselid and Becker (1996) they recognize that such estimates are more susceptible than cross-sectional estimates to attenuation due to measurement error; unlike Huselid and Becker, they make no correction. Thus it is difficult to know whether the weaker support they obtained for the HR–performance relationship is due to them more effectively controlling for omitted variables or whether it is due to downward bias from using a fixed effects model, which exacerbates measurement error problems.[17]

There are (other) costs (beyond measurement error) in using fixed effects. One is that time-invariant variables fall out of the model described (unless suitable intruments can be found); another is that degrees of freedom are lost from the denominator. This is most easily seen in the dummy variable specification where $n-1$ dummy variables are added to the equation (where $n =$ number of firms). This leads to less efficiency. Thus, it is recommended that a test be conducted to determine whether fixed effects belong in the model before using the estimates from the fixed effects model. If not, the recommended model is the error components model (Hausman) and is estimated using generalized least squares (GLS), which accounts for the dependence of the disturbance terms across time.

Control variables: sometimes 'too much of a good thing'

Because omitted variable bias arises from using a model that omits relevant variables, the natural inclination may be to add 'control' variables to a model whenever possible in a regression/ANCOVA approach. However, as Blalock (1961), building on work by Simon (1954) observed, 'the question of when and when not to control for a given variable seems to be more complex than is often recognized' (p. 871). Duncan (1975) likewise cautions against adding control variables 'not for any clearly defined purpose, but simply because it is a "good idea" to look at partial [relationships]' (p. 22).

The problem is that, whether to control for a variable depends on the causal model. Consider, for example, two of the causal models that can be used in a three-variable case. Two variables are HR and performance. Let the third variable be a composite of ability, motivation and opportunity to contribute (AMO). A 'partial mediation' model is:

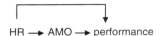

HR → AMO → performance

Another model ('control') is

HR

performance

AMO

Use the hypothetical correlation matrix:

	HR	AMO	Performance
HR	1.0		
AMO	0.40	1.0	
Performance	0.20	0.40	1.0

With the partial mediation model, the direct effect of HR on performance is 0.048 and the indirect effect (via AMO) is 0.152. Thus, the total effect of HR is 0.200. In contrast, using the control specification, the total effect of HR is .048 (direct effect = 0.048, no indirect effect). Thus, using the mediation specification leads to the total effect of HR being estimated as roughly five times larger in magnitude than when using a control specification. (The estimates here can be obtained using LISREL or by using the Alwin and Hauser (1975) approach.)

Summary
There are several approaches that may reduce omitted variable bias – one of which, fixed effects, was addressed here. It was also noted that including more control variables in an attempt to address the possibility of omitted variables does not always make for better estimates. The wisdom of adding control variables depends on the theoretical model.

Simultaneity

In a recursive model, causation runs in one direction. In a non-recursive model, causation is reciprocal (Duncan, 1975). In other words, there is simultaneity. To illustrate, consider the following model and example adapted from Duncan (1975, Chapter 5), which has two exogenous variables, x_1 and x_2, and perf and hr as endogenous variables (variables in standard score form to simplify things):

$$\text{perf} = b_{\text{perf1}}x_1 + b_{\text{perfhr}}\text{hr} + v$$
$$\text{hr} = b_{\text{hr2}}x_2 + b_{\text{hrperf}}\text{perf} + u$$

Thus, in this model, hr → perf and perf → hr.

Ordinary least squares (OLS) estimates of the regression coefficients in this model are biased because the disturbances/residuals are no longer independent of the right-hand side variables in the model (Duncan, 1975, p. 77). For example, given that perf → hr, then v, the disturbance term in the perf equation, must also be related to hr. Thus cov(hr,v) ≠ 0, which will lead to bias in estimating b_{perfhr}. Specifically, Duncan shows that (as applied here) rather than b_{perfhr}, the OLS estimate will equal:

$$b_{\text{perfhr}} + r_{\text{hrv}}/(1 - r^2\text{hr1}).$$

The second part of this equation is referred to as simultaneity bias. One approach to dealing with simultaneity (or endogeneity in a purportedly exogenous variable) is instrumental variables (IV), often estimated using two-stage least squares (2SLS). (As previously noted, IV/2SLS can also be used to address omitted variable and measurement error problems.) Consider again the equations:

$$\text{perf} = b_{\text{perf1}}x_1 + b_{\text{perfhr}}\text{hr} + v$$
$$\text{hr} = b_{\text{hr2}}x_2 + b_{\text{hrperf}}\text{perf} + u$$

The basic idea of instrumental variables is to replace a right-hand side variable, hr, suspected of being correlated with the error term with a predicted value, hr-hat, which is not correlated with the error term. Using 2SLS, hr-hat is obtained by regressing hr on the full set of exogenous variables, which must include at least one instrument. This is the first stage of 2SLS. The second stage is re-estimating the perf-equation by replacing hr with hr-hat. An instrument is a variable that is included in the equation for hr, but is excluded from (or fixed to zero in) the equation for perf and thus influences perf only through hr. A SEM approach such as LISREL (Jöreskog & Sörbom, 2002) can also be used to estimate parameters of simultaneous equation models. For more details on instrumental variables/2SLS and the challenge of finding appropriate instruments, see Gerhart (2007a).

A study by Schneider et al. (2003) uses longitudinal data in an effort to determine whether employee attitudes → business performance versus business performance → employee attitudes. They seem to conclude that it is the latter. See Gerhart (2007a) for some issues to be considered before accepting this conclusion. The use of instrumental variables should be considered as an alternative and perhaps preferred way of addressing the issues in the Schneider et al. study. Finally, I encourage researchers to recognize that causality can run in both directions, as the term 'simultaneity' indicates. It does not have to be one direction or the other.

Longitudinal data and time precedence

As noted earlier, Cook and Campbell (1979) identified time precedence of cause and effect as a necessary condition for causal inference. Longitudinal data are necessary to satisfy this condition. Interestingly, a recent review finds that this condition is not only rarely met in the HR and performance literature, but worse, HR is typically measured after performance (Wright et al., 2005). So, here is clearly a great deal of room for improvement on this front.

Consistent with my earlier discussion, one concern here is that researchers may use control variables in a way that is not consistent with the model they wish to test. Here, the concern is with controlling for prior performance. As Gerhart and Milkovich (1990) noted, if the causal model is something like:

$$hr_{t-2} \to perf_{t-1} \to hr_t \to perf_{t+1}$$

then, yes, controlling for perf at t–1 will reduce the relationship between hr at time t and perf at t+1, especially if hr and perf are stable over time and have stable reciprocal effects on one another over time. But by controlling perf at t–1, one is also removing the earlier effect of hr at t–2, so they warned against over-control.

Controlling for the lagged value of performance almost never yields empirical estimates that correspond to the conceptual model. Indeed, it is a mis-specification to control for the lagged value of performance in a model that seeks to explain differences in the level of performance across firms or units. By including a lagged value, the model in fact becomes a change model. To see this, begin with the model:

$$perf_{t+1} = b_1 perf_t + b_2 hr_t + e_{t+1}$$

Then impose the restriction $b_1 = 1$, and rearrange terms to obtain:

$$perf_{t+1} - perf_t = b_2 hr_t + e_{t+1}$$

Thus, by regressing firm performance at time t+1 on firm performance at time t and HR at time t, the model estimates the effect of HR *level* at t on the *change* in firm performance between times t and t+1. This is fine if this empirical specification coincides with the conceptual model. For example, change in performance would be the appropriate dependent variable if during the period between time t and time t+1 some companies changed their HR practices and the researcher was able to measure HR at these two time periods. However, this is almost never the case in HR and performance research; HR is instead usually measured at a single point in time. In that case, it is not clear that one would expect an unchanging set of HR practices to lead to a change in performance.

Summary

It is unlikely that causation runs in only one direction between HR and performance; simultaneous equation models offer the prospect of a more accurate and nuanced description of this relationship. However, the challenging assumptions of these models (for example, regarding instrumental variables) may be difficult to satisfy.

Causal inference and mediators

Becker and Gerhart (1996) emphasized the importance of specifying and testing intervening causal mechanisms as a way to better understand how HR influences performance, as well as its importance in assessing the credibility/causality of the relationship. However, as Purcell (1999) observed, the field has tended to 'take for granted' that 'often very crude' measures of HR practices are mediated by things like 'worker effort, morale, cooperation, attitudes and behaviour' (p. 29). More recently, workforce ability, motivation and opportunity to contribute (AMO) have been hypothesized as key mediators (Appelbaum et al., 2000; Boxall & Purcell, 2003). Again, however, this hypothesis is largely untested (Gerhart, 2007b).

The classic approach to testing and estimating mediation, described by Alwin and Hauser (1975), begins with the reduced form of the model, which refers to an equation for each endogenous variable that includes only purely exogenous variables on the right-hand side.[18] This is contrasted with the structural model, which includes all right-hand side variables, exogenous or otherwise. The total effect is defined as the coefficient on the exogenous variable in the reduced form equation. The direct effect is defined as the coefficient on the exogenous variable in the structural equation. The indirect effect is defined as the total effect minus the direct effect.

A later paper by Baron and Kenny (1986) uses a similar logic in testing for mediation, but with greater emphasis on statistical significance testing. However, they are careful to note that mediation is not an 'all or nothing' phenomenon, and thus statistical significance testing is not sufficient for assessing the degree of mediation. Rather, one must focus also on the percentage change in the regression coefficient when the mediator is added to the equation (moving from the reduced form to the structural equation), consistent with Alwin and Hauser (1975). Recent work comparing tests of mediation further demonstrates the drawback of relying exclusively on statistical significance tests, in part because of their very poor statistical power in most mediation tests (MacKinnon et al., 2002).

Testing for fit or moderation

Few seem to believe that the 'best practice' or 'universal' model of HR is valid. Most of us find that unlikely and can make plenty of persuasive arguments for why HR practices must display (a) internal/horizontal fit among themselves, (b) external/vertical fit with strategy, and (c) fit with the institutional (including country) environment (Boxall & Purcell, 2003; Paauwe & Boselie, 2003; Dowling et al., 2008)

The fact is, however, that there is precious little (formal research) evidence that (a), (b) or (c) make much difference to business performance (Dyer & Reeves, 1995; Gerhart et al., 1996; Wright & Sherman, 1999; Becker & Huselid, 2006; Gerhart, 2007b). This is not to say that there is no evidence on any of these three aspects of fit – for example, with respect to (c), the regulatory environment may preclude or mandate certain HR practices depending on the country. In the case of horizontal fit, however, a case can be made that there is evidence, but it has been mis-interpreted as supportive evidence (Gerhart, 2007b).

For example, an important study by Ichniowski et al. (1997) used monthly observations on 30 steel finishing lines.[19] Their dependent variable was line uptime and their independent variables were HR practices – either alone, or combined via cluster analysis into HR systems. Their key conclusion was that '[s]ystems of HRM policies determine productivity. Marginal changes in individual policies have little or no effect on productivity. Improving productivity requires substantial changes in a set of HRM policies' (p. 37). However, Gerhart et al. (1996; Gerhart, 2007b) have provided a critique of the Ichniowski et al. (1997) method, which calls into question the conclusion of horizontal fit/synergy/complementarities from their study. Unfortunately, Gerhart (2007b) found that the Ichniowski et al. (1997) method of testing internal fit continues to be used.

The concern here is that unwarranted claims regarding fit/synergy have unwanted consequences for research and policy. From a policy point of view, we do not want to tell companies that they have to 'buy the whole package' of HR system practices to obtain improvement if, in fact, that is not necessary. This general issue is one that very much needs to be addressed more carefully.[20]

Of course, it should be noted that others read the evidence regarding internal fit as being more supportive. In particular, Kepes and Delery (2007) say that 'previous reviews of the fit perspectives in SHRM have had a pessimistic tone and concluded that there was little evidence of the assumption that "fit" leads to organizational success' (p. 386), and they seek to revisit the literature on internal fit, in particular. However, Kepes and Delery never discuss the Ichniowki et al. (1997) methodology. Further, most of their discussion of empirical evidence is to show that 'certain HRM activities fit with each other to form a coherent "bundle"' (p. 397). But as they themselves point out, such evidence does not show that these particular combinations of HR practices actually produce 'synergistic effects' (p. 397) on performance. So they turn to evidence on this point: except for one study, all of the evidence they cite as showing synergistic effects has to do with some element of compensation and one other HR practice. No evidence is presented on synergistic effects of multiple HR system components. Further, many of the studies included in earlier reviews that did not provide support for internal fit are not discussed. Thus, while the Kepes and Delery review is a valuable resource for those studying fit in the HR and performance literature, I do not agree with their overall conclusion – which is 'we dispute claims that there is a scarcity of evidence that supports the notion of internal fit' (p. 400).

Finally, returning to specific methodological issues, there are three other areas where researchers sometimes do not follow recommended practice. First, when testing for interactions by entering a cross-product term, it is necessary to have all lower-order effects in the model that involve those variables. For example, to test a three-way interaction between HR, business strategy and country, one must include not only the three-way cross product but also the three main effects and the three two-way cross-product terms. Second, it is recommended that when testing an interaction, one rules out the possibility that an observed interaction is due to a quadratic effect (MacCallum & Mar, 1995). Third, when plotting an interaction (always recommended), care must be taken to include only values that actually exist in the dataset; so, for example, it is necessary to first verify that there are firms two standard deviations above the mean on HR practices and two standard deviations below the mean on a differentiation business strategy before including such a point in the figure.

Multi-level models and concepts

Sometimes the goal of a paper is to study the effect of HR policy on performance, but it uses a design where there is no organization-level or unit-level variance in HR and data for HR and performance is collected from a single individual. The typical approach in such cases seems to be to regress a perceptual measure of effectiveness (e.g. employee attitude, perceived organization/unit performance) on a perceptual measure of HR practices and N is equal to the number of individual respondents. However, without first demonstrating that (a) there is variance across organizations/units, and (b) that such variance is larger than variance within organizations/units, it is not possible to know whether the observed relationship stems from (a) the HR and performance constructs being related versus (b) common method variance.

One solution is to measure HR and performance using different sources (e.g. survey respondents for HR and archival data for performance). To achieve meaningful variance in observed HR practices, even within a single organization, one possibility is to show that what appears to be a single policy is implemented differently in different parts of the organization, perhaps by supervisor (e.g. Tsui et al., 1997). But to do this one must show that at this supervisor/workgroup level of analysis there is sufficient variance between supervisors/groups relative to within supervisor/group variance (using the appropriate ICC index), and then conduct the study at that level of analysis and not at the person level of analysis.

Hierarchical linear modelling (HLM) (Raudenbush & Bryk, 2000) is increasingly used for multi-level data and has application to the HR and performance literature (Ostroff & Bowen, 2000) where individual data are nested within organizations/units (or supervisors) are used. Typically, data at the person level are nested within units or organizations and thus are not independent, contrary to the assumption made by the classical regression/OLS model. HLM has the advantage of incorporating ICC analyses and of estimating standard errors that are corrected for the dependence of observations nested within units/organizations.[21] Prior to HLM (and related analytic frameworks), the researcher was faced with the choice of analysing data at the individual level (resulting in standard errors that were biased downward) or at the aggregate level (resulting in a smaller sample size and thus larger standard errors). HLM eliminates this trade-off. Another advantage of HLM is simply that it forces the researcher to explicitly address the level of analysis issue.

Conclusion

My goal here has been to identify challenges in estimating effect sizes and drawing causal inferences in research on HR and performance, and to consider possible solutions to these problems. In each of the areas discussed, researchers regularly engage in methodological practices that could be improved and that may result in incorrect conclusions regarding theory and practice.

While there is often a (well-motivated) call for better theory in HR, it is just as important to improve methodology. Some improvements require additional resources (e.g. multiple raters, longitudinal data), but others do not (e.g. presenting meaningful effect size estimates and interpretation, testing for fit correctly, correcting for random measurement error when the relevant reliability information is available, or using alternative estimators). If we are to draw policy inferences from our research, we need to be as confident as possible in our findings and conclusions. Keeping a focus on data and methodology is an important requirement to do so.

Notes

1 I draw freely in the present paper from Gerhart (2007a), which, as noted, deals with many of the same issues. Gerhart (2007a) goes into somewhat greater depth on some of the statistical issues and models raised here.

2 'Performance' often refers to financial or operating performance in the literature. The models discussed here apply equally well to performance as defined by stakeholders other than shareholders (e.g. Brewster, 1999; Paauwe, 2004). Obviously, different stakeholders (shareholders, employees, customers, public) interests are not identical, but there is often a substantial shared interest in the ongoing viability of the organization.

3 Efficiency is only meaningful in conjunction with bias because any constant will be an efficient estimator, but of course is likely to be a biased estimator.

4 Based on Gerhart et al. (2000b, p. 809), $r = 0.10$ is a realistic estimate of the HR–performance correlation when examining the Huselid (1995) study.

5 As Rosnow and Rosenthal (1989) demonstrate, practical significance depends on the area of study, and even 'small' effects (as defined later) can be of practical significance. However, it is nevertheless useful to make use of general standards or conventions for interpreting effect size magnitude and (practical) significance.

6 Sometimes an author claims that when a regression coefficient is not statistically significant, 'if we had used a larger sample size, the coefficient would have reached statistical significance'. This is not necessarily correct, because the regression coefficient varies across samples, meaning it could be smaller in a different sample. So while it is correct that the confidence interval around the coefficient would be smaller in a larger sample, ceteris paribus, it is unlikely that the confidence interval would be centred around the same coefficient estimate in that larger sample.

7 Range enhancement, by contrast, leads to an upward bias in the standardized coefficient.

8 Simply citing research that shows ratio and non-ratio (subjective) measures of firm/unit performance are 'related' (i.e. different from zero) is not sufficient. It is necessary to report the magnitude (e.g. correlation) of the relationship.

9 There are other important assumptions (e.g. homoskedasticity, lack of autocorrelation).

10 Wooldridge (2002, p. 50) observes that in applied econometrics, the term 'endogenous' is used to refer to any right-hand side variable that is correlated with the disturbance term. He also notes, however, that the term 'endogenous' has a more traditional meaning (Alwin & Hauser, 1975): any variable that is explained within a set of

equations, or, in a path model, any variable that has a unidirectional arrow leading into it. Likewise, an exogenous variable is one that is not explained in the system, and in a path diagram has no unidirectional arrows leading into it. To avoid confusion, I use the terms 'exogenous' and 'endogenous' in the latter sense.

11   Roughly speaking, consistency means that in large samples, an estimator's probability density function (or distribution) approaches that of the population parameter as the sample size increases.

12   In the case of more than one x variable, the effects of measurement error are more complex. In fact, in the multivariate case, it is mathematically possible for measurement error to result in upward bias in a regression coefficient. We discuss two-predictor scenarios later in this paper.

13   When using the plant/facility as the level of analysis, which is the typical unit of analysis in industry-level studies (e.g. MacDuffie, 1995; Batt, 2002; Hunter & Lafkas, 2003), evidence suggests that reliability may be significantly better (Gerhart et al., 2000). This finding makes sense because plant practices are easier to observe, both because plants are smaller on average than firms and because there is less likely to be variation in actual HR practices within a plant compared to within a firm with multiple sites (and many employees).

14   As an alternative, a standard econometric approach to correcting for measurement error is the use of instrumental variables, usually using two-stage least squares estimation (discussed later).

15   Interestingly, Wall et al. (2004) note that in 73 of the 369 interviews conducted for Study 2, a respondent was 'unable to answer all questions, with non-response typically involving matters about performance' (p. 106). In such cases, another respondent able to answer these questions was contacted. No such non-response challenge with subjective performance appears to have arisen in Study 1; one wonders whether the issue arose in Study 2 because respondents were asked about specific financial measure, whereas in Study 1 they were only asked for a general assessment of performance.

16   It has long been known that reliability problems are exacerbated by using difference scores (Cronbach & Furby, 1970), though these can be corrected for unreliability using structural equation models (e.g. Gerhart, 1988).

17   Cappelli and Neumark (2001) argue that because they use long panels (i.e. a long time exists between data points), they are able to 'avoid the problem of exacerbating measurement error' (p. 744). As part of this argument, they assume that 'none of the work practices were in place as of the first wave of the panel' (p. 744). However, on p. 741, they report that they find somewhat stronger support for the HR-performance relationship when they use a correction for measurement error. No details are provided on the correction or the results.

18   Recall that endogenous variables have determinants in the model, whereas exogenous variables have no determinants (i.e. are unexplained) in the model.

19   Note that a working paper version of this article was available in 1993, meaning the influence of the study was felt before 1997.

20   A broader issue is whether fit is an overly static concept that has received too much attention to the detriment of related issues, such as 'sustainable fit', which 'can be achieved only by developing a flexible organization' (Wright & Snell, 1998, p. 758). Longitudinal data on how firms are able to respond in HR areas (practices, employee skills, employee behaviours) over time to changes in their competitive environments would be useful here.

21   HLM is not necessary to obtain the correct standard errors. Many statistical packages accomplish the same thing by allowing estimation of robust standard errors.

10
PROGRESS AND PROSPECTS FOR HRM–PERFORMANCE RESEARCH IN SMALL AND MEDIUM-SIZED BUSINESSES

SOPHIE DE WINNE
AND LUC SELS

Introduction

Despite the parallel development of the HRM–performance and small business research traditions, little overlap between both exists (Soriano et al., 2010). In strategic human resource management (SHRM) and HRM–performance research, HRM is seen as a large company phenomenon. The pile of literature on small and medium-sized enterprises (SMEs), in turn, is primarily devoted to management practices in functional domains such as marketing, finance and accounting. In studying determinants of SMEs' survival, success and growth, HRM has been less dominantly present. Only a small number of studies focus on the relationship between multiple HR practices and firm performance in a SME setting.

The lack of research on this topic contrasts sharply with its relevance. First, the statistical predominance and economic importance of SMEs in Europe, the UK and the US calls for research on critical success factors for SMEs' performance. Even though HRM in SMEs seems a contradiction in terms at first sight, there are reasons to believe that HRM can contribute to small business performance. For instance, difficulties of (expanding) SMEs to find qualified employees threaten both the short-run expansion and the long-term continuity of the business (Marchington et al., 2003). Moreover, having a competent workforce is vital because SMEs have less tolerance for inefficiency than larger organizations (Muse et al., 2005). A minimum of HR investments may thus be essential to claim a position in labour markets and to compete with larger players in attracting (sufficient) applicants, a necessary condition to select the best.

Second, the majority of findings from HRM–performance research in large firms points in the direction of a positive relationship (Combs et al., 2006). Yet there are reasons to assume that these results are not necessarily applicable to SMEs. In comparison with larger players, SMEs lack economies of scale. Introducing an HR manager, using assessment centres or organizing training is relatively more expensive for SMEs. To achieve a positive return, the introduction of these practices should yield relatively higher positive results. Thus far, we do not have a clear insight into the necessary critical mass (in terms of the number of employees) needed for HR investments to be profitable. Next, HR decisions in SMEs are usually taken by owners/managers in an informal and personalized manner. This 'small is beautiful' approach has been praised by some authors; yet others claim that it may lead to treating people inconsistently, which might subsequently negatively influence the psychological contract, commitment and motivation of employees (Bowen & Ostroff, 2004; Kotey & Sheridan, 2004). The question as to which approach – formal or informal – is best for SMEs remains unanswered.

Finally, SMEs provide researchers with a unique environment to study the HRM–performance relationship. Several authors have stressed characteristics such as their transparent nature (Aldrich & Auster, 1986) and the small distance between an individual's performance and the company's overall performance (Muse et al., 2005). Both features make it easier to reveal true effects and to study causation issues. Moreover, young SMEs in particular are associated with strong labour market dynamics: they create a lot of jobs, yet at the same time the number of job losses is high due to a high failure rate (European Commission, 2009; USSBA, 2009). Katz et al. (2000) call them 'the fruit flies of management, they live and die quickly' (p. 8). This turbulence and the huge influence of owners/managers (varying in their philosophies, styles, training and experience) on decision-making causes samples of small, young firms to show high variation in performance and HR practices.

The purpose of this chapter is twofold. First, we discuss the progress made thus far in HRM–performance research in SMEs. Based on a review of the small number of relevant empirical articles, we map the commonly accepted arguments, critical shortcomings and main empirical gaps. Second, we develop a research agenda for future HRM–performance research in SMEs, taking both the specificity and heterogeneity of SMEs into account.

HRM–performance research in SMEs: a state-of-the-art

Based on a review of 104 HRM–performance articles in large firms, Boselie et al. (2005) developed a standard causal model for the relationship between HRM and firm performance (Figure 10.1).

It is commonly accepted that HR practices do not directly influence financial performance. HR practices have their most direct impact on employees' attitudes and behaviours (*HRM outcomes*). Changes herein have an effect on operational organizational performance (*internal performance*). Internal performance is also influenced by changes in employees' knowledge, skills and abilities (KSAs) and

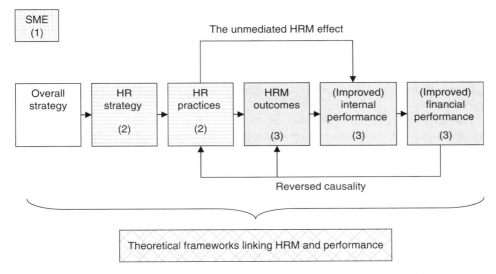

Figure 10.1   Standard causal model for the relationship between HRM and firm performance

Source: based on Boselie et al. (2005)

empowerment (see *unmediated HRM effect*). An increase (or decrease) in internal performance, in turn, contributes to higher level organizational performance constructs such as *financial performance*.

This framework is the starting point of our literature review. We start with an overview of the definitions put forward to delimit the sample of SMEs (1). Next, we describe the conceptualization and measurement of the two main concepts: HRM (2) and firm performance (3). In addition, we study the theoretical frameworks used to link both variables (4). We examine to what extent these concepts and frameworks deviate from previous HRM–performance research in large firms. We end with a summary of the main findings.

Selection of articles

We selected articles based on four inclusion criteria. First, we relied on peer-reviewed journal publications in small business management (e.g. *Small Business Economics*), entrepreneurship (e.g. *Entrepreneurship Theory and Practice*), and HRM (e.g. *Human Resource Management*) to assure a minimum level of quality. Consequently, the overview is not exhaustive, but the selection allows us to capture the main trends regarding HRM–performance research in SMEs. Second, we've chosen articles that focus on small and/or medium-sized businesses, implying that the authors explicitly refer to the small business context in the title or abstract. Third, since articles studying the impact of single HR practices have been subject for debate (Wright & Boswell, 2002), the main subject of study had to be the relationship between multiple HR practices and organizational performance. Finally, we included articles published between 1994 and 2011. In 1994, Arthur published his renowned work that triggered a boom in publications on HRM and firm performance in large firms. Moreover, a citation analysis by Ratnatunga and Romano (1997), based on 725 small business and entrepreneurship articles, indicates that the HRM–performance relationship in SMEs has not been studied before 1994.

The selection resulted in 25 articles (marked with an asterix in the reference list).[1] We distinguish two categories of studies. A first group is exploratory and links multiple HR practices and firm performance on a descriptive level; the authors are mainly interested in (1) the frequency of use of specific HR practices in SMEs and (2) their perceived effectiveness (e.g. Bacon et al, 1996). A second group is explanatory and relies on statistical techniques to study the HRM–performance relationship (Way, 2002). Most studies are quantitative. Some articles combine a quantitative and qualitative approach (Bacon et al., 1996; Cassell et al., 2002; Rowden, 2002).

SMEs: what's in a name?

In all the articles, the focus on SMEs is the main added value. We distinguish two categories of definitions of SMEs. *Qualitative definitions* describe the specific nature of SMEs. One example is the definition of the West Australian Small Business Development Corporation (Holmes & Gibson, 2001):

> [a] small business is a business in which all the main management decisions are made by one or two people without the help of internal staff management expertise, and which has a small share of the total market and a labour force which is small in comparison with the largest units in the same industry.

Studies using qualitative definitions rely on judgment sampling, requiring preliminary contact with the firm and limiting generalization of findings.

Quantitative definitions use one or more of the following criteria: (1) number of employees, (2) sales, receipts or turnover, (3) assets, and (4) percentage of shares owned by other companies (Holmes & Gibson, 2001). One example is the European definition (European Commission, 2003):

> SMEs are enterprises which employ fewer than 250 persons and which have an annual turnover not exceeding 50 million euro and/or an annual balance sheet total not exceeding 43 million euro. Moreover, no more than 25% of shares may be under direct or indirect control of one or more large companies or investors.

Policy-makers develop and use quantitative SME definitions because they need clear and objective indicators for legislative and policy purposes. The choice of criteria and cut-offs is an arbitrary process influenced by information or budgetary limitations and the objective to be reached. This results in a wide variety of definitions, both between and within countries. Since researchers often rely on administrative databases for probability sampling or on public funding, this diversity is also reflected in academic studies.

All articles use quantitative definitions to delimit the sample. One of the selected studies relies on the European definition of SMEs, thereby including all four of the aforementioned criteria (Cassell et al., 2002). Four studies include number of employees and independency of the firm as inclusion criteria (Bacon et al., 1996; Way, 2002; Rauch et al., 2005; Sels et al., 2006). The main reason to include the independency criterion is that satellite firms (i.e. subdivisions or plants of larger groups) are often subject to policies and practices made elsewhere (Bacon et al., 1996). Moreover, performance measures do not necessarily concern the subdivision or plant. Both factors may heavily distort conclusions on the HRM–performance relationship. Most studies exclusively rely on the number of employees to delimit the sample. The upper bounds vary from study to study: some articles use 500 employees as a cut-off, consistent with the definition of the US Small Business Administration; other authors choose 250 employees as the upper boundary, in accordance with the European definition (Aragon-Sánchez & Sánchez-Márin, 2005). Next, we found studies with firms up to 50, 100, 150, 200 or 1000 employees. In addition, there is no agreement on the lower boundary: some authors include very small firms (micro-enterprises) with 1-10 employees (Cassell et al., 2002); others state that HR-related issues are only important in firms with 10, 20, 50 or 100 employees or more.

We conclude that there is no consensus on *how big small is*. This lack of an unambiguous definition hinders generalization, comparability and a clear delimitation of the research field. The choice of criteria and cut-offs is in most cases guided by practical considerations (e.g. sample frame availability) rather than by the research question or an agreed view on the nature of SMEs. The generalization and comparability of findings is moreover influenced by other population characteristics. Some studies focus on relatively 'young firms' (e.g. Rauch et al., 2005), others on 'older firms' (e.g. Cassell et al. 2002). While the liabilities of smallness, such as resource poverty, are present in both groups, established small firms do not necessarily have to cope with the liabilities of newness such as a lack of experience. In addition, the studies cover a wide range of countries and industries (with a bias towards for profit sectors), characterized by different institutional contexts. Each of these factors may influence the relationship between HRM and firm performance, and make firm conclusions difficult.

Human resource management

The *conceptualization of HRM* is consistent across the different articles and similar to definitions in HRM–performance research in large firms. HRM in SMEs involves management decisions and activities regarding the selection, deployment, development and disposal of employees. The explanatory studies also emphasize the strategic character of HRM (e.g. Way, 2002; Hayton, 2003; Rauch et al., 2005; Sels et al., 2006; De Winne & Sels, 2010). They explicitly mention that employees are potential sources of sustained competitive advantage and that HRM is a steering instrument potentially eliciting appropriate worker behaviour in line with strategy. The validity of these conceptualizations within an SME setting is not questioned; there is, however, an ongoing debate about the extent to which large-firm HRM is transferable to small firms. Whereas some authors agree that writings on (strategic) HRM in large firms add to the understanding of HRM in small firms (e.g. Mayson & Barrett, 2006), others plead for a more contextualized approach (e.g. Marlow, 2006). They argue that 'HRM [in SMEs] may be crafted, rather than designed' (Harney & Dundon, 2006, p. 50) and that strategic normative models – and thus a strategic conceptualization of HRM – do not fully capture reality in SMEs. They claim that we first need knowledge about the determinants and configuration of HRM in small firms before we can study the impact of HRM on small business performance.

Regarding the measurement of HRM, the four most studied HR domains are: (1) compensation; (2) staffing, recruitment and selection; (3) performance management; and (4) training and development. These are also the most popular HR domains in HRM–performance research in large firms, although in a different sequence (Boselie et al., 2005). All studies focus on *HR practices*, but they differ in the specific practices they include. Kaman et al. (2001) and Hayton (2003) measure the presence of traditional, bureaucratic HR practices and discretionary, high-commitment HR practices. Whereas Kaman et al. (2001) consider the presence of realistic job previews as an important, high-commitment HR practice, Hayton (2003) does not. In contrast, Hayton (2003) considers formal salary surveys as part of traditional, bureaucratic HR practices, but Kaman et al. (2001) do not include them. Moreover, the studies are inconsistent in *what* has been measured (i.e. presence, coverage, frequency of use or intensity) and *how* it has been measured (i.e. indices, scales or binary variables). Regarding the latter, some authors approach HRM as a 'set of distinct HR practices' (e.g. Carlson et al., 2006), assuming that each HR practice independently contributes to firm performance. Others reduce the set of HR practices to one or more variables using scales (Hayton, 2003; Aragón Sánchez & Sánchez Márin, 2005; Fabi et al., 2010) or additive indices (Way, 2002; Sels et al., 2006). The resulting variables reflect HR systems. However, no consistency exists about the number and kind of HR practices constituting the HR system and about the meaning of the resulting scale or index. Sels et al. (2006), for example, include 18 HR practices related to six HR domains in one index. The resulting *HRM intensity index* is a proxy for the extent to which SMEs engage in HRM. Nguyen and Bryant (2004) use an *HRM formalization index*, consisting of the sum of eight binary variables, ranging from the presence of an HR plan to the use of formal recruitment sources for new employees. This index indicates the extent to which HR practices are formalized.

The lack of consensus on the measurement of HRM hinders a thorough comparison of findings. Moreover, although some authors argue that HRM might be different in small firms, few SME-specific HR measures exist. The basic premise remains that SMEs making a well-considered use of HR practices (similar to the ones used in large firms) will outperform businesses that do not. Furthermore, there is a limited focus on features of the HR strategy and HR function. This is not surprising given the pivotal role of owners/managers. However, the group of SMEs may range from very small independent firms with an authoritarian owner to small subsidiaries of multinational companies with a strategically oriented manager. Therefore, gathering information on HR strategy and the HR function could add to HRM–performance research in SMEs. Finally, some authors argue that a distinction should be made between rhetoric and reality (Paauwe & Boselie, 2005b), since an effective HR system is one in which intended, implemented and perceived HR practices overlap. Because of their transparent nature, SMEs provide researchers with an excellent environment to study the implications of gaps between intended, implemented and perceived HR practices. However, none of the reviewed studies focus on HR practices as *perceived* by workers: all studies claim to focus on *implemented practices*, but since owners/managers or persons in charge of personnel matters are usually the respondent, they may unwittingly address *intended practices*. Indeed, Bacon et al. (1996) compared survey results with observations and interviews on the shop floor, and revealed over-claiming of owners/managers. Rauch et al. (2005), on the other hand, argue that data gathered in small firms may be less biased since the 'political' interests of HR managers in large firms may lead them to represent things in a manner that serves their agenda. The work of Elorza et al. (2011) in Spanish SMEs confirms this hypothesis. The authors found a correlation of 0.75 between the actual HR system (as perceived by managers) and the HR system perceived by employees.

Firm performance

Performance can be *conceptualized* as the result of the way in which someone or something functions. Effectiveness refers to an evaluation of these results (Brewerton & Millward, 2001). An effective organization is one that is performing well according to the criteria on which it is assessed. These criteria depend on the assessor, for example, shareholder, employee, customer or society. In line with research in large firms, the *shareholder's view* dominates in the selected articles.

Two models of effectiveness are central (Cameron, 1986). The *goal model* is present in some of the descriptive articles (e.g. Bacon et al., 1996), assuming that an organization is effective if it accomplishes its stated goals. These authors examine whether HR practices are perceived as contributing to the achievement of the firm's objectives. The *high-performance systems model* is put forward in the explanatory studies (e.g. Way, 2002), arguing that a firm is effective if it is judged excellent compared to other (similar) organizations. Using statistical analyses, these authors examine whether HR practices add to the explanation of why some firms outperform others.

Performance can be conceived as a *chain of different hierarchical levels*, with one level contributing to the next (Dyer & Reeves, 1995). We distinguish four levels: (1) HRM outcomes, (2) operational performance, (3) financial performance and (4) (stock) market performance. A review of the *performance measures* used in the selected studies points to a predominance of non-financial measures of firm performance (e.g. absenteeism, employee turnover, employee satisfaction and product innovation). Most studies, however, explicitly state that HRM outcomes and operational performance are drivers of financial performance (e.g. profitability), thereby acknowledging the shareholder's view. The few studies that examine for several levels of performance (e.g. Way, 2002) generally neglect the inter-relationships between these levels. Only Sels et al. (2006) model the mediating role of HRM outcomes and operational performance between HR practices and financial performance. Finally, since SMEs rarely dominate a market and are usually not quoted on the stock exchange, little attention has been given to measures of (stock) market performance, such as market competitiveness or evolution in share price (e.g. Kerr et al., 2007). However, innovation measures are becoming gradually more important (Hayton, 2003; De Winne & Sels, 2010; Schmelter et al., 2010). This increased attention to innovation can be explained by the fact that innovative small businesses and start-ups are believed to boost innovation in existing industries and create new industries, thereby contributing to employment, wealth creation and competitiveness (De Winne & Sels, 2010). Since knowledge is the basic ingredient for innovation and resides in employees, knowledge-sustaining HR practices can play an important role in driving innovation.

The performance measures can be categorized according to two other dimensions: (1) their objective or subjective nature; and (2) their dynamic or static nature. *Subjective performance indicators* measure the opinion, impression or judgement of the respondent by means of scales. These measures are subject to errors of judgement and common method problems, but allow for inclusion of not-for-profit organizations in the sample. A majority of authors use subjective measures, but their point of reference differs. Some measure perceived importance of HR practices to the firm's operations (Deshpande & Golhar, 1994), whereas others want to know whether HR practices contribute to organizational objectives (Bacon et al., 1996; Cassell et al., 2002; Kerr et al., 2007). In some cases, informants are asked to benchmark the firm's organizational performance against the performance of competitors (Way, 2002; Nguyen & Bryant, 2004; Aragón-Sánchez & Sánchez-Márin, 2005; Patel & Cardon, 2010). *Objective performance indicators* are factual measures, usually represented by continuous variables. To ensure objectivity and avoid common method problems, some authors rely on a secondary database (de Grip & Sieben, 2005; Sels et al., 2006), whereas others have recourse to multiple respondents (Chandler & McEvoy, 2000; Rauch et al., 2005). This, however, does not imply that the measures are error-free. Accounting measures, for example, may still be susceptible to deliberate distortion. All other articles struggle with common method problems. They try to collect objective figures, but rely on one respondent who also answered the questions on the presence of HR practices.

Aragón-Sánchez and Sánchez-Márin (2005), Way (2002) and Ferligoj et al. (1997) use a combination of subjective and objective measures. Previous research has shown that measures of perceived organizational performance correlate positively with objective measures of firm performance (Dess & Robinson, 1984; Wall et al., 2004). Yet others doubt the interchangeable use of objective and subjective measures, especially in a SME setting where owners/managers are often the supplier of both subjective and objective data (Sapienza et al., 1988). In line with this concern, Aragón-Sánchez and Sánchez-Márin (2005) and Way (2002) do not find evidence of positive correlations between both types of measurement.

Static measures are snapshots of a situation at a particular moment. They are used in the majority of studies. This is presumably due to the lack of access to growth-related data. Few authors mention it as a well-considered choice. Only Sels et al. (2006) argue that growth- related measures do not fit SME research, since some SMEs are unwilling to grow. *Dynamic* measures refer to growth-related indicators, measuring the evolution of a variable over a certain timespan. Only four articles rely on growth-related measures: Nguyen and Bryant (2004) measure the perceived rate of profit growth, Rauch et al. (2005) and Rowden (2002) are interested in employment growth, and Carlson et al. (2006) focus on sales growth. Contrary to Sels et al. (2006), Rauch et al. (2005) assume that growth is an objective of every young SME. Carlson et al. (2006) only study growth-oriented family businesses. For these SMEs, growth is indeed an objective.

Some authors argue for the use of time lags, since it takes time before the impact of HR practices becomes visible (Wright & Haggerty, 2005) – especially when looking at financial or growth-related indicators of performance. However, only two studies have built in a time lag measuring HR practices at point (t) and firm performance at point (t+1) (Rauch et al., 2005; Sels et al., 2006). In addition, these studies also make use of longitudinal data (Rauch et al., 2005) or the combination of time lags and a control for past performance (Sels et al., 2006) to tackle the (reversed) causality problem. All other articles use a *post-predictive* (*backward-predictive*) design, measuring HR practices at point (t) and firm performance at point (t–1) or (t); or a *retrospective design,* asking the respondents to go back in time to measure the presence of HR practices (Wright & Haggerty, 2005).

The lack of consensus on the measurement of firm performance further increases the comparability problem. Moreover, we encounter the same methodological problems as HRM–performance research in large firms, such as common method problems and the lack of predictive research designs, objective data on performance, and time lags. Finally, only three studies try to identify performance indicators having inherent meaning for the particular small business context (Rauch et al., 2005; Carlson et al., 2006; Sels et al., 2006), yet each make different choices.

Theoretical frameworks linking HRM and firm performance

The majority of the studies start from a universalistic approach, assuming that *more is better*. Others follow a contingency approach (Chandler & McEvoy, 2002; Aragón-Sánchez & Sánchez-Márin, 2005), stating that *more is better, but only under certain circumstances*. The contingency variables taken into account differ between studies and include strategy (Chandler & McEvoy, 2000; Aragón-Sánchez & Sánchez-Márin, 2005), the level of human capital (Rauch et al., 2005), industry (Hayton, 2003), size (Kaman et al., 2001), and organizational culture (Patel & Cardon, 2010). None of the articles tests a configurational approach in which, next to a vertical fit, the synergistic relationships between HR practices (horizontal fit) are central.

Among the theoretical frameworks used to link HRM and firm performance, the *resource-based view* is mentioned most. However, none of the studies tests the basic assumptions of this theory – for instance, that 'the firm's human resources are unique, rare, inimitable and non-substitutable'. The *behavioural approach* is present in several articles testing the effect of HR practices on voluntary turnover, absenteeism, staff commitment, employee performance and congruence (e.g. Kaman et al., 2001; Sels et al., 2006; Zheng et al., 2006; Teo et al., 2011). Except for Sels et al. (2006) and Teo et al. (2011), none of these studies links employees' behaviour to other performance measures such as operational and financial performance; these studies are characterized by a universalistic approach and none align employees' behaviour with a specific firm strategy and *needed* employees' role behaviour. Sels et al. (2006) build their hypotheses on *human capital theory*. They argue that the potential productivity gains of investments in employees' knowledge, skills and abilities should be offset against costs associated with these investments. It is important – especially in SMEs, which lack economies of scale – to consider both value and cost-increasing effects. Apart from Way (2002), who also pronounces on the return on investment of HR practices in terms of their total effect on labour productivity, this is the only study taking both benefits and costs of HR practices into account. In line with *upper echelon theory*, stating that the firm is a reflection of its top managers (Hambrick & Mason, 1984), five studies take characteristics of owners/managers into account as independent (Ferligoj et al., 1997; Rauch et al., 2005; de Winne & Sels, 2010) or control variables (Aragón-Sánchez & Sánchez-Márin, 2005; Muse et al., 2005). Finally, *institutional, upper echelon, resource dependence* and *political influence theory* are mentioned to explain why SMEs have fewer HR practices compared to large firms. They mainly focus on determinants of HR practices, such as environment, owners/managers, legitimacy on resource markets, etc. Carlson et al. (2006) also mention *agency theory* to explain differences in the use of HR practices between family and non-family firms.

We conclude that the articles are mainly based on strategic normative models and are therefore in line with mainstream HRM–performance research in large firms. Most theories are used as an integrating background or to explain the study's findings. Only a few authors (e.g. Way, 2002; Rauch et al., 2005; Sels et al., 2006) theoretically ground their conceptual model or hypotheses. If no theoretical framework is used, evidence-based arguments to study HRM and firm performance are put forward. Institutional, resource dependency and political perspectives are present in small business literature, as well as upper echelon theory, but are only mentioned to explain the presence or absence of HRM. They are not put forward to theoretically ground the (lack of a) relationship between HRM and small business performance.

What do we know?

The descriptive studies primarily concentrate on the use of HR practices in SMEs and managers' perceptions of their importance and effectiveness. Due to the lack of consistency in measures we need to be careful in interpreting the findings, but we can draw the following conclusions.

First, the percentage of firms using sophisticated HR practices rises with firm size. This is not to say that small firms do not use HR practices; on the contrary, several studies (Bacon et al., 1996; Kaman et al., 2001; Hornsby & Kuratko, 2003) emphasize that the HR practices of small firms are more sophisticated than expected. According to Kerr et al. (2007), SMEs with an HR manager are more likely to have high-performance work systems. Second, the main determinants of HRM seem to be pressing need, rather than strategic considerations or imitative behaviour (Cassell et al., 2002). According to Bacon et al. (1996), adoption of HRM reflects the introduction of formal practices to retain management control along-side (and without destroying) the informal culture and organic nature of management. Finally, training, compensation, recruitment and selection, and performance appraisals are mentioned most in the 'top five' lists of most effective or important HR practices. We must be careful in interpreting this data because these are the topics that are most frequently measured and there is no consistency in the measures used, either for HR practices, or their effectiveness.

The results of the methodologically more sophisticated studies point in the direction of a positive relationship. Articles focusing on *HR systems* (Ferligoj et al., 1997; Kaman et al., 2001; Way, 2002; Hayton, 2003; Nguyen & Bryant, 2004; Rauch et al., 2005; Sels et al., 2006; Kerr et al., 2007; De Winne & Sels, 2010; Fabi et al., 2010; Teo et al., 2011) show that systems of high performance or high-commitment work practices contribute to one or more HR outcomes, operational and/or financial performance. Only Aragon-Sánchez and Sánchez-Márin (2005) do not find evidence of a relationship between the HR system and return on investment, and Sels et al. (2006) fail to provide evidence of an association between HRM intensity and voluntary turnover. Studies introducing *multiple HR practices separately* in the analyses find mixed results. De Grip and Sieben (2005) find a positive impact of training on labour productivity, but no impact of performance evaluation systems and performance-based pay. The results of Zheng et al. (2006) suggest positive effects of motivational HR practices on different HRM outcomes (staff turnover, commitment, congruence and competence); however, they did not find an impact of developmental HR practices. Finally, Schmelter et al. (2010) found positive effects of staff selection, training and development, and rewards on corporate entrepreneurship, but no effect of specialist assignment. These findings imply that not every HR practice contributes to performance and that it might be interesting to study the interrelationships between HR practices in a SME context.

Next, Way (2002) and Sels et al. (2006) conclude that although greater use of HR practices is associated with increased productivity, this effect is offset by increased labour costs. In addition, several studies show that the relationship between HRM and firm performance is moderated by a third variable. Rauch et al. (2005) provide evidence of a moderating impact of employees' human capital on the relationship between HR utilization and development, and employment growth: HR utilization and development is most effective when employees' human capital is high. Patel and Cardon (2010) show that the positive relationship between HR intensity and labour productivity is stronger in SMEs with a high group culture. Hayton (2003) finds that the impact of discretionary HRM on entrepreneurial performance is higher in organizations active in high-technology industries as compared to firms that are active in non-high-technology industries. Chandler and McEvoy (2002) show that total quality management has a positive impact on firm earnings when supported by training and group-based pay, but a negative effect in the absence of these HR practices. This is in line with the hypothesis that firms with a vertical fit between strategy and HRM outperform companies that do not align strategy and HRM.

Katz et al. (2000, p. 8) stated in the introduction of a special issue on HRM and SMEs:

> Let's face it: we can't define what we are very well; we study many different samples; we measure terms differently, and we steal theory from everyone (e.g. organization behaviour, strategy, etc.).

Their assessment still holds. We know very little about the relationship between HRM and firm performance in SMEs, since few studies tackle the topic. The only conclusions one can draw are that (1) the use of HR practices increases with firm size; (2) only a small proportion of SMEs introduce sophisticated HR practices; and (3) the SMEs introducing a configuration of sophisticated or formalized HR practices seem to outperform the ones that do not. The lack of consistency in samples and measures and the lack of attempts to fine-tune hypotheses and measures to a SME setting prevent us from drawing more firm conclusions.

The aforementioned studies are to a large extent a replica of HRM–performance research in large firms. In other words, SMEs are treated as little big firms. But compared to large firms, SMEs are often characterized by high numbers of jobs where employees perform multiple roles with unclear boundaries and job responsibilities (Cardon & Stevens, 2004), easier communication flows, and more opportunities for face-to-face involvement (Wilkinson, 1999). In our opinion, the lack of attention to the specific nature of SMEs might be the biggest threat to further development of this research stream. HRM–performance research should be tuned to the SME context, implying that other issues have to be emphasized. In the next section, we will sketch some avenues for further research.

HRM–performance research in SMEs: some prospects

To structure our research agenda, we rely on two dimensions. The first dimension concerns the distinction between *SME specificity* (i.e. characteristics that distinguish SMEs from large firms, often denoted by the umbrella term *size*) and *SME heterogeneity* (i.e. characteristics that determine differences among SMEs). The second dimension relates to the guises in which the aforementioned characteristics can appear: (1) as *determinants* of HRM, and (2) as *moderators* of the HRM–performance relationship. The framework resulting from the combination of these two dimensions will guide the formulation of suggestions for HRM–performance research in SMEs.

SME specificity and heterogeneity: children are not little grown-ups, and no two are alike

Dandridge (1979) stated that 'children are not little grown-ups' (p. 53). He referred to the idea that SMEs are different from large firms and argues that concepts of organization theory – the study of patterns of formal structure, decision-making, power and communications – are not necessarily applicable to SMEs. His article is a call for small business management theory. Later, d'Amboise and Muldowney (1988) evaluated several attempts to develop small business management theories. They concluded that there was not yet a comprehensive theoretical framework to explain and guide small firms' management.

Today – more than 20 years later – there is still no leading theoretical framework to study small business management. Several theories rooted in economics, psychology or sociology are put forward. The choice depends on the central question or the group of SMEs studied. The same holds for HRM–performance research in SMEs. No theory or perspective offers an all encompassing framework to explain *why* and *how* SMEs implement HRM and to examine the *conditions for successful HRM* (in terms of increased firm performance). Institutional or resource dependence theories are useful to examine the type of HR practices introduced in SMEs operating in different environmental settings (Harney & Dundon, 2006), whereas human capital theory enhances our insights into the conditions for successful investments in the human capital of owners/managers and employees. Agency theory serves as a background to examine principal-agent problems in small family businesses and their consequences for the introduction of HR practices (de Kok et al., 2006), whereas transaction cost theory is appropriate to study the conditions for successful HR outsourcing in SMEs (Klaas et al., 2000).

The lack of a comprehensive small business management theory does not imply that the specific nature of SMEs has been neglected. The importance of *size* is systematically put forward as an argument to study SMEs and highlight the contribution of SME research (Torrès & Julien, 2005). Yet in most HRM–performance studies, neither the measurement of the key concepts nor the conceptualization of the HRM–performance relationship is tuned to a SME setting.

We argue that *size* is an umbrella term for external (environmental) and internal (organizational) factors that determine the specific nature of SMEs. In what follows, we label these characteristics *SME specificity*. In the first two columns of Table 10.1 we list a number of SME specific features, derived from conceptual frameworks of Arthur and Hendry (1990), Bacon and Hoque (2005), Duberley and Walley (1995), and Harney and Dundon (2006). Examples of external factors are market power, institutionalization of social dialogue and legitimacy in labour and financial markets. Examples of internal factors are the number of hierarchical levels, the degree of openness in communication and the presence/absence of economies of scale. These characteristics are (in most cases) different for SMEs compared to large firms.

Torrès and Julien (2005) criticized the *specificity thesis*, stating that research concentrates too much on the distinction between SMEs and large firms. The resulting

Table 10.1 An overview of characteristics that determine SME specificity and SME heterogeneity

	SME specificity		SME heterogeneity	
	External, environmental factors	*Internal, organizational factors*	*External, environmental factors*	*Internal, organizational factors*
	Lack of legitimacy on: - product market (difficult to attract potential customers; low market power) - labour market (difficult to attract potential employees) - financial market (difficult to attract potential financiers) Highly vulnerable to changes in: - product market (entrance of new players, change in customer needs) - labour market (high risk of loosing employees, especially in times of tight labour markets) Difficult access to (external) financial resources Social networks: - highly dependent on social networks	Ownership: - owner is (often) the manager - high ownership concentration - SMEs are often family businesses: ownership and daily management controlled by one family Decision-making and control: - central, by owner/manager - no clear division of responsibilities and tasks between board of directors and manager - usually independent (not part of a larger coordinating organization) Lack of economies of scale Low tolerance for: - inefficiency - discontinuity of production/ service process	Economic climate Competition Industry sector Technology Industrial region Geographical location Lack of legitimacy (e.g. start-up versus established firm) on: - product market (potential customers) - labour market (potential employees) - financial market (potential financiers) National and regional differences in institutional framework/legislation Supply chain relationships with other firms	Managerial characteristics: - objectives/ambition - business-related expectations - strategic vision - human capital, cognitive base - management or leadership style - values/norms/ideology - attitude towards risk Firm history Legal structure Firm age Firm's life cycle stage Firm strategy Part of a larger coordinating organization? Product life cycle Product portfolio Firm's market/customer base

– less dense social networks; strong ties

Legislation can be different for SMEs compared to large firms (e.g. no or less institutionalized social dialogue)

Policy measures can be different for SMEs as compared to large firms (e.g. EU actions to minimise the regulatory burden on SMEs)

Hierarchy:
– few hierarchical levels (no internal market)
Jobs/functions:
– less vertical and horizontal complexity
– broad jobs/less specialization
– multiple roles and responsibilities, ambiguity
Employer–employee relationship:
– direct, face-to-face contacts
Transparency:
– performance of individual employees is highly visible

Unions:
– presence
– coverage
Structural division of labour
Task structure
Number of employees
Workforce skill-mix
Labour/capital intensity
Family business:
– ownership and daily management controlled by one family?
– are employees family members?
Extensiveness of social network

Source: based on the frameworks of Arthur and Hendry (1990), Bacon and Hoque (2005), Duberley and Walley (1995), and Harney and Dundon (2006).

polarized view neglects the heterogeneity among SMEs: a global exporting small business largely differs from a small bakery shop in town. They plead for a contingency approach to study SMEs. We recognize their criticism, and therefore, in the development of our research agenda, we focus on *SME heterogeneity* as well. The third and fourth columns in Table 10.1 give an overview of environmental and organizational factors causing differences *among* SMEs. Examples of external factors are industry, competition and geographical location. Examples of internal factors are the firm's strategy, the owners/managers' leadership style and trade union coverage.

Suggestions for future HRM–performance research in SMEs

Both *SME specificity* and *SME heterogeneity* variables can be modeled as determinants of HRM or as moderators of the HRM–performance relationship (Figure 10.2). Although our primary interest is in factors shaping the relationship between HRM and performance (quadrants II and III), studies of determinants of HRM are necessary and helpful in developing SME-specific HR measures.

Research in quadrants I and II of Figure 10.2 enhances our insights into how HRM and HRM–performance relationships differ between SMEs and large firms. Studies in quadrants III and IV sharpen our insights into how HRM and the HRM–performance relationship differ among SMEs.

In what follows, we elaborate on productive areas for future research. Our main purpose is to introduce a general framework to reflect on HRM–performance research in SMEs rather than to develop an exhaustive list of specific research questions.

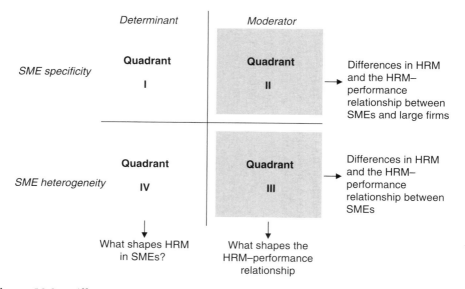

Figure 10.2   Different scenarios

Bridging HRM and HRM–performance research in SMEs

Many studies examine the presence of specific HR practices in SMEs on a descriptive level. Some authors concentrate on differences between SMEs and large firms (e.g. Hornsby & Kuratko, 2003). They conclude that, in general, SMEs implement fewer HR practices than large firms, and that HRM in SMEs is rather informal, intuitive and ad hoc. Others include heterogeneity variables such as industry or product market structure (e.g. Duberley & Walley, 1995; Harney & Dundon, 2006). They conclude that SMEs are indeed heterogeneous when it comes to the adoption of HR practices. The literature review shows that findings of these descriptive studies are not used in HRM–performance research in SMEs. The specificity of SMEs is often mentioned in HRM–performance studies to emphasize their added value, but once HRM and firm performance are conceptualized and their relationship is modelled, the consequences of firm size are largely neglected. HRM–performance research in SMEs replicates research in large firms and only focuses on formalized HR practices. Future studies should bridge both research streams (Figure 10.3).

First, we need case study research to determine the specific nature of small business HRM. The problem thus far is that large-firm HR practices are implicitly or explicitly used as the point of reference to pronounce upon small-firm HRM (e.g. HRM in SMEs is *more* informal, *more* intuitive and *more* reactive). Case studies could, for example, try to enrich SME-specific conceptualizations of HRM by examining the importance of owners/managers' people management skills in small businesses. This is not to say that examining differences in how large and small firms use HR practices is completely irrelevant; for instance, it is possible that some HR practices (e.g. in recruitment and selection) need to be formalized to impact on SMEs' performance, whereas others (e.g. performance appraisal) might be more fruitful in their informal version. Past recruitment research has shown that job applicants' decisions are heavily influenced by the recruitment procedures and HR policies adopted by the organization (Williamson, 2000). A formal recruitment approach and the use of formal and valid selection techniques might be a necessity for SMEs competing with larger firms for the best employees. Performance appraisals, on the other hand, do not necessarily have to be formalized, since employees' behaviours and performance are more visible as compared to employees' behaviour in large firms. It is possible that the benefits of formalized performance appraisals do not outweigh the investment.

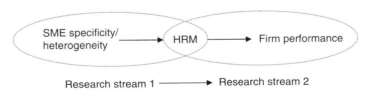

Figure 10.3 Bridging research on SME specificity and heterogeneity as determinants of HRM and research on the HRM–performance relationship

Second, future research should integrate the findings of studies on determinants of HRM in HRM–performance research. From a political perspective, the values, cognitive bases and capacities of the most powerful actors in an organization determine HRM. In SMEs the most powerful actors are owners/managers. Whereas a huge pile of entrepreneurship and small business studies relate characteristics of owners/managers to firm performance (e.g. Maes et al., 2005), most research on HRM and firm performance in SMEs fails to recognize their central role. Yet, the study of De Winne and Sels (2010) showed that 36 per cent of variance in the intensity of use of HR practices can be explained by the owners/managers' human capital and professional networks. The small scale of SMEs enables researchers to interview both owners/managers and employees, thereby creating opportunities to study consequences of gaps between the intentions of owners/managers and the perceptions of employees.

Third, HRM–performance research should focus on more homogeneous groups of SMEs. No doubt the inconclusive findings can be ascribed to the large differences among the SMEs studied. One example is heterogeneity in terms of age. Several studies focus on changes in HRM during a *firm's life cycle* (e.g. Rutherford et al., 2003), concluding that different stages require different HR practices (and different performance measures). Yet HRM–performance research has neglected the life cycle stage. Future HRM–performance research should capture this heterogeneity in terms of life cycle and, at the same time, try to limit heterogeneity regarding other characteristics such as industry, firm strategy, and so on. (see Table 10.1).

Finally, in his literature review on the relationship between training and firm performance, Storey (2004) refers to two explanations as to why small firms provide less training. The *ignorance interpretation* states that small firm owners underestimate the benefits to the business of providing or undertaking training; the *market interpretation* argues that small firms provide less training not because of a lack of awareness of benefits, but rather the reverse. The latter interpretation assumes that small firm owners face higher costs and lower benefits, explaining why small firms provide less training. Storey's (2004) review of research points towards support for the market over the ignorance explanation. Thus far, little is known about the critical mass (in terms of firm size) needed for HR practices to be profitable. Results of Way (2002) and Sels et al. (2006) on firms with less than 100 employees suggest a zero sum game. Muse et al. (2005) also try to explain their conflicting results from a zero effect perspective. Future research might gain insights into the return of investment of several HR practices in SMEs by focusing on both value increasing and cost related effects.

SME specificity and heterogeneity as moderators of the HRM–performance relationship

Future research should concentrate on how economies of scale determine the use of HR practices. In addition, studying the moderating role of scale in the HRM-performance relationship can help to decide at which point HR practices start to be beneficial and increase our insights into the necessary critical mass (in terms of the number of employees) needed for HR investments to be profitable. Strategic HR practices, for example, might have a positive impact on performance in large and

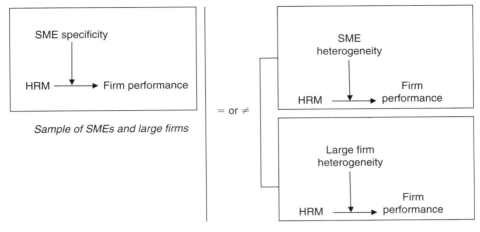

Figure 10.4 Studying the moderating impact of SME specificity on the HRM–performance relationship, and studying the moderating impact of heterogeneity variables on the HRM–performance relationship with a split sample approach

medium-sized firms because growing SMEs need structure and lack the necessary legitimacy on the labour market, but it might have a negative impact in (very) small firms, where formal HR practices can destroy the informal culture. Studying other SME specificity variables, such as the social network structure, as a moderator might be interesting as well to understand differences between SMEs and large firms in terms of HRM. Next, future studies should also study the moderating impact of heterogeneity variables with a split sample approach. This might enhance insights in how this moderating impact can differ between SMEs and large firms. It is possible that some variables have a different impact on the HRM-performance relationship in SMEs as compared to large firms (Figure 10.4).

In what follows, we focus on the moderating impact of three variables: (1) family ownership and management, (2) the presence of social dialogue, and (3) leadership style. We consider *family ownership and management* to be SME-specific variables. The *presence of social dialogue* is a variable that determines both SME specificity (in some European countries, social dialogue is only legally required in large firms) and SME heterogeneity (some SMEs decide to install social dialogue on a voluntary basis). *Leadership style* is a variable that only determines SME heterogeneity.

Our main purpose is to develop different scenarios on the interrelationships between the aforementioned variables and HRM in influencing performance. We develop four scenarios: *powerful connections* (1+1=3), *complements* (1+1=2), *substitutes* (1+1=1) and *deadly combinations* (1+1=0).

Family ownership and management (SME specificity)

According to agency theory, HR practices are instruments to steer managers' and/ or employees' (opportunistic) behaviour. In family businesses, the interests of owners, managers and employees are more likely to be aligned. In many cases employees are family members, increasing the likelihood of everybody pursuing the same goals. This assumption might also hold for employees that are not related (Drummond & Stone, 2007). To the extent that family firms succeed in creating an organizational culture where employees feel they belong to the same family, employees will conform to the objectives put forward by management. We are interested in how family ownership and management moderate the HRM–performance relationship.

1 + 1 = 3. Family ties and HR practices have positive synergistic effects. Family businesses rely on a strong organizational culture. Thanks to this *clan feeling*, family businesses outperform non-family businesses. However, the pool of employees often exists in family and non-family members, which has consequences in terms of unequal treatment (Astrachan & Kolenko, 1994). Thanks to the introduction of HR practices, non-family members are more likely to be treated in the same way as family members, which subsequently decreases feelings of injustice and leads to higher performance. Next, due to strong relational family ties, other issues that are not work-related dominate decision-making. This is pernicious to the functioning of the organization; for example, when owners/managers are reluctant to question a family member's performance or when targets are set based on emotional rather than rational arguments. In these cases, HR practices are a means to take a step back and engage in a more formal and transactional relationship, which is more effective in terms of performance.

1 + 1 = 2. Family ties and HR practices influence firm performance in different manners. The strong clan feeling has a positive impact on the involvement, commitment and motivation of employees, whereas HR practices influence their knowledge and skills. Consequently, family ties serve to create a good atmosphere and ensure that all employees pursue the same objectives (relationship-oriented), whereas HR practices create the conditions under which employees perform well (task-oriented). If the family ties and HR practices are indeed complementary, firm performance will be higher in a family business with HR practices as compared to a family business without HR practices.

1 + 1 = 1. Family ties and HR practices are substitutes. Thanks to the strong clan feeling and kin ties, social control is high. The informal culture, combined with a high level of social control, makes formal HR practices redundant. As mentioned previously, the strong clan feeling can positively influence the employees' involvement, commitment and motivation. Next, in the case of a strong informal culture and social control, employees get a lot of (positive or negative) feedback from the owner/manager and colleagues regarding their behaviour. This allows them to adjust their manner of working (e.g. pursuing training to enhance specific skills) in line with the firm's objectives. In this context, HR practices are not necessarily needed.

1 + 1 = 0. Family ties and HR practices have conflicting effects. Family businesses suffer from internal conflicts and kin ties clash with economic rationality (Edwards & Ram, 2006). HR practices are in these cases instruments to streamline organizational functioning by countering the negative impact on performance of these conflicts. However, if organizational culture is strong, employees may interpret the introduction of HR practices as a signal of distrust, resulting in even more conflicts. Consequently, performance decreases.

Presence of social dialogue/trade unions (SME specificity and heterogeneity)

In 2002, the European Commission developed a guideline on minimum requirements regarding information and consultation of employees (Directive 2002/14/ EG). This guideline applies to firms with 50 employees or more and establishments of larger corporations with at least 20 employees. It boosts debates on the need for institutionalized social dialogue and trade union presence in SMEs. Reactions are polarized: trade unions favour it to protect SME employees, whereas employer organizations reject it to avoid restriction of owners/managers' leeway. A relevant question is how trade union presence and the range and/or quality of social dialogue in SMEs moderate the HRM–performance relationship.

1+1 = 3. Trade unions represent the needs and grievances of employees in their contacts with management. Employees thus believe that trade unions act in their interests during negotiations, for example on the introduction of HR practices. Consequently, workers are more willing to accept HR practices and are more engaged in the process of implementation. This, in turn, has a positive impact on individual and collective performance. One could also examine the moderating impact of content, breath and quality of social dialogue. A rich social dialogue can provide feedback to managers. This might lead to the adjustment or fine-tuning of HR practices and, subsequently, to improved firm performance. Without this feedback loop, firm performance would be lower. Finally, the interaction of management and trade unions/workers in creating high-performance work systems generates path dependency. Consequently, the likelihood of other firms copying the HR practices decreases and the HR practices become a source of sustained competitive advantage in the long term.

1+1 = 2. Trade union presence and HR practices have additive and independent effects on firm performance. HR practices focus on the alignment of employees' behaviour with firm strategy through the reinforcement of motivation, knowledge and skills, whereas trade union presence or a strong social dialogue gives employees a voice and stimulates empowerment. Indirect participation is especially effective to ventilate opinions and grievances that are not expressed through direct participation channels or face-to-face contacts.

1+1 = 1. Trade union presence and HR practices are substitutes. Both are formalized channels through which employees show their grievances and needs. A weekly get-together with employees discussing their work progress and problems is as informative as a formal monthly meeting with one or two workers' representatives. In SMEs – where transparency, open communication and face-to-face contacts are more likely – indirect participation is redundant.

1+1 = 0. Trade union presence and HR practices have conflicting effects. Trade union presence restricts the owners/managers' leeway in implementing HR practices; for instance, if workers' representatives claim that HR practices should be

aligned with previous contractual agreements or with unwritten rules or regulations. This ends in a second best solution: a set of HR practices that is not optimal
and subsequently does not have the desired effects on performance. Moreover,
trade unions tend to emphasize employees' free will to join HR initiatives (e.g.
participation in training). This creates discord between employees that are willing
to participate and the ones that are not. The resulting frustrations end up in bad
performance.

The moderating impact of social dialogue/trade union presence might differ
between large and small firms. One could expect that social dialogue and HR
practices are a powerful connection in large firms because there is less transparency
and direct communication. Since employees feel that their interests are defended,
they will be more open to accept HR practices and more engaged in the process of
implementation (1+1=3). SMEs, on the other hand, are characterized by open
communication and daily face-to-face contacts between employer and employees.
This informal culture is often highly appreciated and replaces a social dialogue.
Therefore, one could expect that the introduction of a formalized social dialogue in
HR-rich SMEs is redundant (1+1=1).

Owners/managers' leadership style (SME heterogeneity)

Owners/managers play a pivotal role in SMEs. They are the main source of
knowledge needed to select the appropriate resources and effectively build and use
the firm's capabilities. In their review of empirical upper echelon studies examining the impact of owners/managers' characteristics on SME performance, Carpenter et al. (2004) concluded that in most cases, psychological and observable
management characteristics are studied; leadership styles are largely neglected. Yet
Chaganti et al. (2002) argue that for a SME to succeed, business strategies and
management systems should match the owners/managers' leadership style. Their
statement raises the question as to how leadership style can moderate the HRM–
performance relationship. According to House (2004), leadership is 'the ability of
an individual to influence, motivate, and enable others to contribute toward the
effectiveness and success of the organizations of which they are members' (p. 15).
HRM can be defined as 'a steering instrument that can elicit appropriate worker
behaviour in line with organizational strategy' (Schuler & Jackson, 1987). Given
the potential strategic contribution of both leadership and HRM, the likelihood of
interrelationships between both concepts is high.

We rely on situational leadership theory to clarify our perspective. Situational
leadership theory posits that there is no single best way to lead: for a group – leader
and subordinates – to perform effectively, there should be an appropriate match
between leadership style and contextual variables. In line with the work of Yukl et al.
(2002), we concentrate on the distinction between task-oriented (with a strong focus
on rewarding good behaviour and punishing bad behaviour) and relationship-
oriented (with a strong focus on good interpersonal relationships) leadership styles.
We assume that the leadership style matches with certain contextual variables
(leader-member relations, task structure and leader position power).

1+1 = 3. The introduction of HR practices does not always get a warm welcome in SMEs, because it damages the informal culture. However, relationship-oriented leaders with high credibility are able to sketch the need for and the potential advantages of HR practices. Consequently, employees are more willing to accept the HR practices and are more motivated to act in accordance with them. This has a positive impact on individual and collective performance, which is absent in the case of a more task-oriented leader or a leader with low credibility. On the other hand, a task-oriented leader needs instruments to encourage 'good' behaviour and punish 'bad' behaviour. Some practices, such as training, performance-based pay and appraisal are very helpful to this end, and can enhance individual and collective performance.

1+1 = 2. According to Greenberg and Baron (2003), leadership and (HR) management are two different things. The primary goal of a leader is to establish the fundamental purpose or mission of an organization and the strategy for attaining it, whereas the primary goal of a manager is to implement this vision. Consequently, leadership concentrates on building good relationships with employees and explaining the mission and strategy in order for employees to pursue the same objectives, thereby increasing chances of successful implementation of strategy. HR practices, in turn, are tools to steer employees' behaviour and to make sure that tasks are well performed. A relationship-oriented leader and HR practices are thus complementary capabilities in striving for high performance.

1+1 = 1. Some research has focused on substitutes for leadership, that is, 'attributes of subordinates, tasks and organizations that provide task guidance and incentives to perform to such a degree that they virtually negate the leader's ability to either improve or impair subordinate performance' (Howell et al., 1990, p. 23). Task-oriented leadership and HR practices are substitutes, since both highlight employees' required task behaviour. This substitutable effect is interesting in a context where owners/managers and employees are often separated (e.g. in the construction sector). In the case of physical distance, it is difficult for the leader to steer and monitor employees (task-oriented leader) and to build a strong relationship (relationship-oriented leader). HR practices formalize contacts (e.g. participation, performance appraisal) and subsequently give managers the opportunity to steer employees' behaviour and/or build a relationship at certain points in time.

1+1 = 0. The effects of leadership style and HR practices might neutralize each other. Employees perform well under supervision of a relationship-oriented leader, who focuses on harmonious interaction. However, the introduction of HR practices and especially strongly formalized control and monitoring systems can have a negative impact on performance. The signal sent by formalized HR practices contradicts the focus on relational harmony.

The moderating impact of leadership style might be different in large firms and SMEs. In a large firm with several relationship-oriented leaders, the likelihood of inconsistent treatment of employees is high. This might subsequently create conflicts between groups of employees, thereby decreasing performance. The presence of HR practices can neutralize this negative effect by formalizing procedures. The combination of relationship-oriented leaders and HR practices is in this case positive in terms of firm performance $(1+1=2)$. In the majority of cases, there is only one owner/manager in SMEs. In the case of a relationship-oriented owner/manager, a consistent treatment of employees is likely. HR practices are redundant in this case $(1+1=1)$.

Where do we need to go?

Previous HRM–performance research in SMEs is to a large extent a replica of HRM–performance research in large firms. The purpose of this research agenda was to develop a framework that might help researchers to go beyond the traditional thinking on SMEs. First, SMEs deviate from large firms in terms of size, that is, number of employees, total sales and assets. However, there are several other environmental and organizational characteristics that determine differences between SMEs and large companies. Some of these features are more relevant to the debate on HRM and HRM–performance in SMEs than size as such. We argue that researchers should take these factors into account and carefully decide on the central question they want to focus on. Second, the group of SMEs is very heterogeneous. To improve our understanding of small-firm HRM and the small-firm HRM–performance relationship, researchers should try to minimize this heterogeneity in studying SME samples. Third, we have shown that both SME specificity and SME heterogeneity variables can be related to HRM and the HRM–performance relationship in different ways. This opens several interesting lines of inquiry and confirms that, to date, little is known about HRM–performance relationships in SMEs.

Note

1   The tables used for analysis (i.e. a chronological overview of the studies and their aim, a detailed overview of the population studied, and a detailed overview of the main findings) can be received upon request by the first author.

11
PROGRESS AND PROSPECTS

DAVID GUEST, PATRICK WRIGHT
AND JAAP PAAUWE

The broad aims of this book have been to draw together and evaluate the evidence about the relationship between human resource management (HRM) and organizational performance. We have also paid attention to outcomes of interest to other stakeholders including, in particular, evidence of any impact of HRM on employee well-being. In this final chapter, we draw together and highlight some of the recurring themes. In addition, reflecting a second aim of the book, we highlight some of the priorities for future theory development and research. Finally, we outline a number of implications for policy and practice. In doing so, we acknowledge that we live in challenging economic times when there is a risk of neglecting the importance of motivating and developing people at work. We would argue that this is precisely the time when a focus on the effective and sustainable management of employees is more important than ever.

In the opening chapter, we set out the case for why HRM is so important in ensuring high performance in organizations and for organizational survival in a highly competitive world. We also emphasized the importance in pluralist societies of taking full account of the concerns of the range of stakeholders including, in particular, the well-being of employees. HRM is inevitably centrally concerned with the management of employees and their role in organizational performance. As well as affecting organizational performance, it is therefore also central to the experience at work of all employees and, through this, to their wider lives and well-being. The potential to pursue the dual goals of high organizational performance and high employee well-being reflects the promise of HRM and is why we believe this should continue to be a major focus of research.

Organizations have choices about how to manage all their resources and these include choices about both the priority they give to managing human resources and the strategy they adopt to manage their employees. Some strategic and contingency perspectives suggest that this is, to some extent, an open choice dependent on both internal and external context. Others argue that the importance of fit between business strategy and human resource strategy severely constrains the choice. However, the reviews of research findings have consistently shown that, irrespective of business strategy and context, there is a positive association between the adoption of more 'progressive', 'high-performance' or 'high-commitment' HR practices and organizational outcomes. The challenge, as successive chapters have indicated, lies in providing a convincing explanation of this association so that we are in a good position to offer evidence-based advice about how organizations should manage employees to achieve the greatest benefits. In their different ways, all the chapters in this book have explored this issue, analysed the problems and suggested ways in which we might fruitfully engage in theory development and research that will advance our knowledge and the utility of our evidence.

A starting point for many of the chapters is the resource-based view of the firm (Barney, 1991). This argues that a basis for competitive advantage is the possession of resources that are valuable, rare, inimitable and non-substitutable. It is further argued that in contemporary organizations, it is often employees that serve as resources par excellence. As Chapter 7 by McMahan and Harris highlights, this has provoked considerable interest in human capital. The chapter raises a number of challenging questions. One is whether human capital is indeed the key resource compared with, for example, access to financial capital; a second is the type of human capital. The analysis and research of Lepak and Snell (1999, 2002) has presented the case for selective investment in key human resources. This is a clear development of the resource-based view that seeks to identify the types of human resource that matter most to organizations seeking competitive advantage. The research of Ployhart et al. (2011) has taken the human capital model in a rather different direction by suggesting that it is the shared perspective, perhaps reflected in similar personality profiles, that reflect the key feature of human capital. This has some similarities with the concept of a strong HR system, reflecting a shared understanding of its purposes and priorities, as highlighted by Bowen and Ostroff's (2004) model – a point we return to later in this chapter.

There are a number of outstanding challenges for a focus on human capital, particularly if it is the kind of selective focus implied in the work of Lepak and Snell. The first is that while the possession of appropriate human capital may be a necessary precondition for high-performance organizations, it does not in itself ensure effective utilization of that human capital. In other words, it is a partial model of HRM. Secondly, one of the main early arguments for HRM – promoted, for example, by Walton (1985) and Pfeffer (1998) – is that a 'high-commitment' model should address the whole workforce rather than operate selectively. Much of the subsequent research has followed this recommendation by collecting data on HR practices applied to the workforce as a whole and this is broadly reflected in the major reviews that show the positive association between HRM and performance. The logic of a human capital perspective, reflected in the work of Lepak and Snell, runs counter to this. In contrast, the Ployhart et al.'s (2011) view of human capital is potentially more inclusive.

A third challenge for the human capital perspective, and one that is relevant to much of the research in this field, is the ethical issue concerning the goals of HRM. The term 'human capital', like the term 'human resource', implies something to be utilized or exploited. The human capital perspective faces ethical challenges on two fronts: the first is the potential advocacy of a focus on selected key human resources while neglecting others; the second is the concern for human resources as a means to organizational ends. This issue is addressed, albeit in rather different ways, in Chapters 2 and 3 by (respectively) Peccei et al. and by Boxall. They suggest that rather than viewing employees as a means to an end, employee well-being can be seen as an end in itself alongside the success of the organization. We anticipate that these various challenges to the human capital model are likely to see it evolve and potentially fragment in the coming decade.

The approach to human capital adopted, for example, by Lepak and Snell, is particularly concerned with internal fit. The question of 'fit' is central to research on HRM and is addressed in Chapter 4 by Paauwe et al. Building on the work of Wood (1999), they note that researchers have typically used the concept of fit in four different ways – but as research has advanced, types of fit have tended to proliferate. Their call is for a more integrated approach and they offer a two-stage model as a means of moving towards integration. This throws out a research challenge, since one of the implications is that data on several types of fit may need to be collected within the same study, preferably tracking down the development of the various fits across time. However, they also offer a set of testable propositions about the potential benefits of achieving an appropriate fit.

It has been argued for some time that for research on HRM and performance to advance, we need to improve our theory about the nature of HRM, the nature of performance and the process whereby they are linked (Guest, 2011). Most of the chapters have addressed one of more of these issues in some detail. Langevin Heavey et al. explored what constitute human resources practices and the ways in which they have been measured in Chapter 8. They convincingly outline major problems of reliability and validity, and point to ways in which our measurement could be improved. In considering which practices we should be measuring, there appears to be some convergence around the AMO model, with its focus on ability, motivation and opportunity to contribute as the core features of the way in which HRM affects employee attitudes and behaviour. However, there is less consensus about the key antecedent HR practices that help to determine ability, motivation and opportunity, and about how to measure them. More specifically, even if we can agree on a practice such as training, we are unsure how much detail is required, in what form it should be provided and from whom it should be collected. Gerhart outlines a range of methodological issues in Chapter 9 and also highlights the challenges of combining the measures. We have not made much advance on the seminal work of Delery and Doty (1996) in exploring additive or multiplicative models for combining practices into an HR system. This matters since, as Becker and Huselid (1998) have powerfully argued, and Wright and Nishii further emphasize in Chapter 6, HRM is distinctive in being viewed as a system of potentially integrated practices; and it is assumed (but not yet clearly demonstrated) that an integrated system of practices yields the best outcomes.

The idea of a system of HR practices is typically captured in the concept of a 'high-performance work system'. In Chapter 3, Boxall provides a critical analysis of this concept and finds it wanting as a general model. His starting point differs from that of some of the other chapters by focusing on the importance of describing practices as they are found in organizations and exploring their rationale. On this basis, he argues, it is possible to identify a range of employment systems in operation of which a high-performance work system is only one. In fact, in Boxall and Purcell (2011), seven systems are described. In his chapter, he places some emphasis on a high involvement system. He also cites the research of Toh et al. (2008), who identify five employment systems and find that the most effective are those that fit with their organizational context. This offers a further perspective on the role of 'fit'. The outline of a variety of systems is a necessary antidote to a universalist best practice view; and it throws up further avenues for research.

Boxall and other contributors offer a number of suggestions for advancing our research on the impact of HR practices. They include the now familiar call for more longitudinal research. As Paauwe (2009) and others have pointed out, we need measurement at several time points for both HR practices and HR outcomes to establish how far HR practices are related to future performance but also to past performance. We might also add the need for longitudinal studies in contexts where there are ongoing changes in HR practices that will permit some analysis of their relative importance. One advantage of this is that it permits some analysis of the influence of other factors such as leadership and organizational culture both as influences on HRM but also as co-variant influences on outcomes. In other words, HRM needs to be put in perspective. Another way of taking this into account is by placing more emphasis on a range of potentially relevant control variables in large-scale, cross-organization studies. At the same time, there is a strong case for combining this approach with in-depth case studies that permit the analysis of complex causal mechanisms and social processes, as well as allowing for the analysis of contextual influences (e.g. Paauwe, 2004; Hesketh & Fleetwood, 2006).

The core outcome implicit in most of the chapters in this book has been organizational performance. This has, perhaps, been insufficiently addressed as a problematic outcome. One of the puzzling findings of the meta-analysis by Combs et al. (2006) was that the association between HRM and distal financial performance indicators was stronger than the association with the somewhat more proximal measures of productivity. A possible explanation is that our measures of productivity may be less reliable and valid; however, the financial indicators are many and varied, and there is no consensus about the most appropriate financial indicator of organizational performance. The picture is further clouded by studies that focus on the workplace level of analysis and make comparisons within a single large organization or studies that focus on public sector, healthcare and other not-for-profit organizations where financial indicators are less relevant. There has been surprisingly little theoretical and analytic work exploring the most appropriate outcomes to use in measuring the impact of HRM on organizational performance. As Wright and Nishii note in Chapter 6, Dyer and Reeves (1995) identified four types of performance, namely employee, organizational, financial and market value. This list can be extended. There is a general assumption that the association will be stronger for more proximal outcomes such as labour turnover and productivity than for distal outcomes such as financial performance, but as we note above, this has not been consistently supported by research findings. This is an area that would benefit from further conceptual and empirical work.

One issue that is addressed, most notably in Chapter 2 by Peccei et al., is the potential for mutually beneficial outcomes for both the organization and its employees. They provide a systematic review of those studies, limited in number, that explore outcomes for both parties. They find evidence for mutual benefit when the employee outcomes focus on satisfaction and organizational commitment. However, the very few studies that address both organizational performance and aspects of well-being are much more equivocal. The measures of well-being are often poor and seem to focus mainly on indicators of stress. In these cases, there is sometimes evidence that increased use of HR practices is associated with higher levels of stress. Set against this, there is evidence from a range of studies focusing on employee outcomes that reveal a positive association between HRM and employee well-being (e.g. Appelbaum et al, 2000; Guest, 2002; Boxall & Macky, 2009) which suggest that on balance the outcomes of more HRM for employees are generally positive.

Embedded in the analysis of mutual outcomes is an interest in different types of HRM. This is characterized by Peccei et al. in Chapter 2 as reflecting an optimistic or pessimistic view, or as a high road or low road approach. In this context, behavioural commitment (Salancik, 1977) becomes relevant. If individuals freely choose to become committed to certain kinds of behaviour that lead to positive outcomes for both organization and individual, then mutual gains are feasible. However, if workers are compelled to engage in certain kinds of behaviour (perhaps by a regime of performance management), then mutual benefits are far less certain, although the organizational outcomes might be positive. Boxall, in his analysis of the 'state of the art' of HRM research in Chapter 3, reaches the view that, on balance, HRM can result in benefits for employees. There is therefore still the need for a clearer model that needs to be more fully drawn out of 'good' HRM. Alongside this, we need a clearer statement of what the alternatives look like and in particular what an integrated 'low road' HR strategy entails. This would open the way for more coherent testing of alternative models, ideally related to relevant contextual features. In this way, research could move beyond the current focus on whether more or less HR practices are present.

Chapter 2 by Peccei et al. begins to address the process whereby HRM and performance are linked. Although they do not make it explicit, there is an assumption that high performance results either from engaging capable employees and providing opportunities to contribute so that they display high motivation resulting in positive attitudes and behaviour. Or employees' performance is 'managed', through the use of clear goals and incentives to ensure high performance. This is part of the now well-established linkage model that is also reflected, in a somewhat different way, in Chapter 5 by Guest and Bos-Nehles, which focuses on implementation. They argue that too much attention has been paid to identifying the presence of HR practices at the expense of consideration of whether the practices are effectively implemented. This issue is also highlighted in Chapter 6 by Wright and Nishii and is reflected in the gap, also identified by Khilji and Wang (2006), between intended and implemented practices.

Guest and Bos-Nehles outline four stages of implementation and present a model within which to identify factors that are likely to influence the implementation process. This draws attention to those responsible for management of human resources and suggests that the role of line managers should receive more attention. They also raise questions about the part that HR managers can realistically play. They suggest that more research is needed to establish the conditions under which line managers will be more likely to ensure effective implementation. In this context, they and others cite the model of a 'strong' HR system outlined by Bowen and Ostroff (2004). This suggests that senior managers must take a lead in ensuring that HR practices are consistent, and communicate a clear and relevant message both to line managers and to employees. The research of Nishii et al. (2008) has reinforced the importance of the communication process and the attributions made by employees in shaping their response to the HR practices. There is scope to develop research on the symbolic and signalling role of HR practices, and how such processes are managed and perceived. There is also a need for further research exploring the relative importance of the content versus the implementation of HR practices (e.g. Guest & Conway, 2011), and for testing and further development of Bowen and Ostroff's (2004) complex model.

In Chapter 6 Wright and Nishii present an integrative model that seeks to take account of many of the issues highlighted here. Their starting point is the need to understand sources of variation and potential error when exploring the HRM–performance relationship. By emphasizing issues such as the gap between intended and implemented practices, they demonstrate the need to be clear about what constitutes the primary focus of attention in research. As they illustrate, if the main interest lies in intended HR practices, data should be collected at a senior managerial level; if it is implemented or experienced practices, then employees will provide a more accurate account. They argue convincingly that research needs to be conducted within an analytic framework that (1) takes account of processes whereby HRM might influence performance and (2) recognizes the need to integrate different levels of analysis. In doing so, they build on the earlier work of Ostroff and Bowen (2000).

Much of the research on HRM and performance has been conducted in large organizations. Chapter 10 by de Winne and Sels reminds us that most organizations are small and form an important part of the economy and source of employment. They review research on HRM in small and medium-sized enterprises, and conclude that many of the issues are similar to those reported in larger organizations – and confirm, unsurprisingly, that size is a factor in determining the presence of more HR practices. However, they also argue strongly that this is too simplistic and that an array of additional factors have to be taken into account to explain variation in the adoption of HRM across SMEs. One might also argue that the role of leadership may exert a more visible role in shaping the HR system in SMEs and it is perhaps in such contexts that the Bowen and Ostroff model is most likely to be directly relevant and actionable.

De Winne and Sels systematically analyse the wide range of contextual factors, both internal and external to SMEs, that can help to determine the presence of HR practices. Several other chapters highlight the importance of context and contingencies, and we need to acknowledge some of the contextual limitations of the bulk of existing research. In addition to the focus on large organizations, it is notable that most of the research reported in this book, and broadly representative of the wider body of research, is conducted in western, industrialized countries and in private sector organizations. In recent years, a growing amount of research on aspects of HRM has begun to be reported from China, Taiwan, South Korea and other Asian countries. The findings generally lend strong support to the association between HRM and performance. A focus on the public sector and not-for-profit organizations may be more relevant in Europe than in North America. A distinctive challenge in such contexts is the identification and measurement of outcomes: some financial indicators may be relevant, but profit will not be. To expand our research into these different kinds of organization, more thought needs to be given to the kinds of outcome that are relevant. A recent example of this has been provided by Messersmith et al. (2011) in their study of local authorities. There is a growing body of research exploring HRM and performance in the healthcare sector, where patient outcomes are a key indicator of performance (see, for example, Stanton et al, 2010; Veld et al., 2010). With an ageing population, more people are going to require health and social care, and the quality of the service provided by staff is already a major and increasing concern. In such contexts, the contribution of effective HRM is going to be crucial.

One differentiating feature of public sector organizations is that with their different and often more visible accountabilities, they may be required to demonstrate good employment practices. Other outcomes may include transparency, legitimacy and accountability. As Paauwe (2004) has observed, institutional requirements such as these can lead to a certain homogenization in the HR practices in place. In these contexts, the key differentiation is more likely to be the way in which the practices are implemented. As research becomes more nuanced, there is a strong case for focusing attention on a wider range of organizational contexts and exploring some of the boundary conditions for the effective use of HRM. One way of progressing this, reflecting a call by a number of observers, is to adopt a broader institutional framework with a multiple stakeholder perspective that gives greater emphasis to the role of HRM in promoting outcomes such as legitimacy, fairness, sustainability and mutual benefits.

An area that has perhaps been underplayed in many of the chapters concerns the role of the social partners. This may reflect the decreasing influence of trade unions in many organizations and their minor role in the USA. Whatever the reasons, much of the research on HRM and performance, particularly in the USA, adopts a unitarist perspective, focusing only on organizational outcomes and/or assuming that a good organizational outcome is invariably a good outcome for its employees. However, European legislation based on a pluralist perspective has enshrined rights of consultation and communication for employee representatives, and trade unions have played a major role in promoting legislation designed to enhance the quality of working life. Some of the outcomes of this legislation feed in to a 'high-commitment' model of HRM, if not always a 'high-performance' model. This raises the broader question, also under-developed in research, of what factors lead to the introduction of more HR practices and what role the social partners can play. As already indicated, future research might usefully explain how HR practices come about; how, by whom and for what reasons they are introduced; and what institutional and other pressures affect the presence of more or less HRM in organizations. In doing so, we might build a more explicitly pluralist perspective.

Embedded in all the chapters, but highlighted in particular by Gerhart in Chapter 9, is a call for improved methodology. Gerhart systematically addresses a range of issues on which research has generally been found wanting and sets out a series of guidelines for better research. These includes giving more thought to ways of measuring outcome variables to allow for estimates of effect sizes, on the grounds that this is a more useful indicator than statistical significance. He also emphasizes the need to use multiple raters of HR practices to improve the generally low reliability in many studies and the need, noted above, to give more thought to omitted variables. He joins Wright and Nishii in calling for more multi-level analysis. The credibility of the research on HRM and performance depends on the quality of the research methods, so it is important that his call for improved methods of data collection and analysis is heeded. At the same time, we acknowledge that Gerhart focuses on quantitative studies. Elsewhere, we have argued that these need to be complemented by more qualitative research and here, too, the need to adopt careful methods of data collection and analysis remain paramount. In this respect we can think of using a multiple-respondent approach (e.g. Guest & King, 2004), fully recording and transcribing interviews, using thematic content analysis (Eisenhardt, 1989; Boyatzis, 1998; Hyde et al., 2009), making sure to do this in a systematic and replicable way with the help of software packages such as Nvivo 9, and achieving intersubjectivity by double-checking the coding process by different researchers/authors.

The study of the relationship between HRM, performance and other outcomes is important as a topic of theoretical and empirical interest. However, it is also a highly practical issue, and the research findings have potentially major implications for policy and practice. As interest grows in evidence-based management (Rousseau & Barends, 2011), it is notable that many of the more robust findings appear to fall under the broad umbrella of HRM. These relate to topics such as the role of tests of cognitive ability, the benefits of structured questionnaires in selection and the impact of providing clear goals, as well as the more general statement of the association between HRM and performance (Rynes et al., 2007). However, as other research has indicated, many managers, including HR managers, are unaware of the evidence or choose not to believe it. As the research in this book has confirmed, despite a lot of encouraging progress – and while there are still many gaps to be filled before we can be fully confident that more high quality and effectively implemented HRM invariably leads to higher performance – we can be more certain that research findings demonstrate that an association exists. On this basis, we can generally recommend that a full use of HRM is good for organizations, good for those who work in them and good for their customers.

Building on this analysis, there are a number of practical implications. One concerns the responsibilities of senior and line managers for implementing HRM effectively. Chapter 1, by Paauwe et al., and Chapter 5, by Guest and Bos-Nehles, both address the role of the HR manager and outline its potential limitations in managing change and HR implementation. As several chapters note, and Bowen and Ostroff (2004) have also highlighted, senior management have a key role in setting the HR strategy and the climate within which it is enacted. They cannot leave this to the HR function. Some line managers find inherent difficulties in dealing with employees, particularly problematic and challenging employees. They need support from the wider management system. The need to recognize that HR practices are best viewed as a system is also highly relevant to all managers – particularly if they are tempted to focus on one kind of practice, whether it is performance-related pay or employee engagement, as a kind of solution or panacea in the face of organizational challenges.

In this book we have highlighted a vibrant field of theory and research, and an important area of policy and practice with the potential to affect organizational performance and individual well-being. The idea of an integrated approach to HRM is relatively recent and research has advanced rapidly over the past 25 years. Most of the chapters in this book have been written by a combination of established researchers who have helped to shape the field up to now and promising younger academics who can take the field forward in the future. What we have shown is that there is a solid research base but still many unanswered questions. We hope that the emerging generation of researchers can successfully address them.

REFERENCES

The articles selected for the literature review in Chapter 10 are indicated by an asterisk.

Abrahamson, E. (1991) Managerial fads and fashions: the diffusion and rejection of innovations. *Academy of Management Review*, 16(3), 586–612.

*Ahmad, S. and Schroeder, R.G. (2003) The impact of human resource management practices on operational performance: recognizing country and industry differences. *Journal of Operational Management*, 21(1), 19–43.

*Akdere, M. (2009) A multi-level examination of quality-focused human resource practices and firm performance: evidence from the US healthcare industry. *International Journal of Human Resource Management*, 20(9), 1945–64.

Aldrich, H. and Auster, E. (1986) Even dwarfs started small: liabilities of age and size and their strategic implications. In B. Staw and L. Cummings (eds) *Research in Organizational Behaviour* (pp. 165–98). Greenwich, Conn.: JAI Press.

Allen, T.D., Freeman, D.M., Russell, J.E.A., Reizenstein, R.C. and Rentz, J.O. (2001) Survivor reactions to organizational downsizing: does time ease the pain? *Journal of Occupational and Organizational Psychology*, 74(2), 145–64.

Allen, M.R. and Wright, P. (2007) Strategic management and HRM. In P. Boxall, J. Purcell and P. Wright (eds) *The Oxford Handbook of Human Resource Management* (pp. 88–107). Oxford, UK: Oxford University Press.

Alwin, D.F. and Hauser, R.M. (1975) The decomposition of effects in path analysis. *American Sociological Review*, 40(1), 37–47.

Alwin, D.H. (1974) Approaches to the interpretation of relationships in multitrait-multimethod matrix. In H.L. Costner (ed.) *Sociological Methodology* (pp. 79–105). San Francisco: Jossey Bass.

Appelbaum, E. (2002) The impact of new forms of work organization on workers. In G. Murray, J. Belanger, A. Giles and P.A. Lapointe (eds) *Work Employment Relations in the High-Performance Workplace*. London: Continuum.

Appelbaum, E., Bailey, T., Berg, P. and Kalleberg, A. (2000) *Manufacturing Advantage: Why High-Performance Work Systems Pay Off*. Ithaca, NY: Cornell University Press.

Appelbaum, E. and Batt, R. (1994) *The New American Workplace*. Ithaca, NY: ILR Press.

Appelbaum, E., Bernhardt, A. and Murnane, R. (eds) (2003) *Low-Wage America: How Employers are Reshaping Opportunity in the Workplace*. New York: Russell Sage Foundation.

Appelbaum, S.H. and Grigore, M.L. (1997) Organizational change and job redesign in integrated manufacturing: a macro-organizational to micro-organizational perspective. *Journal of European Industrial Training*, 21(2), 51–62.

*Aragón-Sánchez, A. and Sánchez-Marín, G. (2005) Strategic orientation, management characteristics and performance: a study of Spanish SMEs. *Journal of Small Business Management*, 43(3), 287–308.

Arthur, J.B. (1992) The link between business strategy and industrial relation systems in American steel minimills. *Industrial and Labor Relations Review*, 45(3), 488–506.

Arthur, J.B. (1994) Effects of human resource systems on manufacturing performance and turnover. *Academy of Management Journal*, 37(3), 670–87.

Arthur, M.B. and Hendry, C. (1990) Human resource management and the emergent strategy of small to medium sized business units. *International Journal of Human Resource Management*, 1(3), 233–50.

Astrachan, J.H. and Kolenko, T.A. (1994) A neglected factor explaining family business success: human resource practices. *Family Business Review*, 7(3), 251–62.

Atkinson, J. (1984) Manpower strategies for flexible organizations. *Personnel Management*, 16(8), 28–31.

Bach, S., Givan, R.K. and Forth, J. (2009) The public sector in transition. In W. Brown, A. Bryson, J. Forth and K. Whitfield (eds) *The Evolution of the Modern Workplace* (pp. 307–31). Cambridge, UK: Cambridge University Press.

*Bacon, N., Ackers, P., Storey, J. and Coates, D. (1996) It's a small world: managing human resources in small business. *International Journal of Human Resource Management*, 7(1), 82–100.

Bacon, N. and Hoque, K. (2005) HRM in the SME sector: valuable employees and coercive networks. *International Journal of Human Resource Management*, 16(11), 1976–99.

Bakker, A.B. and Demerouti, E. (2007) The job demands-resources model: state of the art. *Journal of Managerial Psychology*, 22(3), 309–28.

Bakker, A.B. and Demerouti, E. (2008) Towards a model of work engagement. *Career Development International*, 13(3), 209–23.

Bailey, T. (1993) *Discretionary Effort and the Organization of Work: Employee Participation and Work Reform Since Hawthorne*. Unpublished manuscript, Teachers College, Columbia University, New York.

Baird, L. and Meshoulam, I. (1988) Managing two fits of strategic human resource management. *Academy of Management Review*, 13(1), 116–28.

Barker, J. (1993). Tightening the iron cage: Concertive control in self-managing teams. *Administrative Science Quarterly*, 38, 408–437.

Barney, J. (1991) Firm resources and sustained competitive advantage. *Journal of Management*, 17(1), 99–120.

Barney, J.B. (2001) Resource-based theories of competitive advantage: a ten-year retrospective on the resource-based view. *Journal of Management*, 27(6), 643–50.

Baron, R.M. and Kenny, D.A. (1986) The moderator mediator variable distinction in social psychological research. *Journal of Personality and Social Psychology*, 51(6), 1173–82.

Baron, J.N. and Kreps, D.M. (1999) *Strategic Human Resources: Frameworks for General Managers*. Danvers, MA: John Wiley & Sons, Inc.

Barrick, M.R., Stewart, G.L., Neubert, M.J. and Mount, M.K. (1998) Relating member ability and personality to work-team processes and team effectiveness. *Journal of Applied Psychology*, 83(3), 377–91.

Barry, B. and Stewart, G.L. (1997) Composition, process, and performance in self-managed groups: the role of personality. *Journal of Applied Psychology*, 82(1), 62–78.

Barsade, S.G. and Gibson, D.E. (1998) Group emotion: a view from top and bottom. In D.H. Gruenfeld et al. (eds) *Composition: Research on Managing Groups and Teams* (pp. 81–102). Stamford, CT: JAI Press.

Baruch, Y. and Hind, P. (1999) Perpetual motion in organizations: effective management and the impact of the new psychological contracts on 'survivor syndrome. *European Journal of Work and Organizational Psychology*, 8(2), 295–306.

Batt, R. (2000) Strategic segmentation in front-line services: matching customers, employees and human resource systems. *International Journal of Human Resource Management*, 11(3), 540–61.

Batt, R. (2002) Managing customer services: human resource practices, quit rates, and sales growth. *Academy of Management Journal*, 45(3), 587–97.

Batt, R. (2007) Service strategies: marketing, operations and human resource practices. In P. Boxall, J. Purcell and P. Wright (eds) *The Oxford Handbook of Human Resource Management*. Oxford, UK: Oxford University Press.

Becker, B. and Gerhart, B. (1996) The impact of human resource management on organizational performance: progress and prospects. *Academy of Management Journal*, 39(4), 779–801.

Becker, B.E. and Huselid, M.A. (1998) High performance work systems and firm performance: a synthesis of research and managerial implications. In K.M. Rowland and G.R. Ferris (eds) *Research in Personnel and Human Resource Management* (pp. 53–101). Greenwich, CT: JAI Press.

Becker, B. E., Huselid, M. A., & Ulrich, D. (2001). *The HRD Scorecard: Linking People, Strategy, and Performance*. Boston: Harvard Business School Press.

Becker, B.E. and Huselid, M.A. (2006) Strategic human resource management: where do we go from here? *Journal of Management*, 32(6), 898–925.

Becker, B.E., Huselid, M.A., Pickus, P.S. and Spratt, M.F. (1997) HR as a source of shareholder value: research and recommendations. *Human Resource Management*, 36(1), 39–48.

Becker, G.S. (1962) Investment in human capital: a theoretical analysis. *The Journal of Political Economy*, 70(55), 9–49.

Becker, G.S. (1964) *Human Capital*. New York: Columbia University Press.

Beer, M., Spector, B., Lawrence, P.R., Mills, D.Q. and Walton, R.E. (1984) *Managing Human Assets*. New York: Free Press.

Belanger, J., Giles, A. and Murray, G. (2002) Towards a new production model: potentialities, tensions and contradictions. In G. Murray, J. Belanger, A. Giles and P. Lapointe (ed.) *Work and Employment Relations in the High-performance Workplace*. London and New York: Continuum.

Bell, B.S. and Kozlowski, S.W.J. (2008) Active learning: effects of core training design elements on self-regulatory processes, learning and adaptability. *Journal of Applied Psychology*, 93(2), 296–316.

Bell, S.T. (2007) Deep-level composition variables as predictors of team performance: a meta-analysis. *Journal of Applied Psychology*, 92(3), 395-415.

Beltrán-Martín, I., Roca-Puig, V., Escrig-Tena, A. and Bou-Llusar, J.C. (2008) Human resource flexibility as a mediating variable between high performance work systems and performance. *Journal of Management*, 34(5), 1009–44.

Bennett, N., Ketchen Jr., D.J. and Schultz, E.B. (1998) An examination of factors associated with the integration of human resource management and strategic decision making. *Human Resource Management*, 37(1), 3–16.

Bettencourt, L.A & Brown, S.W. (1997). Contact employees: Relationships among workplace fairness, job satisfaction and prosocial service behaviors. *Journal of Retailing*, 73, 39–61.

Bhattacharya, M., Gibson, D.E. and Doty, D.H. (2005) The effects of flexibility in employee skills, employee behaviors and human resource practices on firm performance. *Journal of Management*, 31(4), 622–40.

Blalock, H.M. (1961) Evaluating the relative importance of variables. *American Sociological Review*, 26(6), 866–74.

Blasi, J. and Kruse, D. (2006) US high-performance work practices at century's end. *Industrial Relations*, 45(4), 547–78.

Blau, P.M. (1964) *Exchange and Power in Social Life*. New York: John Wiley & Sons, Inc.

Blyton, P. and Turnbull, P. (1992) *Reassessing Human Resource Management*. London: Sage.

Bond, C.F., Wiitala, W.L. and Richard, F.D. (2003) Meta-analysis of raw mean differences. *Psychological Methods*, 8(4), 406–18.

Bond, S. and Wise, S. (2003) Family leave policies and devolution to the line. *Personnel Review*, 32(1), 58–72.

Bondarouk, T., Looise, J.K. and Lempsink, B. (2009) Framing the implementation of HRM innovation: HR professionals versus line managers in a construction company. *Personnel Review*, 38(5), 472–91.

Boon, C., den Hartog, D.N., Boselie, P. and Paauwe, J. (2010) The relationship between perceptions of HR practices and employee outcomes: examining the role of person-organization and person-job fit. *International Journal of Human Resource Management*, 22(1), 138–62.

Boon, C., Paauwe, J., Boselie, P. and den Hartog, D. (2009) Institutional pressures and HRM: developing institutional fit. *Personnel Review*, 38(5), 492–508.

Bos-Nehles, A.C. (2010) *The Line Makes the Difference: Line Managers as Effective HR Partners*. Zutphen: CPI Wöhrmann Print Service.

Boselie, P., Brewster, C. and Paauwe, J. (2009) In search of balance – managing the dualities of HRM: an overview of the issues. *Personnel Review*, 38(5), 461–71.

Boselie, P., Dietz, G. and Boon, C. (2005) Commonalities and contradictions in HRM and performance research. *Human Resource Management Journal*, 15(3), 67–94.

Boselie, P., Paauwe, J. and Jansen, P. (2001) Human resource management and performance: lessons from the Netherlands. *International Journal of Human Resource Management*, 12(7), 1107–25.

Boselie, P., Paauwe, J. and Richardson, R. (2003) Human resource management, institutionalization and organizational performance: a comparison of hospitals, hotels and local government. *International Journal of Human Resource Management*, 14(8), 1407–29.

Boyatzis, R.E. (1998) *Transforming Qualitative Information: Thematic Analysis and Code Development* (2nd edn). London: Sage.

Bowen, D.E. and Ostroff, C. (2004) Understanding HRM–firm performance linkages: the role of the 'strength' of the HRM system. *Academy of Management Review*, 29(2), 203–21.

Bowers, D. and Franklin, J. (1972) Survey-guided development: using human resources measurement in organizational change. *Journal of Contemporary Business*, 1, 43–55.

Boxall P., Ang, S.H. and Bartram, T. (2011) Analysing the 'black box' of HRM: uncovering HR goals, mediators and outcomes in a standardised service environment. *Journal of Management Studies*, 48(7), 1504–32.

Boxall, P. and Macky, K. (2009) Research and theory on high-performance work systems: progressing the high involvement stream. *Human Resource Management Journal*, 19(1), 3–23.

Boxall, P. and Purcell, P. (2003) *Strategy and Human Resource Management* (1st edn). Basingstoke: Palgrave Macmillan.

Boxall, P. and Purcell, P. (2008) *Strategy and Human Resource Management* (2nd edn). Basingstoke: Palgrave Macmillan.

Boxall, P. and Purcell, J. (2010) An HRM perspective on employee participation. In A. Wilkinson, P. Gollan, M. Marchington and D. Lewin (eds) *The Oxford Handbook of Participation in Organizations* (pp. 29–51). Oxford, UK: Oxford University Press.

Boxall, P. and Purcell, J. (2011) *Strategy and Human Resource Management* (3rd edn). Basingstoke: Palgrave Macmillan.

Boxall, P., Purcell, J. and Wright, P. (2007) Human resource management: scope, analysis, and significance. In P. Boxall, J. Purcell and P. Wright (eds) *The Oxford Handbook of Human Resource Management*. Oxford, UK: Oxford University Press.

Boxall, P. and Steeneveld, M. (1999) Human resource strategy and competitive advantage: a longitudinal study of engineering consultancies. *Journal of Management Studies*, 36(4), 443–63.

Boyer, K., Keong Leong, G., Ward, P. and Krajewski, L. (1997) Unlocking the potential of advanced manufacturing technologies. *Journal of Operations Management*, 15(4), 331–47.

Brandl, J. and Pohler, D. (2010) The human resource department's role and conditions that affect its development: explanations from Austrian CEO's. *Human Resource Management*, 49(6), 1025–46.

Brent-Smith, D.B. (2008) *The People Make the Place: Dynamic Linkages Between Individuals and Organizations*. New York: Taylor and Francis Group.

Bretz, R.D. and Judge, T.A. (1994) The role of human resource systems in job applicant decision processes. *Journal of Management*, 20(3), 531–51.

Brewster, C. (1999) Different paradigms in strategic HRM: questions raised by comparative research. In P. Wright, L. Dyer, J. Boudreau and G. Milkovich (eds) *Strategic Human Resources Management in the Twenty-first Century*. Supplement to G.R. Ferris (ed.) *Research in Personnel and Human Resources Management*. Stanford, CT: JAI Press.

Brewster, C. (2007) Comparative HRM: European views and perspectives. *International Journal of Human Resource Management*, 18(5), 769–87.

Brewster, C. and Larsen, H.H. (1992) Human resource management in Europe: evidence from ten countries. *International Journal of Human Resource Management*, 3(3), 409–34.

Brewster, C. and Larsen, H.H. (2000) Responsibility in human resource management: the role of the line. In C. Brewster and H.H. Larsen (eds) *Human Resource Management in Northern Europe* (pp. 195–218). Oxford, UK: Blackwell.

Brewerton, P.M. and Millward, L.J. (2001) Assessing performance in organizations. In P.M. Brewerton and L.J. Millward (eds) *Organizational Research Methods: A Guide for Students and Researchers* (pp. 122–42). London: Sage Publications.

Brief, A.P. (1997). *Attitudes in and around organizations*. Thousand Oaks, CA.: Sage.

Bryson, A., Forth, J. and Kirby, S. (2005) High-involvement management practices, trade union representation and workplace performance in Britain. *Scottish Journal of Political Economy*, 52(3), 451–91.

Buyens, D. and de Vos, A. (2001) Perceptions of the value of the HR function. *Human Resource Management Journal*, 11(3), 70–89.

Cain, G.G. and Watts, H.W. (1970) Problems in making policy inferences from the Coleman report. *American Sociological Review*, 35(2), 228–42.

Caldwell, R. (2001) Champions, adapters, consultants and synergists: the new change agents in HRM. *Human Resource Management Journal*, 11(3), 39–52.

Cameron, K. (1986) Effectiveness as paradox: consensus and conflict in conceptions of organizational effectiveness. *Management Science*, 32(5), 539–53.

Campbell, D.T. and Fiske, D.W. (1959) Convergent and discriminant validation by the multitrait-multimethod matrix. *Psychological Bulletin*, 56(2), 81–105.

Campion, M.A. and McClelland, C.L. (1993) Follow-up and extension of the interdisciplinary costs and benefits of enlarged jobs. *Journal of Applied Psychology*, 78(3), 339–51.

Cannon-Bowers, J.A., Salas, E. and Converse, S.A. (1993) Shared mental models in expert decision-making. In N.J. Castellan (ed.) *Individual and Group Decision-making* (pp. 221–46). Hillsdale, NJ: LEA.

Cappelli, P. and Neumark, D. (2001) Do high performance work practices improve establishment-level outcomes? *Industrial and Labor Relations Review*, 54(4), 737–75.

Cardon, M. and Stevens, C. (2004) Managing human resources in small organizations: what do we know? *Human Resource Management Review*, 14(3), 295–323.

*Carlson, D.S., Upton, N. and Seaman, S. (2006) The impact of human resource practices and compensation design on performance: an analysis of family-owned SMEs. *Journal of Small Business Management*, 44(4), 531–43.

Carmeli, A. and Schaubroeck, J. (2005) How leveraging human resource capital with its competitive distinctiveness enhances the performance of commercial and public organizations. *Human Resource Management*, 44(4), 391–412.

Carmeli, A. and Tishler, A. (2004a) The relationship between intangible organizational elements and organizational performance. *Strategic Management Journal*, 25(13), 1257–78.

Carmeli, A. and Tishler, A. (2004b) Resources, capabilities, and the performance of industrial firms: a multivariate analysis. *Managerial and Decision Economics*, 25(6/7), 299–315.

Carpenter, M.A., Geletkanycz, M.A. and Sanders, W.G. (2004) Upper echelons research revisited: antecedents, elements and consequences of top management team composition. *Journal of Management*, 30(6), 749–78.

Carr, J.Z., Schmidt, A.M., Ford, J.K. and DeShon, R.P. (2003) Climate perceptions matter: a meta-analytic path analysis relating molar climate, cognitive and affective states, and individual level work outcomes. *Journal of Applied Psychology*, 88(4), 605–19.

*Cassell, C., Nadin, S., Gray, M. and Clegg, C. (2002) Exploring human resource management practices in small and medium sized enterprises. *Personnel Review*, 31(5/6), 671–93.

Chaganti, R., Cook, R. and Smeltz, W. (2002) Effects of styles, strategies, and systems on the growth of small businesses. *Journal of Developmental Entrepreneurship*, 7(2), 175–92.

*Chandler, G., Keller, C. and Lyon, D.W. (2000) Unraveling the determinants and consequences of an innovation-supportive organizational culture. *Entrepreneurship: Theory and Practice*, 25(3), 59–76.

*Chandler, G. and McEvoy, G. (2000) Human resource management, TQM and firm performance in small and medium-sized enterprises. *Entrepreneurship Theory & Practice*, 25(1), 43–57.

Child, J. and Partridge, B. (1982) *Lost Managers: Supervisors in Industry and Society*. Cambridge, UK: Cambridge University Press.

Chuang, C.H. and Liao, H. (2010) Strategic human resource management in service context: taking care of employees and customers. *Personnel Psychology*, 63(1), 153–96.

Cohen, J. (1992) A power primer. *Psychological Bulletin*, 112(1), 155–9.

Cohen, J. (1994) The earth is round (p <.05). *American Psychologist*, 49(12), 997–1003.

Cohen, J. and Cohen, P. (1983) *Applied Multiple Regression/correlation Analysis for the Behavioral Sciences*. Hillsdale, NJ: Erlbaum.

Colbert, B.A. (2004) The complex resource-based view: implications for theory and practice in strategic human resource management. *Academy of Management Review*, 29(3), 341–58.

Coleman (1990)

Collins, C.J. and Clark, K.D. (2003) Strategic human resource practices, top management team social networks, and firm performance: the role of human resource practices in creating organizational competitive advantage. *Academy of Management Journal*, 46(6), 740–51.

Collins, C.J. and Smith, K.G. (2006) Knowledge exchange and combination: the role of human resource practices in the performance of high-technology firms. *Academy of Management Journal*, 49(3), 544–60.

*Collings, D.G., Demirbag, M., Mellahi, K. and Tatoglu, E. (2010) Strategic orientation, human resource management practices and organizational outcomes: evidence from Turkey. *International Journal of Human Resource Management*, 21(14), 2589–613.

Combs, J., Liu, Y., Hall, A. and Ketchen, D. (2006a) How much do high-performance work practices matter? A meta-analysis of their effects on organizational performance. *Personnel Psychology*, 59(3), 501–28.

Committee on Science, Engineering, and Public Policy (1995) *On Being a Scientist: Responsible Conduct in Research* (2nd edn). Washington, DC: National Academy of Sciences; National Academy of Engineering; Institute of Medicine.

Cook, T.D. and Campbell, D.T. (1979) *Quasi-experimentation*. Chicago: Rand McNally.

Cooke, W.N. (2007) Integrating human resource and technological capabilities: the influence of global business strategies on workplace strategy choices. *Industrial Relations*, 46(2), 241–70.

Cordery, J. and Parker, S.K. (2007) Work organization. In P. Boxall, J. Purcell and P. Wright (eds) *The Oxford Handbook of Human Resource Management*. Oxford, UK: Oxford University Press.

Crawford, E.R., LePine, J.A. & Rich, B.L. (2010). Linking job demands and resources to employee engagement and burnout: A theoretical extension and meta-analytic test. *Journal of Applied Psychology*, 95, 834–848.

Cronbach, L.J. and Furby, L. (1970) How should we measure change – or should we? *Psychological Bulletin*, 74(1), 68–80.

Cronbach, L.J., Gleser, G.C., Nanda, H. and Rajaratnam, N. (1972) *The Dependability of Behavioral Measurements: Theory of Generalizability of Scores and Profiles*. New York: John Wiley & Sons, Inc.

Cropanzano, R. & Wright, T.A. (2001). When a "happy" worker is really a "productive" worker. A review and further refinements of the happy-productive worker thesis. *Consulting Psychology Journal*, 53, 182–199.

Crook, T.R., Todd, S.Y., Combs, J.G., Woehr, D.J. & Ketchen, D.J. (2011). Does human capital matter? A meta-analysis of the relationship between human capital and firm performance. *Journal of Applied Psychology*, 96, 443–456.

Croon, M. and van Veldhoven, M. (2007) Predicting group-level outcome variables from variables measured at the individual level: a latent variable multilevel model. *Psychological methods*, 12(1), 45–57.

Cunningham, I. and Hyman, J. (1995) Transforming the HRM vision into reality: the role of line managers and supervisors in implementing change. *Employee Relations*, 17(8), 5–20.

Cunningham, I. and Hyman, J. (1999) Devolving human resources responsibilities to the line. *Personnel Review*, 28(1/2), 9–27.

D'Amboise, G. and Muldowney, M. (1988) Management theory for small business: attempts and requirements. *Academy of Management Journal*, 13(2), 226–40.

Dandridge, T.C. (1979) Children are not 'little grown-ups': small business needs its own organizational theory. *Journal of Small Business Management*, 17(2), 53–7.

Danna, K. and Griffin, R.W. (1999) Health and well-being in the workplace: a review and synthesis of the literature. *Journal of Management*, 25(3), 357–84.

Darlington, R.B. (1990) *Regression and Linear Models*. New York: McGraw-Hill.

Das, A. and Narasimhan, R. (2001) Process-technology fit and its implications for manufacturing performance. *Journal of Operations Management*, 19(5), 521–40.

Datta, D.K., Guthrie, J.P. and Wright, P.M. (2005) Human resource management and labor productivity: does industry matter? *Academy of Management Journal*, 48(1), 135–45.

De Cieri, H., Wolfram-Cox, J. and Fenwick, M. (2007) A review of international human resource management: integration, interrogation, imitation. *International Journal of Management Reviews*, 9(4) 281–302.

*De Grip, A. and Sieben, I. (2005) The effect of human resource management on small firms' productivity and employees' wages. *Applied Economics*, 37(9), 1047–54.

De Kok, J., Uhlaner, L.M. and Thurik, R. (2006) Professional HRM practices in family owned-managed enterprises. *Journal of Small Business Management*, 44(3), 441–60.

De Menezes, L., Wood, S. and Gelade, G. (2010) The integration of human resource and operation management practices and its link with performance: a longitudinal latent class study. *Journal of Operations Management*, 28(6), 455–71.

*De Winne, S. and Sels, L. (2010) Interrelationships between human capital, HRM and innovation in Belgian start-ups aiming at an innovation strategy. *International Journal of Human Resource Management*, 21(11), 1860–80.

De Wit, B. and Meyer, R. (1998) *Strategy: Process, Content, Context: An International Perspective* (2nd edn). London: Thomson.

De Witte, H. (1999) Job insecurity and psychological well-being: review of the literature and exploration of some unresolved issues. *European Journal of Work and Organizational Psychology*, 8(2), 155–77.

De Witte, H. (2005) Job insecurity: review of the international literature on definitions, prevalence, antecedents and consequences, *South-African Journal of Industrial Psychology*, 31(4), 1–6.

Dean, J.W. and Snell, S.A. (1991) Integrated manufacturing and job design: moderating effects of organizational inertia. *Academy of Management Journal*, 34(4), 776–804.

Deephouse, D.L. (1999) To be different, or to be the same? It's a question (and theory) of strategic balance. *Strategic Management Journal*, 20(2), 147–66.

Delaney, J.T. and Huselid, M.A. (1996) The impact of human resource management practices on perceptions of organizational performance. *Academy of Management Journal*, 39(4), 949–69.

Delbridge, R., Hauptmeier, M. and Sengupya, S. (2011) Beyond the enterprise: broadening the horizons of International HRM. *Human Relations*, 64(4), 483–505.

Delbridge, R. and Keenoy, T. (2010) Beyond managerialism? *International Journal of Human Resource Management*, 21(6), 799–817.

Delbridge, R. and Turnbull, P. (1992) Human resource maximisation: the management of labour under just-in-time manufacturing systems. In P. Blyton and P. Turnbull (eds) *Reassessing Human Resource Management*. London: Sage.

Delery, J. and Doty, D. (1996) Modes of theorizing in strategic human resource management: tests of universalistic, contingency and configurational performance predictions. *Academy of Management Journal*, 39(4), 802–35.

Delery, J. and Shaw, J. (2001) The strategic management of people in work organizations: review, synthesis, and extension. *Research in Personnel and Human Resources Management*, 20, 165–97.

Delery, J.E. (1998) Issues of fit in strategic human resource management: implications for research. *Human Resource Management Review*, 8(3), 289–310.

Delmotte, J. (2008) *Evaluating the HR Function: Empirical Studies on HRM Architecture and HRM System Strength*. Leuven: K.U. Leuven.

Demerouti, E., Bakker, A.B., Nachreiner, F. & Schaufeli, W.B. (2001). The job demands-resources model of burnout. *Journal of Applied Psychology*, 86, 499–512.

Den Hartog, D.N., Boselie, P. and Paauwe, J. (2004) Performance management: a model and research agenda. *Applied Psychology*, 53(4), 556–69.

*Deshpande, S.P. and Golhar, D.Y. (1994) HRM practices in large and small manufacturing firms: a comparative study. *Journal of Small Business Management*, 32(2), 49–56.

Dess, G. and Robinson, R.B. (1984) Measuring organizational performance in the absence of objective measures. *Strategic Management Journal*, 5(3), 265–73.

DiMaggio, P. and Powell, W. (1983) The iron cage revisited: Institutional isomorphism and collective rationality in organizational fields. *American Sociological Review*, 48(2), 147–60.

Dorenbosch, L. (2009) *Management by Vitality*. Dissertation, Tilburg University.

Doty, D.H. and Glick, W.H. (1998) Does common methods variance really bias results? *Organizational Research Methods*, 1(4), 374–406.

Dowling, P.J., Festing, M. and Engle, A.D. (2008) *International Human Resource Management* (5th edn). London: Thomson.

Dreher, G.F. and Bretz, R.D. (1991) Cognitive ability and career attainment: moderating effects of early career success. *Journal of Applied Psychology*, 76(3), 392–7.

Drucker, P.F. (1954) *The Practice of Management*. New York: Harper & Brothers.

Drummond, I. and Stone, I. (2007) Exploring the potential of high performance work systems in SMEs. *Employee Relations*, 29(2), 192–207.

Duberley, J.P. and Walley, P. (1995) Assessing the adoption of HRM by small and medium-sized manufacturing organizations. *International Journal of Human Resource Management*, 6(4), 891–909.

Duncan, O.D. (1975) *Introduction to Structural Equation Models*. New York: Academic Press.

Dyer, L. and Reeves, T. (1995) Human resource strategies and firm performance: what do we know and where do we need to go? *International Journal of Human Resource Management*, 6(3), 656–70.

Edwards, A. and Kurvilla, S. (2005) International HRM: national business systems, organizational politics and the international division of labour in MNCs. *International Journal of Human Resource Management*, 16(1), 1–21.

Edwards, J.R. (1991) Person-job fit: A conceptual integration, literature review, and methodological critique. In C.L. Cooper and I.T. Robertson (eds) *International Review of Industrial and Organizational Psychology* (pp. 283–357). New York: John Wiley & Sons, Inc.

Edwards, M. (2010) An integrative review of employer branding and OB theory. *Personnel Review*, 39(1), 5–23.

Edwards, P. and Ram, M. (2006) Surviving on the margins of the economy: working relationships in small, low-wage firms. *Journal of Management Studies*, 43(4), 895–916.

Edwards, P. and Wright, M. (2001) High-involvement work systems and performance outcomes: the strength of variable, contingent and context-bound relationships. *International Journal of Human Resource Management*, 12(4), 568–85.

Eisenberger, R., Rhoades, L. and Cameron, J. (1999) Does pay for performance increase or decrease perceived self-determination and intrinsic motivation? *Journal of Personality and Social Psychology*, 77(5), 1026–140.

Eisenhardt, K.M. (1989) Building theories from case study research. *Academy of Management Review*, 14(4), 532–50.

Ellis, A.P.J., Bell, B.S., Ployhart, R.E., Hollenbeck, J.R. and Illgen, D.R. (2005) An evaluation of generic teamwork skills training with action teams: effects of cognitive and skill-based outcomes. *Personnel Psychology*, 58(3), 641–72.

Elorza, U., Aritzeta, A. and Ayestarián, S. (2011) Exploring the black box in Spanish firms: the effect of the actual and perceived system on employees' commitment and organizational performance. *International Journal of Human Resource Management*, 22(7), 1401–22.

European Commission (2003) Commission recommendation of 6 May 2003 concerning the definition of micro, small and medium-sized enterprises (notified under document number C(2003) 1422). *Official Journal* L124/36-L124/41.

European Commission (2009) *European SMEs Under Pressure. Annual Report on EU Small and Medium-sized Enterprises 2009*. EIM Business & Policy Research.

Evans, R. and Davis, W. (2005) High-performance work systems and organizational performance: the mediating role of internal social structure. *Journal of Management*, 31(5), 758–75.

Evans, P. and Genadry, N. (1999) A duality-based perspective for strategic human resource management. In P. Wright, L. Dyer, J. Boudreau and G. Milkovich (eds) *Strategic Human*

Resources Management in the Twenty-first Century. Supplement to G.R. Ferris (ed.) *Research in Personnel and Human Resources Management*. Stanford, CT: JAI Press.

*Fabi, B., Lacoursière, R., Raymond, L. and St-Pierre, J. (2010) HRM capabilities as a determinant and enabler of productivity for manufacturing SMEs. *Human Systems Management*, 29(3), 115–25.

Farndale, E. and Paauwe, J. (2007) Uncovering competitive and institutional drivers of HRM practices in multinational corporations. *Human Resource Management Journal*, 17(4), 355–75.

Feldman, M.S. and Pentland, B.T. (2003) Reconceptualizing organizational routines as a source of flexibility and change. *Administrative Science Quarterly*, 48(1), 94–119.

Feldman, M.S. and Rafaeli, A. (2002) Organizational routines as sources of connections and understandings. *Journal of Management Studies*, 39(3), 309–31.

*Ferligoj, A., Prasnikar, J. and Jordan, V. (1997) Competitive advantage and human resource management in SMEs in a transitional economy. *Small Business Economics*, 9(6), 503–14.

Ferris, G.R., Arthur, M.M., Berkson, H.M., Kaplan, D.M., Harrell-Cook, G. and Frink, D.D. (1998) Toward a social context theory of the human resource management–organization effectiveness relationship. *Human Resource Management Review*, 8(3), 235–64.

Ferris, G.R., Hochwarter, W.A., Buckley, M.R., Harrell-Cook, G. & Frink, D.D. (1999). Human resource management: Some new directions. *Journal of Management*, 25, 385–415.

Fey, C. F. and Bjorkman, I. (2001) The effect of human resource management practices on MNC subsidiary performance in Russia. *Journal of International Business Studies*, 32(1), 59–75.

Fisher, C.D. (2010) Happiness at work. *International Journal of Management Reviews*, 12(4), 384–412.

Fombrun, C., Tichy, N.M. and Devanna, M.A. (1984) *Strategic Human Resource Management*. New York: John Wiley & Sons, Inc.

Foulkes, F.K. (1980) *Personnel Policies in Large Non-union Companies*. Englewood Cliffs, NJ: Prentice-Hall.

Francis, H. and Keegan, A. (2006) The changing face of HRM: in search of balance. *Human Resource Management Journal*, 16(3), 231–334.

Francis, H., Keegan, A. and Wilson, L. (2005) Thinking critically about the thinking performer, *CIPD Professional Standards Conference*. Keele University.

Fredrickson, B.L. (2001). The role of positive emotions in positive psychology: The broaden-and-build theory of positive emotions. *American Psychologist*, 56, 218–226.

Fredrickson, B.L. (2004). The broaden-and-build theory of positive emotions. *Phil. Trans. Royal Society London*, August, 1367–1377.

Fredrickson, B.L. & Branigan, C. (2005). Positive emotions broaden the scope of attention and thought-action repertoires. *Cognition and Emotion*, 19, 313–332.

Fucini, J. and Fucini, S. (1990) *Working for the Japanese: Inside Mazda's American Auto Plant*. New York: Free Press.

Fulmer, I., Gerhart, B. and Scott, K. (2003) Are the 100 best better? An empirical investigation of the relationship between being a 'great place to work' and firm performance. *Personnel Psychology*, 56, 965–91.

Gallie, D. (2007) *Employment Regimes and the Quality of Work*. Oxford, UK: Oxford University Press.

Gardner, T. and Wright, P. (2010) The HR–firm performance relationship: is it only in the mind of the beholder? *International Journal of Human Resource Management*/Center for Advanced Human Resource Studies, Cornell University, Ithaca, NY.

Gardner, T.M., Wright, P.M. and Moynihan, L.M. (2011) The impact of motivation, empowerment, and skill-enhancing practices on aggregate voluntary turnover: the mediating effect of collective affective commitment. *Personnel Psychology*, 64, 315–50.

Geare, A., Edgar, F. and Deng, M. (2006) Implementation and consumption of HRM: stakeholder differences. *Research and Practice in Human Resource Management*, 14(2), 34–48.

Gelade, G.A. and Ivery, M. (2003) The impact of human resource management and workclimate on organizational performance. *Personnel Psychology*, 56(2), 383–404.

Gellatly, I.R. and Irving, P.G. (2001) Personality, autonomy, and contextual performance of managers. *Human Performance*, 14(3), 231–45.

Gennard, J. and Kelly, J. (1997) The unimportance of labels: the diffusion of the personnel/HRM function. *Industrial Relations Journal*, 28(1), 27–42.

George, J.M. (1996) Group affective tone. In M.A. West (ed.) *Handbook of Workgroup Psychology*. Chichester: John Wiley & Sons, Ltd.

George, J.M. & Brief, A.P. (1992). Feeling good-doing good: A conceptual analysis of the mood at work-organizational spontaneity relationship. *Psychological Bulletin*, 112, 310–329.

Gerhart, B. (1988) Sources of variance in incumbent perceptions of job complexity. *Journal of Applied Psychology*, 73(2), 154–62.

Gerhart, B. (1999) Human resource management and firm performance: measurement issues and their effect on causal and policy inferences. In P. Wright, L. Dyer, J. Boudreau and G. Milkovich (eds) *Strategic Human Resources Management in the Twenty-first Century*. Supplement to G.R. Ferris (ed.) *Research in Personnel and Human Resources Management*. Stanford, CT: JAI Press.

Gerhart (2001)

Gerhart, B. (2004) Research on human resources and effectiveness: selected methodological challenges, international seminar on *HRM: What's next?* Rotterdam, The Netherlands: Erasmus University.

Gerhart, B. (2007a) Modeling human resource management–performance linkages. In P. Boxall, J. Purcell and P. Wright (eds) *The Oxford Handbook of Human Resource Management*. Oxford, UK: Oxford University Press.

Gerhart, B. (2007b) Horizontal and vertical fit in human resource systems. In C. Ostroff and T. Judge (eds) *Perspectives on Organizational Fit* (SIOP Organizational Frontiers Series). New York: Lawrence Erlbaum Associates, Taylor & Francis Group.

Gerhart, B. and Fang, M. (2005) National culture and human resource management: assumptions and evidence. *International Journal of Human Resource Management*, 16(6), 975–90.

Gerhart, B. and Milkovich, G.T. (1990) Organizational differences in managerial compensation and firm performance. *Academy of Management Journal*, 33(4), 663–91.

Gerhart, B., Trevor, C. and Graham, M. (1996) New directions in employee compensation research. In G.R. Ferris (ed.) *Research in Personnel and Human Resources Management* (pp. 143–203). Stanford, CT: JAI Press.

Gerhart, B., Wright, P.M. and McMahan, G.C. (2000a) Measurement error in research on the human resources and firm performance relationship: further evidence and analysis. *Personnel Psychology*, 53(4), 855–72.

Gerhart, B., Wright, P., McMahan, G. and Snell, S. (2000b) Measurement error in research on human resources and firm performance. How much error is there and how does it influence size estimates? *Personnel Psychology*, 53(4), 803–34.

Gersick, C.J. and Hackman, J.R. (1990) Habitual routines in task-performing groups. *Organizational Behavior and Human Decision Processes*, 47(1), 65–97.

Gibson, J. W. and Tesone, D.V. (2001) Management fads: emergence, evolution and implications for managers. *Academy of Management Executive*, 15(4), 122–33.

Gittell, J.H., Seidner, R. & Wimbush, J. (2010). A relational model of how high-performance work systems work. *Organization Science*, 21, 490–506.

Gittleman, M., Horrigan, M. and Joyce, M. (1998) 'Flexible' workplace practices: evidence from a nationally representative survey. *Industrial and Labor Relations Review*, 52(1), 99–115.

*Godard, J. (1998) Workplace reforms, managerial objectives and managerial outcomes: the perceptions of Canadian IR/HRM managers. *International Journal of Human Resource Management*, 9(1), 18–40.

*Godard, J. (2001) Beyond the high-performance paradigm? An analysis of variation in Canadian managerial perceptions of reform programme effectiveness. *British Journal of Industrial Relations*, 39(1), 25–52.

Godard, J. (2004) A critical assessment of the high performance paradigm. *British Journal of Industrial Relations*, 42(2), 439–78.

Godard, J. (2010) What is best for workers? The implications of workplace and human resource management practices revisited. *Industrial Relations*, 49(3), 466–88.

Godard, J. and Delaney, J. (2000) Reflections on the 'high performance' paradigm's implications for industrial relations as a field. *Industrial and Labor Relations Review*, 53(3), 482–502.

Golden, K.A. and Ramanujam, V. (1985) Between a dream and a nightmare: on the integration of the human resource management and strategic business planning processes. *Human Resource Management*, 24(4), 429–52.

*Golhar, D. and Deshpande, S. (1997) HRM practices of large and small Canadian manufacturing firms. *Journal of Small Business Management*, 35(3), 30–8.

Gong, Y., Law, K.S., Chang, S. and Xin, K.R. (2009) Human resource management and firm performance: the differential role of managerial affective and continuance commitment. *Journal of Applied Psychology*, 94(1), 263–75.

Gooderham, P., Nordhaug, O. and Ringdal, K. (1999) Institutional and rational determinants of organizational practices: human resource management in European firms. *Administrative Science Quarterly*, 44(3), 507–31.

Gospel, H. and Pendleton, A. (2003) Finance, corporate governance and the management of labour: a conceptual and comparative analysis. *British Journal of Industrial Relations*, 42(3), 557–82.

Gospel, H. and Pendleton, A. (2005) *Corporate Governance and Labour Management: An International comparison*. Oxford, UK: Oxford University Press.

*Gould-Williams, J. (2003) The importance of HR practices and workplace trust in achieving superior performance: a study of public-sector organizations. *International Journal of Human Resource Management*, 14(1), 28–54.

Gouldner, A.W. (1960). The norm of reciprocity: A preliminary statement. *American Sociological Review*, 25, 161–178.

Graham, M.E. and Tarbell, L.M. (2006) The importance of the employee perspective in the competency development of human resource professionals. *Human Resource Management*, 45(3), 337–55.

Grant, A.M., Christianson, M.K. and Price, R.H. (2007) Happiness, health, or relationships? Managerial practices and employee well-being tradeoffs. *Academy of Management Perspectives*, 21(3), 51–63.

Gratton, L., Hope Hailey, V., Stiles, P. and Truss, C. (1999) Linking individual performance to business strategy: the people process model. *Human Resource Management*, 38(1), 17–31.

Gratton, L. and Truss, C. (2003) The three-dimensional people strategy: putting human resources policies into action. *Academy of Management Executive*, 17(3), 74–86.

Green, F. (2006) *Demanding Work: The Paradox of Job Quality in the Affluent Economy*. Princeton: Princeton University Press.

Greenberg, J. and Baron, R. (2003) Leadership in organizations. In J. Greenberg and R. Baron, *Behavior in Organizations* (8th edn) (pp. 469–512). Canada: Prentice Hall.

Greene, W.H. (1993) *Econometric Analysis*. New York: Macmillan Publishing Company.

Groysberg, B., Lee, L. and Nanda, A. (2008) Can they take it with them? The portability of star knowledge workers' performance. *Management Science*, 54(7), 1213–30.

Guest, D. (1997) Human resource management and performance: a review and research agenda. *International Journal of Human Resource Management*, 8(3), 263–76.

Guest, D. (1999) Human resource management – the workers' verdict. *Human Resource Management Journal*, 9(3), 5–25.

Guest, D. (2001) Human resource management: when research confronts theory. *International Journal of Human Resource Management*, 12(7), 1092–106.

Guest, D. (2002) Human resource management, corporate performance and employee well-being: building the worker into HRM. *Journal of Industrial Relations*, 44(3), 335–58.

Guest, D. (2007) Human resource management and the worker: towards a new psychological contract? In P. Boxall, J. Purcell and P. Wright (eds) *The Oxford Handbook of Human Resource Management*. Oxford, UK: Oxford University Press.

Guest, D. (2011) Human resource management and performance: still searching for some answers. *Human Resource Management Journal*, 21(1), 3–13.

Guest, D. and Bryson, A. (2009) From industrial relations to human resource management: the changing role of the personnel function. In W. Brown, A. Bryson, J. Forth and K. Whitfield (eds) *The Evolution of the Modern Workplace* (pp. 120–50). Cambridge, UK: Cambridge University Press.

Guest, D. and Clinton, M. (2007) *Human Resource Management and University Performance*. London, UK: Leadership Foundation for Higher Education.

Guest, D. and Conway, N. (2011) The impact of HR practices, HR effectiveness and a 'strong' HR system on organizational outcomes: a stakeholder perspective. *International Journal of Human Resource Management*, 22(8), 1686–702.

Guest, D.E. & Hoque, K. (1994). The good, the bad and the ugly: Employment relations in non-union workplaces. *Human Resource Management Journal*, 5, 1–14.

Guest, D. and Hoque, K. (1996) National ownership and HR practices in greenfield sites. *Human Resource Management Journal*, 6(4), 50–74.

Guest, D., Isaksson, K. and De Witte, H. (2010) *Employment Contracts, Psychological Contract and Employee Well-being*. Oxford, UK: Oxford University Press.

Guest, D. and King, Z. (2004) Power, innovation and problem-solving: the personnel managers' three steps to heaven? *Journal of Management Studies*, 41(3), 401–23.

Guest, D., Michie, J., Sheehan, M. and Conway, N. (2003) Human resource management and corporate performance in the UK. *British Journal of Industrial Relations*, 41(2), 291–314.

Guest, D., Michie, J., Sheehan, M., Conway, N. and Metochi, M. (2000) *Effective People Management*. London: CIPD.

Guest, D.E. (1987) Human resource management and industrial relations. *Journal of Management Studies*, 24(5), 503–21.

*Guest, D.E. and Peccei, R. (2001) Partnership at work: mutuality and the balance of advantage. *British Journal of Industrial Relations*, 39(2), 207–36.

Guthrie, J.P. (2000) Alternative pay practices and employee turnover: an organization economics perspective. *Group & Organization Management*, 25(4), 419–39.

Guthrie, J.P. (2001) High-involvement work practices, turnover, and productivity: evidence from New Zealand. *Academy of Management Journal*, 44(1), 180–92.

Guy, F. (2003) High-involvement work practices and employee bargaining power. *Employee Relations*, 25(5), 453–69.

Hackman, J.R. and Lawler, E.E. (1971) Employee reactions to job characteristics. *Journal of Applied Psychology*, 55(3), 259–86.

Hackman, J.R. and Oldham, G.R. (1976. Motivation through the design of work: a test of a theory. *Organizational Behavior and Human Performance*, 16(2), 250–79.

Hackman, J.R. and Oldham, G.R. (1980) *Work Redesign*. Reading, MA: Addison-Wesley.

Halbesleben, J.R.B. (2006). Sources of social support and burnout: A meta-amnlytic test of the conservation of resources model. *Journal of applied Psychology*, 91, 1134–1145.

Hall, L. and Torrington, D. (1998) Letting go or holding on – the devolution of operational personnel activities. *Human Resource Management Journal*, 8(1), 41–55.

Hall, P. and Soskice, D. (2001) An introduction to varieties of capitalism. In P. Hall and D. Soskice (eds) *Varieties of Capitalism: The Institutional Foundations of Comparative Advantage*. Oxford, UK: Oxford University Press.

Hambrick, D.C. (2007) The field of management's devotion to theory: too much of a good thing? *Academy of Management Journal*, 50(6), 1346–52.

Hambrick, D.C. and Mason, P.A. (1984) Upper echelons: the organization as a reflection of its top managers. *Academy of Management Review*, 9(2), 193–206.

Hanges, P.J., Lord, R.G. and Dickson, M.W. (2000) An information-processing perspective on leadership and culture: a case for connectionist architecture. *Applied Psychology: An International Review*, 49(1), 133–61.

Harney, B. and Dundon, T. (2006) Capturing complexity: developing an integrated approach to analysing HRM in SMEs. *Human Resource Management Journal*, 16(1), 48–73.

Harris, C.M., McMahan, G.C. and Wright, P.M. (2009) Strategic human resource management 2.0: relationships among human capital, social capital, behaviors, and performance. Presented at the Academy of Management Conference, Chicago, IL.

Harris, L. (2001) Rewarding employee performance: line managers' values, beliefs and perspectives. *International Journal of Human Resource Management*, 12(7), 1182–92.

Harris, L., Doughty, D. and Kirk, S. (2002) The devolution of HR responsibilities – perspectives from the UK's public sector. *Journal of European Industrial Training*, 26(5), 218–29.

Harter, J.K., Schmidt, F.L. and Hayes, T. (2002) Business-unit-level relationship between employee satisfaction, employee engagement, and business outcomes: a meta-analysis. *Journal of Applied Psychology*, 87(2), 268–79.

Harzing, A.W. (2001) Who's in charge? An empirical study of executive staffing practices in foreign subsidiaries. *Human Resource Management*, 40(2), 139–58.

Hatch, N.W. and Dyer, J.H. (2004) Human capital and learning as a source of sustainable competitive advantage. *Strategic Management Journal*, 25, 1122–78.

Hatfield, E., Cacioppo, J.T. & Rapson, R.L. (1994). *Emotional contagion*. Cambridge: Cambridge University Press.

Hausman, J.A. (1978) Specification tests in econometrics. *Econometrica*, 46(6), 1251–71.

*Hayton, J.C. (2003) Strategic human capital management in SMEs: an empirical study of entrepreneurial performance. *Human Resource Management*, 42(4), 375–91.

Heckman, J.J. (1979) Sample selection bias as a specification error. *Econometrica*, 47(1), 53–61.

Heinsman, D.T. and Shadish, W.R. (1996) Assignment methods in experimentation: when do nonrandomized experiments approximate answers from randomized experiments? *Psychological Methods*, 1(2), 154–69.

Helfat, C.E. and Peteraf, M.A. (2003) The dynamic resource-based view: capability lifecycles. *Strategic Management Journal*, 24(10), 997–1010.

Hellriegel, D. and Slocum, J.W. (1974) Organizational climate: measures, research and contigencies. *Academy of Management Journal*, 17(2), 255–80.

Hesketh, A. and Fleetwood, A. (2006) Beyond measuring the human resource management–organisational performance link: a critical realist meta-theory. *Organization*, 13(5), 677–700.

Hill, G.W. (1982) Group versus individual performance: are N + 1 heads better than one? *Psychological Bulletin*, 91(3), 517–39.

Hitt, M.A., Bierman, L., Shimizu, K. and Kochhar, R. (2001) Direct and indirect effects of human capital on strategy and performance in professional service firms: a resource-based perspective. *Academy of Management Journal*, 44(1), 13–28.

Hitt, M.A., Bierman, L., Uhlenbruck, K. and Shimiz, K. (2006) The importance of resources in the internationalization of professional service firms: the good, the bad, and the ugly. *Academy of Management Journal*, 49(6), 1137–57.

Hitt, M.A. and Ireland, R.D. (1985) Corporate distinctive competence, strategy, industry, and performance. *Strategic Management Journal*, 6(3), 273–93.

Hobfoll, S.E. (1989). Conservation of resources: A new attempt at conceptualizing stress. *American Psychologist*, 44, 513–524.

Hobfoll, S. (2001) The influence of culture, community, and the nested-self in the stress process: advancing conservation of resources theory. *Applied Psychology: An International Review*, 50(3), 337–70.

Hobfoll, S. (2002). Social and psychological resources and adaptation. *Review of General Psychology*, 6, 307–324.

Hobfoll, S. (2011) Conservation of resource caravans and engaged settings. *Journal of Occupational and Organizational Psychology*, 84(1), 16–122.

Hobfoll, S. & Freedy, J. (1993). Conservation of resources: A general stress theory applied to burnout. In W.B. Schaufeli, C. Maslach and T. Marek (Eds.), *Professional burnout: Recent developments in theory and research*, pp. 115–129. New York: Taylor & Francis.

Hoffman, D., Griffin, M. and Gavin, M. (2000) The application of hierarchical linear modeling to organizational research: multilevel theory, research, and methods in organizations: foundations, extensions, and future directions. In K. Klein and S. Kozlowski (eds) *Multilevel Theory, Research, and Methods in Organizations*. San Francisco, CA: Jossey-Bass.

Hofstede, G. (1980) *Culture's Consequences: International Differences in Work-related Values*. London: Sage.

Holmes, S. and Gibson, B. (2001) *Definition of Small Business. Final Report*. The University of Newcastle.

Hope Hailey, V., Farndale, E. and Truss, C. (2005) The HR department's role in organizational performance. *Human Resource Management Journal*, 15(3), 49–66.

Hope Hailey, V., Gratton, L., McGovern, P., Stiles, P. and Truss, K. (1997) A chameleon function? HRM in the '90s. *Human Resource Management Journal*, 7(3), 5–18.

*Hoque, K. (1999) Human resource management and performance in the UK hotel industry. *British Journal of Industrial Relations*, 37(3), 419–43.

*Hornsby, J. and Kuratko, D. (2003) Human resource management in US small businesses: a replication and extension. *Journal of Developmental Entrepreneurship*, 8(1), 73–92.

House, R.J. (2004) *Culture, Leadership, and Organizations: The GLOBE Study of 62 Societies*. Thousand Oaks: Sage Publications.

Howell, J., Bowen, D., Dorfman, P., Kerr, S. and Podsakoff, P. (1990) Substitutes for leadership: effective alternatives to ineffective leadership. *Organizational Dynamics*, 19(1), 20–38.

Hunter, J. and Hunter, R. (1984) Validity and utility of alternative predictors of job performance. *Psychological Bulletin*, 96(1), 72–98.

Hunter, J.E. (1986) Cognitive ability, cognitive aptitudes, job knowledge, and job performance. *Journal of Vocational Behavior*, 29(3), 340–62.

Hunter, L.W. and Lafkas, J.J. (2003) Opening the box: information technology, work practices, and wages. *Industrial and Labor Relations Review*, 56(2), 224–43.

Huselid, M.A. (1995) The impact of human resource management practices on turnover, productivity, and corporate financial performance. *Academy of Management Journal*, 38(3), 635–72.

Huselid, M.A. and Becker, B.E. (1996) Methodological issues in cross-sectional and panel estimates of the human resource-firm performance link. *Industrial Relations*, 35(3), 400–22.

Huselid, M.A. and Becker, B.E. (2000) Comments on 'Measurement error in research on human resources and firm performance: how much error is there and how does it influence effect size estimates?' by Gerhart, Wright, McMahan and Snell. *Personnel Psychology*, 53(4), 835–54.

Huselid, M.A., Becker, B.E. and Beatty, R.W. (2005) *The Workforce Scorecard: Managing Human Capital to Execute Strategy*. Boston: Harvard Business Press.

Huselid, M.A., Jackson, S.E. and Schuler, R.S. (1997) Technical and strategic human resource management effectiveness as determinants of firm performance. *Academy of Management Journal*, 40(1), 171–88.

Hutchison, S., Kinney, N. and Purcell, J. (2002) Bringing policies to life: discretionary behavior and the impact on business performance. Paper presented at the Bath Conference, University of Bath School of Management, 10–11 April.

Hutchinson, S. and Purcell, J. (2010) Managing ward managers for roles in HRM in the NHS: overworked and under-resourced. *Human Resource Management Journal*, 20(4), 357–74.

Hyde, P., Harris, C., Boaden, R. and Cortvriend, P. (2009) Human relations management, expectations and healthcare: a qualitative study. *Human Relations*, 62(5), 701–25.

Ichniowski, C., Shaw, K. and Prennushi, G. (1997) The effects of human resource management practices on productivity: a study of steel finishing lines. *The American Economic Review*, 87(3), 291–313.

Isen A.M. (2000). Positive affect and decision-making. In M. Lewis and J.M. Haviland-Jones (Eds.), *Handbook of positive emotions*, 2nd edition, pp. 417–435. New York: Guilford.

Isen, A.M., Daubman. K.A. & Novicki, G.P. (1987). Positive affect facilitates creative problem solving. *Journal of Personality and Social Psychology*, 52, 1122–1131.

Jackson, S. and Schuler, R. (1995) Understanding human resource management in the context of organizations and their environments. *Annual Review of Psychology*, 46, 237–64.

James, L.R., Choi, C.C., Ko, C.H.E., McNeil, P.K., Minton, M.K., Wright, M.A. and Kim, K. (2008) Organizational psychological climate: a review of theory and research. *European Journal of Work and Organizational Psychology*, 17(1), 5–32.

James, L.R., Joyce, W.F. and Slocum, J.W. (1988) Comment: organizations do not cognize. *Academy of Management Review*, 13(1), 129–32.

Johnson, M., Christensen, C. and Kagermann, H. (2008) Reinventing your business model. *Harvard Business Review*, December, 59–68.

Jones, D., Kalmi, P. and Kauhanen, A. (2010) How does employee involvement stack up? The effects of human resource management policies on performance in a retail firm. *Industrial Relations*, 49(1), 1–21.

Jöreskog, K.G. and Sörbom, D. (2002) *LISREL 8.52*. Chicago: Scientific Software.

Judge, A.J., Thoreson, T.J., Bono, J.E. and Patton, G.K. (2001) The job satisfaction-job performance relationship: a qualitative and quantitative review. *Psychological Bulletin*, 127 (3), 376–407.

Judge, T.A., Cable, D.M., Boudreau, J.W. and Bretz, R.D. (1995) An empirical investigation of the predictors of executive career success. *Personnel Psychology*, 48(3), 485–519.

Judge, T.A., Klinger, R.L. and Simon, L.S. (2010) Time is on my side: time, general mental ability, human capital, and extrinsic career success. *Journal of Applied Psychology*, 97(1), 92–107.

Kalleberg, A.L. and van Buren, M.E. (1996) Is bigger better? Explaining the relationship between organization size and job rewards. *American Sociological Review*, 61(1), 47–66.

*Kaman, V., McCarthy, A.M., Gulbro, R.D. and Tucker, M.L. (2001) Bureaucratic and high commitment human resource practices in small service firms. *Human Resource Planning*, 24(1), 33–44.

Kanter, R. (1983) *The Change Masters*. New York, NY: Allen & Unwin.

Karasek, R. and Theorell, T. (1990) *Healthy Work: Stress, Productivity and the Reconstruction of Working Life*. New York: Basic Books.

Karasek, R.A. (1979) Job demands, job decision latitude, and mental strain: implications for job redesign. *Administrative Science Quarterly*, 24(2), 285–308.

*Katou, A. and Budhwar, P.S. (2006) Human resource management systems and organizational performance: a test of a mediating model in the Greek manufacturing context. *International Journal of Human Resource Management*, 17(7), 1223–53.

Katz, J., Aldrich, H., Welbourne, T. and Williams, P. (2000) Guest editor's comments. Special issue on human resource management and the SME: toward a new synthesis. *Entrepreneurship Theory and Practice*, 25(1), 7–10.

Katz, J. and Darbishire, O. (2000) *Converging Divergences: Worldwide Changes in Employment Systems*. Ithaca: Cornell University Press.

Kaufman, B. (1993) *The Origins and Evolution of the Field of Industrial Relations in the United States*. Ithaca: ILR Press.

Kaufman, B. (2010) SHRM theory in the post-Huselid era: why it is fundamentally misspecified. *Industrial Relations*, 49(2), 286–313.

Kaufman, B.E. (2004) What unions do: insights from economic theory. *Journal of Labor Research*, 25(3), 351–82.

Keegan, A. and Boselie, P. (2006). The lack of impact of dissensus inspired analysis on developments in the field of human resource management. *Journal of Management Studies*, 43, 1491–511.

Kehoe, R. and Collins, C. (2008) Exploration and exploitation business strategies and the contingent fit of alternative HR systems. *Research in Personnel and Human Resources Management*, 27, 149–76.

Kehoe, R.R. and Wright, P.M. (2010) The impact of high performance human resource practices on employees' attitudes and behaviors. *Journal of Management*, published online before print, 8 April.

Kehoe, R.R. & Wright, P.M. (2010). The impact of high performance human resource practices on employees' attitudes and behaviours. *Journal of Management*.

Keenoy, T. (1990) HRM: A case of the wolf in sheep's clothing? *Personnel Review*, 19(2), 3–9.

Keenoy, T. (1997). HRMism and the language of re-presenattion. *Journal of Management Studies*, 34, 825–841.

Keenoy, T. and Schwan, R., (1990) Review article human resource management: rhetoric, reality and contradiction. *The International Journal of Human Resource Management*, 1(3), 363–84.

Kelley, M. (2000) The participatory bureaucracy: a structural explanation for the effects of group-based employee participation programs on productivity in the machined products sector. In C. Ichniowski, D. Levine, C. Olson and G. Strauss (eds) *The American Workplace: Skills, Compensation and Employee Involvement*. Cambridge, UK: Cambridge University Press.

Kelley, M. and Harrison, B. (1992) Unions, technology, and labor management cooperation. In L. Mishel and Voos, P. (eds) *Unions and Economic Competitiveness* (pp. 247–86). Armonk, N.Y.: M.E. Sharpe.

Kepes, S. and Delery, J. (2007) HR systems and the problem of internal fit. In P. Boxall, J. Purcell and P. Wright (eds) *The Oxford Handbook of Human Resource Management*. Oxford, UK: Oxford University Press.

Kerlinger F. (1973) *Foundations of Behavioral Research* (2nd edn). New York: Holt, Rinehart and Winston, Inc.

*Kerr, G., Way, S.A. and Thacker, J. (2007) Performance, HR practices and the HR manager in small entrepreneurial firms. *Journal of Small Business and Entrepreneurship*, 20(1), 55–68.

Kersley, B., Alpin, C., Forth, J., Bryson, A., Bewley, H., Dix, G. and Oxenholme, S. (2006) *Inside the Workplace: Findings from the 2004 Workplace Employment Relations Survey*. London, UK: Routledge.

Khilji, S.E. and Wang, X. (2006) 'Intended' and 'implemented' HRM: the missing linchpin in strategic human resource management research. *International Journal of Human Resource Management*, 17(7), 1171–89.

Kirk, R.E. (1996) Practical significance: a concept whose time has come. *Educational and Psychological Measurement*, 56(5), 746–59.

Kirkpatrick, D.L. (1959/1960) Techniques for evaluating training programs. *Journal of the American Society of Training Directors*, in four parts: 13(11), 3–9, 13(12), 21–6, 14(1), 13–18 and 14(2), 28–32.

Klaas, B., McClendon, J. and Gainey, T. (2000) Managing HR in the small and medium enterprise: the impact of professional employer organizations. *Entrepreneurship Theory & Practice*, 25(1), 107–24.

Kmenta, J. (1971) *Elements of Econometrics*. New York: MacMillan.

Kochan, T. (2007) Social legitimacy of the HR profession: a US perspective. In P. Boxall, J. Purcell and P. Wright (eds) *The Oxford Handbook of Human Resource Management* (pp. 599–619). Oxford, UK: Oxford University Press.

Kochan, T.A. and Osterman, P. (1994) *The Mutual Gains Enterprise: Forging a Winning Partnership Among Labor, Management, and Government*. Cambridge, MA: Harvard Business School Press.

Konzelmann, S., Forrant, R. and Wilkinson, F. (2004) Work systems, corporate strategy and global markets: creative shop floors or 'a barge mentality'? *Industrial Relations Journal*, 35 (3), 216–32.

Kooij, D. (2010) Motivating older workers: a lifespan perspective on the role of perceived HR practices. Dissertation, Free University Amsterdam.

Kopelman, R.E., Brief, A.P. and Guzzo, R.A. (1990) The role of climate and culture in productivity. In Schneider, B. (ed.) *Organizational Climate and Culture*. San Francisco, CA: Jossey-Bass.

Korczynski, M. (2001) The contradictions of service work: call centre as customer-oriented bureaucracy. In A. Sturdy, I. Grugulis and H. Willmott (eds) *Customer Service: Empowerment and Entrapment*. Basingstoke: Palgrave Macmillan.

Kotey, B. and Sheridan, A. (2004) Changing HRM practices with firm growth. *Journal of Small Business and Enterprise Development*, 11(4), 474–85.

Kotha, S. and Swamidass, P. (2000) Strategy, advanced manufacturing technology and performance: evidence from US manufacturing firms. *Journal of Operations Management*, 18(3), 257–77.

Koys, D. (2001) The effects of employee satisfaction, organizational citizenship behavior, and turnover on organizational effectiveness: a unit-level, longitudinal study. *Personnel Psychology*, 54(1), 101–114.

Kozlowski, S.W.J. and Bell, B.S. (2003) Work groups and teams in organizations. In W.C. Borman, D.R. Ilgen and R.J. Klimoski (eds) *Handbook of Psychology (Vol. 12): Industrial and Organizational Psychology* (pp. 333–75). New York: John Wiley & Sons, Inc.

Kozlowski, S.W.J. and Hattrup, K. (1992) A disagreement about within-group agreement: disentangling issues of consistency versus consensus. *Journal of Applied Psychology*, 77(2), 161–7.

Kozlowski, S.W.J. and Klein, K.J. (2000) A multilevel approach to theory and research in organizations: contextual, temporal, and emergent processes. In K.J. Klein and S.W.J. Kozlowski (eds) *Multilevel Theory, Research, and Methods in Organizations: Foundations, Extensions, and New Directions* (pp. 3–90). San Francisco, CA: Jossey-Bass.

Kristof-Brown, A.L., Zimmerman, R.D. and Johnson, E.C. (2005) Consequences of individuals' fit at work: a meta-analysis of person-job, person-organization, person-group, and person-supervisor fit. *Personnel Psychology*, 58(2), 281–342.

Kroon, B. and Jaap Paauwe, J. (2013) Structuration of precarious employment systems in economically constrained firms: The case of Dutch Agriculture. In: *Human Resource Management Journal (forthcoming)*.

Kroon, B., van de Voorde, F.C. and van Veldhoven, M.J.P.M. (2009) Cross-level effects of high performance work practices: two counteracting mediating mechanisms compared. *Personnel Review*, 38(5), 509–25.

Kulik, C.T. and Bainbridge, H.T. (2006) HR and the line: the distribution of HR activities in Australian organizations. *Asia Pacific Journal of Human Resources*, 44(4), 240–56.

Landsbergis, P Cahill, J. and Schnall, P. (1999) The impact of lean production and related new systems of work organization on worker health. *Journal of Occupational Health Psychology*, 4(2), 108–30.

Larsen, H.H. and Brewster, C. (2003) Line management responsibility for HRM: what is happening in Europe? *Employee Relations*, 25(3), 228–44.

Larson, R. and Finkelstein, S. (1999) Integrating strategic, organizational, and human resource perspectives on mergers and acquisitions: a case survey of synergy realization. *Organization Science*, 10(1), 1–26.

Lawler, E. (1986) *High Involvement Management*. San Francisco: Jossey-Bass.

Lawler, E. and Mohrmann, S. (2003) *Creating a Strategic Human Resources Organization: An Assessment of Trends and New Directions*. Stanford, CA: Stanford University Press.

Leana, C. and van Buren, H. (1999) Organizational social capital and employment practices. *Academy of Management Review*, 24(3), 538–55.

Legge, K. (1978) *Power, Innovation and Problem-Solving in Personnel Management*. London, UK: McGraw-Hill.

Legge, K. (1995) *Human Resource Management: Rhetorics and Realities*. Basingstoke, London: Palgrave MacMillan.

Legge, K. (2000) Silver bullet or spent round? Assessing the meaning of the 'high commitment management'/performance relationship. In J. Storey (ed.) *Human Resource Management: A Critical Text* (2nd edn). London: Thompson Learning.

Legge, K. (2005). Human Resource Management: Rhetoric and Realities, Anniversary Edition, London: Palgrave.

Lengnick-Hall C. and Lengnick-Hall, M. (1988) Strategic human resources management: a review of the literature and a proposed typology. *Academy of Management Review*, 13(3), 454–70.

Lepak, D., Liao, H., Chung, Y. and Harden, E. (2006) A conceptual review of human resource management systems in strategic human resource management research. *Research in Personnel and Human Resources Management*, 25, 217–71.

Lepak, D. and Snell, S. (2002) Examining the human resource architecture: the relationships among human capital, employment and resource configurations. *Journal of Management*, 28(4), 517–43.

Lepak, D.P., Maronne, J.A. and Takeuchi, R. (2004) The relativity of HR systems: conceptualizing the impact of desired employee contributions and HR philosophy. *International Journal of Technology Management*, 27(6/7), 639–55.

Lepak, D.P. and Snell, S.A. (1999) The human resource architecture: toward a theory of human capital allocation and development. *Academy of Management Review*, 24(1), 31–48.

Lewin, K. (1951) *Field Theory in Social Science*. New York, NY: Harper & Row.

Liao, H., Toya, K., Lepak, D. and Hong, Y. (2009) Do they see eye to eye? Management and employee perspectives of high-performance work systems and influence processes on service quality. *Journal of Applied Psychology*, 94(2), 371–91.

Lindell, M.K. and Whitney, D.J. (2001) Accounting for common method variance in cross-sectional research designs. *Journal of Applied Psychology*, 86(1), 114–21.

Lopez-Cabrales, A., Perez-Luno, A. and Cabrera, R.V. (2009) Knowledge as a mediator between HRM practices and innovative activity. *Human Resource Management*, 48(4), 485–503.

Lopez-Cabrales, A., Valle, R. and Herreo, I. (2006) The contribution of core employees to organizational capabilities and efficiencies. *Human Resource Management*, 45(1), 81–109.

Lowe, J. (1992) Locating the line: the front line supervisor and human resource management. In P. Blyton and P. Turnbull (eds) *Reassessing Human Resource Management* (pp. 148–68). London: Sage.

MacCallum, R.C. and Mar, C.M. (1995) Distinguishing between moderator and quadratic effects in multiple regression. *Psychological Bulletin*, 118(3), 405–21.

MacDuffie, J.P. (1995) Human resource bundles and manufacturing performance: organizational logic and flexible production systems in the world auto industry. *Industrial and Labor Relations Review*, 48(2), 197–221.

MacKinnon, D.P., Lockwood, C.M., Hoffman, J.M., West, S.G. and Sheets, V. (2002) A comparison of methods to test mediation and other intervening variable effects. *Psychological Methods*, 7(1), 83–104.

Macky, K. and Boxall, P. (2007) The relationship between high-performance work practices and employee attitudes: an investigation of additive and interaction effects. *International Journal of Human Resource Management*, 18(4), 537–67.

Macky, K. and Boxall, P. (2008) High-involvement work processes, work intensification and employee well-being: a study of New Zealand worker experiences. *Asia Pacific Journal of Human Resources*, 46(1), 38–55.

Maertz Jr., C.P., Griffeth, R.W., Campbell, N.S. and Allen, D.G. (2007) The effects of perceived organizational support and perceived supervisor support on employee turnover. *Journal of Organizational Behavior*, 28(8), 1059–75.

Maes, J., Sels, L. and Roodhooft, F. (2005) Modeling the link between management practices and financial performance: evidence from small construction companies. *Small Business Economics*, 25(1), 17–34.

March, J.G. & Simon, H.A. (1958). *Organizations*. New York: John Wiley & Sons.

Marchington, M. (2001) Employee involvement at work. In J. Storey (ed.) *Human Resource Management: A Critical Text* (2nd edn) (pp. 232–52). Padstow, UK: Thomson Learning.

Marchington, M., Carroll, M. and Boxall, P. (2003) Labour scarcity and the survival of small firms: a resource-based view of the road haulage industry. *Human Resource Management Journal*, 13(4), 5–22.

Marchington, M. and Grugulis, I. (2000) 'Best practice' human resource management: perfect opportunity or dangerous illusion? *International Journal of Human Resource Management*, 11(6), 1104–25.

Marlow, S. (2006) Human resource management in smaller firms: a contradiction in terms? *Human Resource Management Review*, 16(4), 467–77.

Martocchio, J.J. and Judge, T.A. (1997) Relationships between conscientiousness and learning in employee training: mediating influences of self-description and self-efficacy. *Journal of Applied Psychology*, 82(5), 764–73.

Maslach, C., Schaufeli, W.B. & Leiter, M.P. (2001). Job burnout. *Annual Review of Psychology*, 57, 397–422.

Maxwell, G. and Farquharson, L. (2008) Senior managers perceptions of the practice of human resource management. *Employee Relations*, 30(3), 304–22.

Mayson, S. and Barrett, R. (2006) The 'science' and 'practice' of HRM in small firms. *Human Resource Management Review*, 16(4), 447–55.

McConville, T. (2006) Devolved HRM responsibilities, middle-managers and role dissonance. *Personnel Review*, 35(6), 637–53.

McGovern, P. (1999) HRM policies and management practices. In L. Gratton, V. Hope Hailey, P. Stiles and C. Truss (eds) *Strategic Human Resource Management* (pp. 133–52). Oxford, UK: Oxford University Press.

McGovern, P., Gratton, L., Hope Hailey, V., Stiles P. and Truss, C. (1997) Human resource management on the line? *Human Resource Management Journal*, 7(4), 12–29.

McHenry, J.J., Hough, L.M., Toquam, J.L., Hanson, M. and Ashworth, S. (1990) Project A validity results: the relationship between predictor and criterion domains. *Personnel Psychology*, 43(2), 335–54.

McMahan, G.C., Virick, M. and Wright, P.M. (1999) Alternative theoretical perspectives for strategic human resource management revisited: progress, problems, and prospects. In P. Wright, L. Dyer, J. Boudreau and Milkovich, G. (eds) *Research in Personnel and Human Resource Management* (pp. 99–122). Greenwich, CT: JAI Press.

Messersmith, J., Patel, P. and Lepak, D. (2011) Unlocking the black box: exploring the link between high-performance work systems and performance. *Journal of Applied Psychology*, 99(6), 1105–18.

Meyer, J.P., Stanley, D.J., Herscovitch, L., & Topolnytsky, L. (2002). Affective, continuance, and normative commitment to the organization: A meta-analysis of antecedents, correlates, and consequences. *Journal of Vocational Behavior*, 61, 20–52.

Meyer, J.P. and Allen, N.J. (1997) *Commitment in the Workplace*. London: Sage.

Miles, R.E. and Snow, C.C. (1978) *Organizational Strategy, Structure, and Process*. New York: McGraw-Hill.

Miles, R.E. and Snow, C.C. (1984) Fit, failure and the hall of fame. *California Management Review*, 26, 10–28.

Miles, R.E. and Snow, C.C. (1994) *Fit, Failure, and the Hall of Fame: How Companies Succeed or Fail*. New York: Free Press.

Mintzberg, H. (1978) Patterns in strategy formation. *Management Science*, 24(9), 934–48.

Mintzberg, H. (1995). *Structure in fives: Designing effective organizations*. Englewood Cliffs, N.J.: Prentice-Hall.

Mintzberg, H., Ahlstrand, B. W. and Lampel, J. B. (2008) *Strategy Safari: The Complete Guide Through the Wilds of Strategic Management*. London: Financial Times/Prentice Hall.

Mirvis, P.H. (1997) Human resource management: leaders, laggards, and followers. *Academy of Management Executive*, 11(2), 43–56.

Morgan, S.J. (2009) *The Human Side of Outsourcing: Psychological Theory and Management Practice*. Chichester: John Wiley & Sons, Ltd.

Mossholder, K., Richardson, H. and Settoon, R. (2011) Human resource systems and helping in organizations: a relational perspective. *Academy of Management Review*, 36(1), 33–52.

*Muse, L., Rutherford, M., Oswald, S. and Raymond, J. (2005) Commitment to employees: does it help or hinder small business performance? *Small Business Economics*, 24(2), 97–111.

Nadler, D.A. and Tushman, M.L. (1980) A model for diagnosing organizational behavior. *Organizational Dynamics*, 9(2), 35–51.

Neal, A., Patterson, M.A. and West, M.G. (2005) Do organizational climate and competitive strategy moderate the relationship between human resource management and productivity? *Journal of Management*, 31(4), 492–512.

Nehles, A.C., van Riemsdijk, M.J., Kok, I. and Looise, J.C. (2006) Implementing human resource management successfully: the role of first-line managers. *Management Review*, 17 (3), 256–73.

Neuman, G.A. and Wright, J. (1999) Team effectiveness: beyond skills and cognitive ability. *Journal of Applied Psychology*, 84(3), 376–89.

Ng, T.W., Eby, L.T., Sorensen, K.L. and Feldman, D.C. (2005) Predictors of objective and subjective career success: a meta-analysis. *Personnel Psychology*, 58(2), 367–408.

*Nguyen, T.V. and Bryant, S.E. (2004) A study of the formality of human resource management practices in small and medium-size enterprises in Vietnam. *International Small Business Journal*, 22(6), 595–618.

*Nishii, L.H., Lepak, D.P. and Schneider, B. (2008) Employee attributions of the 'why' of HR practices: their effects on employee attitudes and behaviors, and customer satisfaction. *Personnel Psychology*, 61(3), 503–45.

Nishii, L. and Wright, P. (2008) Variability within organizations: implications for strategic human resources management. In D.B. Smith (ed.) *The People Make the Place*. Mahwah, N. J.: Erlbaum.

Nunnaly, J. and Bernstein, I. (1994) *Psychometric Theory*. New York, NY: McGraw-Hill.

O'Reilly, C.A. and Chatman, J.A. (1994) Working smarter and harder: a longitudinal study of managerial success. *Administrative Science Quarterly*, 39(4), 603–27.

O'Reilly, C.A., Chatman, J.A. and Caldwell, M.M. (1991) People and organizational culture: a Q-sort approach to assessing person-organization fit. *Academy of Management Journal*, 34 (3), 487–516.

Oldham, G.R. (1976) Job characteristics and internal motivation: the moderating effect of interpersonal and individual variables. *Human Relations*, 29(6), 559–69.

Ones, D., Viswesvaran, C. and Schmidt, F. (1993) Comprehensive meta-analysis of integrity test validities: findings and implications for personnel selection and theories of job performance. *Journal of Applied Psychology*, 78(4), 679–703.

Organ, D.W. (1988) *Organizational Citizenship Behavior: The Good Soldier Syndrome*. Lexington, MA: Lexington Books.

Organ, D.W., Podsakoff, P.M. and MacKenzie, S.B. (2006) *Organizational Citizenship Behavior: Its Nature, Antecedents and Consequences*. Beverly Hills, CA: Sage.

*Orlitzky, M. and Frenkel, S. (2005) Alternative pathways to high-performance workplaces. *International Journal of Human Resource Management*, 16(8), 1325–48.

Osterman, P. (1987) Choice of employment systems in internal labor markets. *Industrial Relations*, 26(1), 48–63.

Osterman, P. (1994) How common is workplace transformation and who adopts it? *Industrial and Labor Relations Review*, 47(2), 173–88.

Ostroff, C. (1993) Comparing correlations based on individual and aggregated data. *Journal of Applied Psychology*, 78(4), 569–82.

Ostroff, C. and Bowen, D.E. (2000) Moving HR to a higher level: HR practices and organizational effectiveness. In K. Klein and S. Kozlowski (eds) *Multilevel Theory, Research, and Methods in Organizations* (pp. 211–66). San Francisco, CA: Jossey-Bass.

Ostroff, C., Kinicki, A.J. and Clark, M.A. (2002) Substantive and operational issues of response bias across levels of analysis: an example of climate-satisfaction relationships. *Journal of Applied Psychology*, 87(2), 355–68.

Paauwe, J. (2004) *HRM and Performance: Achieving Long-term Viability*. Oxford, UK: Oxford University Press.

Paauwe, J. (2009) HRM and performance: achievements, methodological issues and prospects. *Journal of Management Studies, 46* (1), 129–42.

Paauwe, J. and Boselie, J.P. (2003) Challenging 'strategic HRM' and the relevance of institutional setting. *Human Resource Management Journal*, 13(3), 56–70.

Paauwe, J. and Boselie, P. (2005a) Best practices . . . in spite of performance: just a matter of imitation? *International Journal of Human Resource Management*, 16(6), 987–1003.

Paauwe, J. and Boselie, P. (2005b) HRM and performance: what next? *Human Resource Management Journal*, 15(5), 68–83.

Paauwe, J. and Boselie, J.P. (2007) Human resource management and societal embeddedness. In P. Boxall, J. Purcell and P. Wright (eds) *The Oxford Handbook of Human Resource Management*. Oxford, UK: Oxford University Press.

Paauwe, J. and Farndale, E. (2008) De Nederlandse HR-functie voor het voetlicht: een vergelijking tussen Nederlandse en Americkaanse/Britse HR-rollen. *Maandblad voor Accountancy en Bedrijfseconomie*, 82(7/8), 345–56.

Paauwe, J. and Richardson, R. (1997) Introduction to special issue on HRM and performance. *International Journal of Human Resource Management*, 8(3), 257–62.

Panayotopoulou, L., Bourantas, D. and Papalexandris, N. (2003) Strategic human resource management and its effects on firm performance: an implementation of the competing values framework. *The International Journal of Human Resource Management*, 14(4), 680–99.

Parent-Thirion, A., Fernádez Macías, E., Hurley, J. and Vermeylen, G. (2007) *Fourth European Working Conditions Survey*. Luxembourg: Office for Official Publication of the European Communities.

*Park, H.J., Mitsuhashi, H., Fey, C.F. and Bjorkman, I. (2003) The effect of human resource management practices on Japanese MNC subsidiary performance: a partial mediating model. *International Journal of Human Resource Management*, 14(8), 1391–406.

Parker, C.P., Baltes, B.B., Young, S.A., Huff, J.W., Altmann, R.A. and Lacost, H.A. (2003) Relationships between psychological climate perceptions and work outcomes: a meta-analytic review. *Journal of Organizational Behavior*, 24(4), 389–416.

*Patel, P.C. and Cardon, M.S. (2010) Adopting HRM practices and their effectiveness in small firms facing product-market competition. *Human Resource Management*, 49(2), 265–90.

Patterson, M.G., West, M.A., Shackleton, V.J., Dawson, J.F., Lawthom, R., Maitlis S., Robinson, D.L. and Wallace, A.M. (2005) Validating the organisational climate measure: links to managerial practices, productivity and innovation. *Journal of Organisational Behavior*, 26(4), 379–408.

*Paul, A.K. and Anantharaman, R.N. (2003) Impact of people management practices on organizational performance: analysis of a causal model. *International Journal of Human Resource Management*, 14, 1246–66.

Peccei, R. (2004) *Human Resource Management and the Search for the Happy Workplace*. Rotterdam: Erasmus Research Institute of Management (ERIM).

Peccei, R. and Rosenthal, P. (2001) Delivering customer-oriented behaviour through empowerment: an empirical test of HRM assumptions. *Journal of Management Studies*, 38(6), 831–57.

Peccei, R., van de Voorde, K. and van Veldhoven, M. (2012) HRM, well-being and performance: a theoretical and empirical review. In J. Paauwe, D. Guest and P. Wright (eds) *HRM and Performance: What's Next*. Oxford, UK: Blackwell Publishing Ltd.

Perry-Smith, J.Y. and Blum, T.C. (2000) Work-family human resource bundles and perceived organizational performance. *Academy of Management Journal*, 43(6), 1107–17.

Peters, T. and Waterman, R. (1982) *In Search of Excellence*, New York: Harper and Row.

Pfeffer, J. (1994) *Competitive Advantage through People*. Boston: Harvard Business School Press.

Pfeffer, J. (1998) *The Human Equation: Building Profits by Putting People First*. Boston: Harvard Business School Press.

Pfeffer, J. (2007) A modest proposal: how we might change the process and product of managerial research. *Academy of Management Journal*, 50(6), 1334–45.

Pfeffer, J. and Sutton, R.I. (2006) *Hard Facts, Dangerous Half-truths, and Total Nonsense: Profiting from Evidence-based Management*. Boston: Harvard Business School Publishing.

Phillips, J.M. and Gully, S.M. (1997) Role of goal orientation, ability, need for achievement, and locus of control in the self-efficacy and goal-setting process. *Journal of Applied Psychology*, 82(5), 792–802.

Pierce, J.L., Dunham, R.B. and Blackburn, R.S. (1979) Social systems structure, job design, and growth need strength: a test of a congruency model. *Academy of Management Journal*, 22(2), 223–40.

Pil, F.K. and Leana, C. (2009) Applying organizational research to public school reform: the effects of teacher human and social capital on student performance. *Academy of Management Journal*, 52(6), 1101–24.

Ployhart, R., Van Iddekinge, C. and MacKenzie, W. (2011) Acquiring and developing human capital in service contexts: the interconnectedness of human capital resources. *Academy of Management Journal*, 54, 353–68.

Ployhart, R.E. and Moliterno, T.P. (2011) Emergence of the human capital resource: a multilevel model. *Academy of Management Review*, 36(1), 127–50.

Ployhart, R.E., Weekley, J.A. and Baughman, K. (2006) The structure and function of human capital emergence: a multilevel examination of the attraction-selection-attrition model. *Academy of Management Journal*, 49(4), 661–77.

Ployhart, R.E., Weekley, J.A. and Ramsey, J. (2009) The consequences of human resource stocks and flows: a longitudinal examination of unit service orientation and unit effectiveness. *Academy of Management Journal*, 52, 996–1015.

Porter, M.E. (1985) *Competitive Advantage: Creating and Sustaining Superior Performance*. New York: Free Press.

Pugh, S.D (2001). Service with a smile: Emotional contagion in the service encounter. *Academy of Management Journal*, 44, 1018–1027.

Purcell, J. (1999) Best practice and best fit: chimera or cul-de-sac? *Human Resource Management Journal*, 9(3), 26–41.

Purcell, J. (2003) *Older and Wiser: Reflections on the Search for the HRM Holy Grail*. Keynote address for 3rd Dutch HRM Network Conference, University of Twente, Enschede, The Netherlands.

Purcell, J. and Hutchinson, S. (2007) Front-line managers as agents in the HRM–performance causal chain: theory, analysis and evidence. *Human Resource Management Journal*, 17(1), 3–20.

Purcell, J. and Kinnie, N. (2007) HRM and business performance. In P. Boxall, J. Purcell and P. Wright (eds) *The Oxford Handbook of Human Resource Management*. New York: Oxford University Press.

Purcell, J., Kinnie, N., Hutchinson, S., Swart, J. and Rayton, B. (2003) *Understanding the People and Performance Link: Unlocking the Black Box*. London: CIPD.

Quinn, R.E. and Rohrbaugh, J. (1983) A spatial model of effectiveness criteria: toward a competing values approach to organizational analysis. *Management Science*, 29(3), 363–77.

Ramamoorthy, N. and Carroll, S.J. (1998) Individualism/collectivism orientations and reactions toward alternative human resource management practices. *Human Relations*, 51(5), 571–88.

Ramsay, H., Scholarios, D. and Harley, B. (2000) Employees and high-performance work systems: testing inside the black box. *British Journal of Labour Relations*, 38(4), 501–31.

Ratnatunga, J. and Romano, C. (1997) A 'citation classics' analysis of articles in contemporary small enterprise research. *Journal of Business Venturing*, 12(3), 197–212.

Rauch, A., Frese, M. and Utsch, A. (2005) Effects of human capital and long-term human resources development and utilization on employment growth of small-scale businesses: a causal analysis. *Entrepreneurship Theory and Practice*, 29(6), 681–98.

Raudenbush, S.W. and Bryk, A.S. (2002) *Hierarchical Linear Models*. Thousand Oaks, CA: Sage.

Ree, M. J., & Earles, J. A. (1991). Predicting training success: Not much more than g. *Personnel Psychology, 44*, 321-332.

Ree, M.J., Earles, J.A. and Teachout, M.S. (1994) Predicting job performance: not much more than g. *Journal of Applied Psychology*, 70, 518–24.

Renwick, D. (2000) HR–line work relations: a review, pilot case and research agenda. *Employee Relations*, 22(2), 179–205.

Renwick, D. (2003) Line manager involvement in HRM: an inside view. *Employee Relations*, 25(3), 262–80.

Richard, O. and Johnson, N. (2001) Strategic human resource management effectiveness and firm performance. *International Journal of Human Resource Management*, 12(2), 299–310.

Richard, O. and Johnson, N. (2004) High performance work practices and human resource management effectiveness: substitutes of complements? *Journal of Business Strategies*, 21 (2), 133–48.

*Riordan, C.M., Vandenberg, J. and Richardson, H.A. (2005) Employee involvement climate and organizational effectiveness. *Human Resource Management*, 44(4), 471–88.

Rogers, E.W. and Wright, P.M. (1998) Measuring organizational performance in strategic human resource management: problem, prospects, and performance information markets. *Human ResourceManagement Review*, 8(3), 311–31.

Rosenbaum, P. and Rubin, D. (1983) The central role of the propensity score in observational studies for causal effects. *Biometrika*, 70(1), 41–55.

Rosenthal, P. (2004) Management control as an employee resource: the case of front-line service workers. *Journal of Management Studies*, 41(4), 601–22.

Rosnow, R.L. and Rosenthal, R. (1989) Statistical procedures and the justification of knowledge in psychological science. *American Psychologist*, 44(10), 1276–84.

Roth, K. and O'Donnell, S. (1996) Foreign subsidiary compensation strategy: an agency theory perspective. *Academy of Management Journal*, 39(3), 678–703.

Rousseau, D. and Barends, D. (2011) Becoming an evidence-based HR practitioner. *Human Resource Management Journal*, 21(3), 221–35.

Rousseau, D.M. (1995) *Psychological Contracts in Organizations: Understanding Written and Unwritten Agreements*. Thousand Oaks, CA: Sage Publications.

Rousseau, D.M. (2001) Schema, promise and mutuality: the building blocks of the psychological contract. *Journal of Occupational and Organizational Psychology*, 74(4), 511–41.

Rousseau, D.M. (2006) Is there such a thing as evidence-based management? *Academy of Management Review*, 31(2), 256–69.

*Rowden, R. (2002) High performance and human resource characteristics of successful small manufacturing and processing companies. *Leadership & Organization Development Journal*, 23(2), 79–83.

Rush, M.C., Thomas, J.C. and Lord, R.G. (1977) Implicit leadership theory: a potential threat to the internal validity of leader behavior questionnaires. *Organizational Behavior and Human Performance*, 20(1), 93–110.

Rutherford, M.W., Butler, P.F. and McMullen, P.R. (2003) Human resource management problems over the life cycle of small to medium-sized firms. *Human Resource Management*, 42(4), 321–36.

Ryan, A.M., Schmit, M.J. and Johnson, R. (1996) Attitudes and effectiveness: examining relations at an organizational level. *Personnel Psychology*, 49(4), 853–82.

Rynes, S., Giluk, T. and Brown, K. (2007) The very separate worlds of academic and practitioner periodicals in human resource management: implications for evidence-based management. *Academy of Management Journal*, 50(5), 987–1008.

Salancik, G. (1977) Commitment and control of organizational behaviour and belief. In B. Staw and G. Salancik (eds) *New Directions in Organizational Behavior* (pp.1–54). Chicago, Ill: St Clair Press.

Salancik, G. and Pfeffer, J. (1977) An examination of need-satisfaction theories of job attitudes. *Administrative Science Quarterly*, 22(3), 521–40.

Salanova, M., Schaufeli, W.B., Xanthopoulou, D. and Bakker, A.B. (2010) Gain spirals of resources and work engagement. In A.B. Bakker and M.P. Leiter (eds) *Work Engagement: A Handbook of Essential Theory and Research*. New York: Psychology Press.

Sapienza, H.J., Smith, K.G. and Gannon, M.J. (1988) Using subjective evaluations of organizational performance in small business research. *American Journal of Small Business*, 12(3), 45–53.

Schalk, M.J.D., van Veldhoven, M., de Lange, A.H., de Witte, H., Kraus, K. Stamov-Roβnagel C. et al. (2010) Moving European research on work and ageing forward: overview and agenda. *European Journal of Work and Organizational Psychology*, 19(1), 76–101.

Schaufeli, W.B. and Bakker, A.B. (2004) Job demands, job resources, and their relationship with burnout and engagement: a multi-sample study. *Journal of Organizational Behavior*, 25(3), 293–315.

Schein, E. (1986) *Organizational Culture and Leadership* (2nd edn). San Francisco, CA: Jossey Bass.

*Schmelter, R., Mauer, R., Börsch, C. and Brettel, M. (2010) Boosting corporate entrepreneurship through HRM practices: evidence from German SMEs. *Human Resource Management*, 49(4), 715–41.

Schmidt, F.L. (1996) Statistical significance testing and cumulative knowledge in psychology: implications for training of researchers. *Psychological Methods*, 1(2), 115–29.

Schneider, B. (1980) The service organization: climate is crucial. *Organizational Dynamics*, 9 (2), 52–65.

Schneider, B. (1987) The people make the place. *Personnel Psychology*, 40, 437–54.

Schneider, B., Hanges, P.J., Smith, B. and Salvaggio, A.N. (2003) Which comes first: employee attitudes or organizational financial and market performance. *Journal of Applied Psychology*, 88(5), 836–51.

Schneider, B., Salvaggio, A.N. and Subirats, M. (2002) Climate strength: a new direction for climate research. *Journal of Applied Psychology*, 87(2), 220–9.

Schneider, B., White, S.S. and Paul, M.C. (1998) Linking service climate and customers perceptions of service quality: test of a causal model. *Journal of Applied Psychology*, 83(2), 150–63.

Schuler, S., and Jackson, S. (1987) Linking competitive strategies with human resource management practices. *Academy of Management Executive*, 1(3), 207–19.

Schwab, D.P. (1980) Construct validity in organizational behavior. *Research in Organizational Behavior*, 2, 3–43.

Schwarz, N. (1996) *Cognition and Communication: Judgmental Biases, Research Methods and the Logic of Conversation*. Hillsdale, NJ: Erlbaum.

Schwarz, N., Groves, R.M. and Schuman, H. (1999) *Survey Methods*. Ann Arbor, MI: Institute for Social Research.

Schwarz, N. and Hippler, H.J. (1991) Response alternatives: the impact of their choice and ordering. In P. Biemer, R. Groves, N. Mathiowetz and S. Sudman (eds) *Measurement Errors in Surveys*. Chichester: John Wiley & Sons, Ltd.

Scotti, D., Harmon, J., Behnson, S. J. and Messina. D. J. (2007) Links among high-performance work environment, service quality, and customer. *Journal of Healtcare Management*, 57(2).

Seidler, J. (1974) On using informants: a technique for collecting quantitative data and controlling measurement error in organization analysis. *American Sociological Review*, 39 (6), 816–31.

*Sels, L., De Winne, S., Maes, J., Faems, D., Delmotte, J. and Forrier, A. (2006) Unravelling the HRM–performance link: value-creating and cost-increasing effects of small business HRM. *Journal of Management Studies*, 43(2), 319–42.

Sewell, G. and Wilkinson, B. (1992) Empowerment or emasculation: shopfloor surveillance in a total quality organisation. In P. Blyton and P. Turnbull (eds) *Reassessing Human Resource Management*. London: Sage.

Shah, R. and Ward, P. (2003) 'Lean manufacturing: context, practice bundles, and performance. *Journal of Operations Management*, 21, 129–49.

Shaw, J.B. (1990) A cognitive categorization model for the study of intercultural management. *Academy of Management Review*, 15(4), 626–45.

Shaw, J.D., Gupta, N. and Delery, J.E. (2001) Congruence between technology and compensation systems: implications for strategy implementation. *Strategic Management Journal*, 22(4), 379–86.

Short, J., Payne, G. and Ketchen, D. (2008) Research on organizational configurations: past accomplishments and future challenges. *Journal of Management*, 34(6), 1053–79.

Siebert, W. and Zubanov, N. (2009) Searching for the optimal level of employee turnover: a study of a large UK retail organization. *Academy of Management Journal*, 52(2), 294–313.

Siehl, C. and Martin, J. (1990) Organizational culture: a key to financial performance? In B. Schneider (ed.) *Organizational Climate and Culture*. San Fransisco: Jossey Bass.

Simon, H.A. (1954) Spurious correlation: a causal interpretation. *Journal of the American Statistical Association*, 49(267), 467–79.

Simon, H.A. (1979) Rational decision making in business organizations. *American Economic Review*, 69(4), 493–513.

Skinner, W. (1981) Big hat, no cattle: managing human resources. *Harvard Business Review*, 59(5), 106–14.

Snell, S. and Dean, J. (1994) Integrated manufacturing and human resource management: the moderating effects of jobs and organizational inertia. *Academy of Management Journal*, 34(4), 1109–40.

Snell, S.A. and Dean, J.W. (1992) Integrated manufacturing and human resource management: a human capital perspective. *Academy of Management Journal*, 35(3), 467–504.

Soriano, D.R., Dobón, S.R. and Tansky, J. (2010) Guest editors' note: Linking entrepreneurship and human resources in globalization. *Human Resource Management*, 49(2), 217–23.

Spector, P.E., Cooper, C.L., Sanchez, J.I., O'Driscoll, M., Sparks, K., Bernin, P. et al. (2001) Do national levels of individualism and internal locus of control relate to well-being: an ecological level international study. *Journal of Organizational Behavior*, 22(8), 815–32.

Spector, P.E., Cooper, C.L., Sanchez, J.I., O'Driscoll, M., Sparks, K., Bemin, P. et al. (2002) A 24 nation/territory study of work locus of control in relation to well-being at work: how generalizable are western findings. *Academy of Management Journal,* 45, 453–66.

Spector, P.E. and Jex, S.M. (1998) Development of four self-report measures of job stressors and strain: interpersonal conflict at work scale, organizational constraints scale, quantitative workload inventory, and physical symptoms inventory. *Journal of Occupational Health Psychology,* 3(4), 356–67.

Spreitzer, G., Sutcliffe, K., Dutton, J., Sonenshein, S. & Grant, A.M. (2005). A socially embedded model of thriving at work. *Organization Science,* 16, 537–549.

Stanton, P., Young. S., Bartram T. and Leggat, S.G. (2010) Singing the same song: translating HRM messages across management hierarchies in Australian hospitals. *The International Journal of Human Resource Management,* 20(4), 567–81.

Staw, B.M. (1996). Organizational psychology and the pursuit of the happy/productive worker. *California Management Review,* 27, 40–55.

Steers, R.M. and Spencer, D.G. (1977) The role of achievement motivation in job design. *Journal of Applied Psychology,* 62(4), 472–9.

Steffy, B. and Mauer, S. (1998) Conceptualizing and measuring the economic effectiveness of human resource activities. *Academy of Management Review,* 13(2), 271–86.

Steiner, I.D. (1972) *Group Process and Productivity.* New York: Academic Press.

Stewart, T. (1996) Taking on the last bureaucracy. *Fortune,* January, no 15, 113(1), 105–107.

Stewart, G.L. (2006) A meta-analytic review of the relationship between team design feature and team performance. *Journal of Management,* 32(1), 29–54.

Stiglitz, J. (2010) *Freefall: Free Markets and the Sinking of the Global Economy.* London: Allen Lane.

Storey, D. (2004) Exploring the link, among small firms, between management training and firm performance: a comparison between the UK and other OECD countries. *International Journal of Human Resource Management,* 15(1), 112–30.

Storey, J. (1992) *Developments in the Management of Human Resources.* Oxford, UK: Blackwell.

Subramaniam, M. and Youndt, M.A. (2005) The influence of intellectual capital on the types of innovative capabilities. *Academy of Management Journal,* 48(3), 450–63.

Subramony, M. (2009) A meta-analytic investigation of the relationship between HRM bundles and firm performance. *Human Resource Management,* 48(5), 745–68.

Sun, L., Aryee, S. and Law, K. (2007) High performance human resource practices, citizenship behavior, and organizational performance: a relational perspective. *Academy of Management Journal,* 50(3), 558–77.

Talacchi S. (1960) Organization size, individual attitudes and behavior: an empirical study. *Administrative Science Quarterly,* 5(3), 398–420.

Takeuchi, R., Lepak, D., Wang, H. and Takeuchi, K. (2007) An empirical examination of the mechanisms mediating between high-performance work systems and the performance of Japanese organizations. *Journal of Applied Psychology,* 92(4), 1069–83.

*Teo, S.T.T., Le Clerc, M. and Galang, M.C. (2011) Human capital enhancing HRM systems and frontline employees in Australian manufacturing SMEs. *International Journal of Human Resource Management,* 22(12), 2522–38.

Thompson, J. (1967) *Organizations in Action.* New York, NY: McGraw-Hill.

Thoms, P., Moore, K.S. and Scott, K.S. (1996) The relationship between self-efficacy for participating in self-managed work groups and the big five personality dimensions. *Journal of Organizational Behavior,* 17(4), 349–62.

Toh, S., Morgeson, F. and Campion, M. (2008) Human resource configurations: investigating fit with the organizational context. *Journal of Applied Psychology,* 93(4), 864–82.

Torrès, O. and Julien, P.A. (2005) Specificity and denaturing of small business. *International Small Business Journal,* 24(3), 355–77.

*Truss, C. (2001) Complexities and controversies in linking HRM with organizational outcomes. *Journal of Management Studies*, 38(8), 1121–49.

Truss, C. and Gratton, L. (1994) Strategic human resource management: a conceptual approach. *The International Journal of Human Resource Management*, 5(3), 663–86.

Tsui, A.S. (1984) A role set analysis of managerial reputation. *Organizational Behavior and Human Performance*, 34(1), 64–96.

Tsui, A.S. (1987) Defining the activities and effectiveness of the human resource department: a multiple constituency approach. *Human Resource Management*, 26(1), 35–69.

Tsui, A.S. (1990) A multiple-constituency model of effectiveness: an empirical examination at the human resource subunit level. *Administrative Science Quarterly*, 35(3), 458–83.

Tsui, A.S. and Milkovich, G.T. (1987) Personnel department activities: constituency perspective and preferences. *Personnel Psychology*, 40(3), 519–37.

Tsui, A.S., Pearce, J.L., Porter, L.W. and Hite, J.P. (1995) Choice of employee-organization relationship: influence of external and internal organizational factors. In G.R. Ferris (ed.) *Research in Personnel and Human Resource Management*. Greenwich, CT: JAI Press.

Tsui, A.S., Pearce, J.L., Porter, L.W. and Tripoli, A.M. (1997) Alternative approaches to the employee-organization relationship: does investment in employees pay off ? *Academy of Management*, 40(5), 1089–1121.

Tukey, J.W. 1991. The philosophy of multiple comparisons. *Statistical Science*, 6, 100–116.p. 154.

Turban, D.B. and Keon, T.L. (1993) Organizational attractiveness: an interactionist perspective. *Journal of Applied Psychology*, 78(2), 184–93.

Tziner, A. and Eden, J.C. (1985) Effects of crew composition on crew performance: does the hole equal the sum of its parts? *Journal of Applied Psychology*, 70, 85–93.

Ulrich, D. (1997) *Human Resource Champions: The Next Agenda for Adding Value and Delivering Results*. Boston, MA: Harvard Business School Press.

USSBA (United States Small Business Administration) (2009) *The Small Business Economy. A Report to the President*. Washington: United States Government Printing Office.

Van de Voorde, K. (2010) *HRM, Employee Well-being and Organizational Performance: A Balanced Perspective* (Dissertation, Tilburg University).

Van de Voorde, K., Paauwe, J. and van Veldhoven, M. (2010a) Predicting business unit performance using employee surveys: monitoring HRM-related changes. *Human Resource Management Journal*, 20(1), 44–63.

Van de Voorde, K., Paauwe, J. and van Veldhoven, M. (2011) Employee well-being and the HRM-organizational performance relationship: a review of quantitative studies. *International Journal of Management Reviews*.

Van de Voorde, K., van Veldhoven, M.J.P.M. and Paauwe, J. (2010b) Time precedence in the relationship between organizational climate and organizational performance: a cross lagged study at the business unit level. *International Journal of Human Resource Management*, 21(10), 1712 –32.

Van de Voorde, K., van Veldhoven, M. and Paauwe, J. (forthcoming) Competing perspectives on employee well-being in the HRM–performance relationship: a review of quantitative studies. *International Journal of Management Reviews*.

*Van den Berg, R.J., Richardson, H.A. and Eastman, L.J. (1999) The impact of high involvement work processes on organizational effectiveness: a second-order latent variable approach. *Group and Organizational Management*, 24(3), 300–39.

Van Iddekinge, C.H., Putka, D.J., Raymark, P.H. and Eidson C.E. (2005) Modeling error variance in job specification ratings: the influence of rater, job, and organization-level factors. *Journal of Applied Psychology*, 90(2), 323–34.

Van Gestel, N., & Nyberg, D. (2009). Translating national policy changes into local HRM practices. *Personnel Review,* 38(5): 544–559.

Van Veldhoven, M. (2001) *Te moe voor het paradijs. Werkstress: tussen weten en doen [Too Tired for Paradise. Job Stress: Between Knowledge and Action].* Leuven: Acco.

*Van Veldhoven, M. (2005) Financial performance and the long-term link with HR practices, work climate and job stress. *Human Resource Management Journal,* 15(4), 30–53.

Van Veldhoven, M., Broersen, S. and Fortuin, R. (1999) *Werkstress in beeld: psychosociale arbeidsbelasting en werkstress in Nederland [Job Stress in Figures: Psychosocial Workload and Job Stress in The Netherlands].* Amsterdam: SKB.

Van Vianen, A.E.M. (2000) Person-organization fit: the match between newcomers' and recruiters' preferences for organizational culture. *Personnel Psychology,* 53(1), 113–49.

*Vanhala, S. and Tuomi, K. (2006) HRM, company performance and employee well-being. *Management Revue,* 17(3), 241–55.

*Varma, A., Beatty, R.W., Schneier, C.E. and Ulrich, D.O. (1999) High performance work systems: exciting discovery or passing fad? *Human Resource Planning,* 22, 26–37.

Veld, M., Paauwe, J. and Boselie, P. (2010) HRM and strategic climates in hospitals: does the message come across at the ward level? *Human Resource Management Journal,* 20(4), 339–56.

Verburg, R.M., den Hartog, D.N. and Koopman, P.L. (2007) Configurations of human resource management practices: a theoretical model and empirical test of internal fit. *International Journal of Human Resource Management,* 18(2), 184–208.

Vroom, V. (1964) *Work and Motivation.* New York: John Wiley & Sons, Inc.

Wall, T., Michie, J., Patterson, M., Wood, S.J., Sheehan, M., Clegg, C.W. and West, M. (2004) On the validity of subjective measures of company performance. *Personnel Psychology,* 57(1), 95–118.

Wall, T. and Wood, S. (2005) The romance of human resource management and business performance, and the case for big science. *Human Relations,* 58(4), 429–62.

Walton, R. (1985) From control to commitment in the workplace. *Harvard Business Review,* 63(2), 77–84.

Warr, P. (2007) *Work, Happiness, and Unhappiness,* London: Lawrence Erlbaum.

Warr, P.B. (1987) *Work, Unemployment, and Mental Health.* Oxford, UK: Clarendon Press.

Watson, T. (1986) *Management, Organization and Employment Strategy: New Directions in Theory and Practice.* London: Routledge.

Watson, T. (2005) Organizations, strategies and human resourcing. In J. Leopold, L. Harris and T. Watson (eds) *The Strategic Managing of Human Resources.* Harlow: Pearson Education.

Watson Wyatt (2002) *Human Capital Index®: Human Capital as a Lead Indicator of Shareholder Value – Research Report,* February.

*Way, S. (2002) High performance work systems and intermediate indicators of firm performance within the US small business sector. *Journal of Management,* 28(6), 765–85.

Weick, K.E. (1995) *Sensemaking in Organizations.* Thousand Oaks, CA: Sage Publications.

White, M., Hill, S., McGovern, P., Mills, C. and Smeaton, D. (2003) High-performance management practices, working hours and work-life balance. *British Journal of Industrial Relations,* 41(2), 175–95.

Whitener, E.M. (2001) Do 'high commitment' human resource practices affect employee commitment? *Journal of Management,* 27, 515–35.

Whittaker, S. and Marchington, M. (2003) Devolving HR responsibility to the line – threat, opportunity or partnership? *Employee Relations,* 25(3), 245–261.

Wilkinson, A. (1999) Employment relations in SMEs. *Employee Relations,* 21(3), 206–17.

Wilkinson, L. and the Task Force on Statistical Inference (1999) Statistical methods in psychology journals. *American Psychologist,* 54(8), 594–604.

Williams, W.M. and Sternberg, R.J. (1988) Group intelligence: why some groups are better than others. *Intelligence*, 12(4), 351–77.

Williamson, O. (2000) Employer legitimacy and recruitment success in small businesses. *Entrepreneurship Theory and Practice*, 25(1), 27–42.

Willmott, H. (1993) Strength is ignorance; slavery is freedom: managing culture in modern organisations. *Journal of Management Studies*, 30(s1), 515–52.

Wise, L.L., McHenry, J. and Campbell, J.P. (1990) Identifying optimal predictor composites and testing for generalizability across jobs and performance factors. *Personnel Psychology*, 43(2), 355–66.

Womack, J., Jones, D. and Roos, D. (1990) *The Machine that Changed the World: The Triumph of Lean Production*. New York: Rawson Macmillan.

Wood, S. (1999) Human resource management and performance. *International Journal of Management Reviews*, 1(4), 397–413.

Wood, S., van Veldhoven, M., Croon, M. and de Menezes, L.M. (2012) Enriched job design, high involvement management and organizational performance: the mediating roles of job satisfaction and well-being. *Human Relations*, 65(4): 419.

Wood, S. and Wall, T. (2007) Work enrichment and employee voice in human resource management-performance studies. *International Journal of Human Resource Management*, 18(7), 1335–72.

Woodrow, C. and Guest, D. (2011) When 'good' HR gets bad results: a case of failure to implement policies to prevent bullying and harassment. *Human Resource Management Journal*, under review.

Wooldridge, J.M. (2002) *Econometric Analysis of Cross Section and Panel Data*. London: Princeton University Press.

Wright, P. and Boswell, W. (2002) Desegregating HRM: a review and synthesis of micro and macro human resource management research. *Journal of Management*, 28(3), 247–76.

Wright, P. and Haggerty, J. (2005) Missing variables in theories on strategic human resource management: time, cause and individuals. *Management Revue*, 16(2), 164–73.

Wright, P.M., Dunford, B.B. and Snell, S.A. (2001a) Human resources and the resource based view of the firm. *Journal of Management*, 27(6), 701–21.

Wright, P.M. and Gardner, T. (2004) The human resource–firm performance relationship: methodological and theoretical challenges. In D. Holman, T. Wall, C. Clegg, P. Sparrow and A. Howard (eds) *The New Workplace: A Guide to the Human Impact of Modern Work Practices* (pp. 311–30). London: John Wiley & Sons, Ltd.

Wright, P.M. and Gardner, T.M. (2003a) Theoretical and empirical challenges in studying the HR practice – firm performance relationship. In D. Holman, T.D. Wall, C. Clegg, P. Sparrow and A. Howard (eds) *The New Workplace: People, Technology and Organization*. Chichester: John Wiley & Sons, Ltd.

Wright, P.M. and Gardner, T.M. (2003b) The human resource-firm performance relationship: methodological and theoretical challenges. In P. Sparrow and A. Howard (eds) *The New Workplace: A Guide to the Human Impact of Modern Working Practices*. Chichester: John Wiley & Sons, Ltd.

Wright, P.M., Gardner, T.M. and Moynihan, L.M. (2003) The impact of HR practices on the performance of business units. *Human Resource Management Journal*, 13(3), 21–36.

Wright, P.M., Gardner, T.M., Moynihan, L.M. and Allen, M.R. (2005) The relationship between HR practices and firm performance: Examining the causal order. *Personnel Psychology*, 58(2), 409–46.

Wright, P.M., Gardner, T.M., Moynihan, L.M., Park, H.J., Delery, J.R. and Gerhart, B. (2001a) Measurement error in research on human resources and firm performance: additional data and suggestions for future research. *Personnel Psychology*, 54, 875–901.

Wright, P.M., Kacmar, K.M., McMahan, G.C. and DeLeeuw, K.L. (1995a) P=f(M x A): cognitive ability as a moderator of the relationship between personality and job performance. *Journal of Management*, 21, 1129–39.

Wright, P.M. and McMahan, G.C. (1992) Theoretical perspectives for strategic human resource management. *Journal of Management*, 18(2), 295–320.

Wright P.M. and McMahan, G.C. (2011) Exploring human capital: putting 'human' back into strategic human resource management. *Human Resource Management Journal.*

Wright, P.M., McMahan, G.C. and McWilliams, A. (1994) Human resources and sustained competitive advantage: a resource-based perspective. *International Journal of Human Resource Management*, 5(2), 301–26.

Wright, P.M., McMahan, G.C., Snell, S.A. and Gerhart, B. (2001b) Comparing line and HR executives' perceptions of HR effectiveness: Services, roles, and contributions. *Human Resource Management*, 40(2), 111–23.

Wright, P.M. and Sherman, W.S. (1999) Failing to find fit in strategic human resource management: theoretical and empirical problems. In P. Wright, L. Dyer, J. Boudreau and G. Milkovich (eds) *Strategic Human Resources Management in the Twenty-First Century.* Supplement to G.R. Ferris (ed.) *Research in Personnel and Human Resources Management.* Stanford, CT: JAI Press.

Wright, P.M., Smart, D.L. and McMahan, G.C. (1995b) Matches between human resources and strategy among NCAA basketball teams. *Academy of Management Journal*, 38(4), 1052–74.

Wright, P.M. and Snell, S.A. (1998) Toward a unifying framework for exploring fit and flexibility in strategic human resource management. *Academy of Management Review*, 23(4), 756–72.

Wright, P., Snell, S. and Jacobsen, P. (2004) Current approaches to HR strategies: inside-out vs. outside-in. *Human Resource Planning*, 27, 36–46.

Yammarino, F. and Markham, S. (1992) On the application of within and between analysis: are absence and affect really group-based phenomena? *Journal of Applied Psychology*, 77(2), 168–76.

Youndt, M. and Snell. S. (1995) Human resource management and firm performance: testing a contingency model of executive controls. *Journal of Management*, 21(4), 711–37.

Youndt, M.A., Snell, S.A., Dean, J.W. and Lepak, D.P. (1996) Human resource management, manufacturing strategy, and firm performance. *Academy of Management Journal*, 39(4), 836–66.

Youndt, M.A., Subramaniam, O. and Snell, S.A. (2004) Intellectual capital profiles: an examination of investment and returns. *Journal of Management Studies*, 41, 335–61.

Yukl, G., Gordon, A. and Taber, T. (2002) A hierarchical taxonomy of leadership behavior: integrating a half century of behavior research. *Journal of Leadership and Organizational Studies*, 9(1), 15–32.

Zaccaro, S. J. and McCoy, M. C. (1988) The effects of task and interpersonal cohesiveness on performance of a disjunctive group task. *Journal of Applied Social Psychology*, 18(10), 837–51.

*Zheng, C., Morrison, M. and O'Neill, G. (2006) An empirical study of high performance HRM practices in Chinese SMEs. *International Journal of Human Resource Management*, 17(10), 1772–803.

Zohar, D. (1980) Safety climate in industrial organizations. Theoretical and applied implications. *Journal of Applied Psychology*, 65(1), 96–102.

Zohar, D. (2000) A group-level model of safety climate: testing the effect of group climate on microaccidents in manufacturing jobs. *Journal of Applied Psychology*, 85(4), 587–96.

Zohar, D. and Luria, G. (2005) A multilevel model of safety climate: cross-level relationships between organization and group-level climates. *Journal of Applied Psychology*, 90(4), 616–28.

INDEX